D0239084

Describing Language

Describing Language

David Graddol
Jenny Cheshire
and
Joan Swann

Open University Press
Milton Keynes · Philadelphia

Open University Press
12 Cofferidge Close
Stony Stratford
Milton Keynes MK11 1BY England

and
242 Cherry Street
Philadelphia PA 19106. USA

First Published 1987. Reprinted 1989

British Library Cataloguing in Publication Data

Graddol, David
  Describing language.
  1. Linguistics
  I. Title II. Cheshire, Jenny III. Swann, Joan,
  410 P121

  ISBN 0-335-15980-X
  ISBN 0-335-15979-6 Pbk

Library of Congress Cataloging in Publication Data

Graddol, David.
  Describing language.

  Bibliography: p.
  Includes index.
  1. Language and languages. 2. Linguistics.
  I. Cheshire, Jenny. II. Swann, Joan. III. Title.
  P121.G69 1987   400   86-18272
  ISBN 0-335-15980-X
  ISBN 0-335-15979-6 (soft)

Text design by Carlton Hill
Typeset by Mathematical Composition Setters, Ltd., Salisbury, England
Printed in Great Britain

Contents

Preface

A book such as this shows the work of several hands. It draws on materials which have been written by various authors for undergraduate language courses at the Open University, and it contains much new material which has been improved by comments and ideas from many colleagues. The broad division of labour between the three authors was as follows. Jenny Cheshire contributed most of Chapters 3 and 4; Joan Swann wrote substantial parts of Chapters 1, 4 and 7; and David Graddol was responsible, more or less, for the rest, and for the coordination of the book.

Some sections trade upon materials written by various people for earlier Open University courses. In particular, the section on the Quirk *et al*. grammar in Chapter 3 is largely taken from material by Pam Czerniewska in course PE232 *Language development* (originally published in 1981) and the subsections in Chapter 7 on *Cohesion*, *Quantitative approaches*, and *Story grammars* from material by Tony Pugh in E263 *Language in use* (originally published in 1981). Acknowledgement must also be made for the more diffuse incorporation of work by David Langford, Eric Lunzer, Barbara Mayor, Bernadette Robinson and Michael Stubbs. Various chapters have benefited greatly from the comments (at some time or another) of James Britton, Penelope Brown, John Green, James Hurford, Angus McIntosh, Harold Rosen, Gordon Wells, colleagues at the Open University and many students throughout the UK. Relentless production schedules have alas prevented us from taking into account all the revisions which have properly been urged upon us.

David Graddol
Jenny Cheshire
Joan Swann

Introduction

This book is designed as a practical and accessible introduction to various areas of linguistic description. The audience is first and foremost those Open University students following undergraduate and postgraduate courses which require some technical background in linguistics. It is not, however, in any way intended to form an introduction to linguistic theory. It should be found useful by anyone who wishes to refer to technical literature involving linguistic description, who requires a basic conceptual framework and technical vocabulary with which to talk about language, or who has a requirement to make elementary but principled descriptions and analyses of real data, such as classroom interaction or counselling sessions.

The selection and treatment of material is eclectic and practical in orientation, both in the sense that the content is more concerned with methods of usefully describing real linguistic data than with making interesting theoretical points, and in the sense that the selection is designed to be helpful, in a practical manner, to an inexperienced student approaching the literature for the first time.

The book is quite definitely not designed to be read on its own, chapter by chapter. We envisage that students will refer to particular chapters, either as set course reading or as the need arises, and have therefore avoided making too many links from one chapter to another. The organisation, however, caters for the specific reading requirements of Open University students, and may not entirely suit other users. For this reason cross-references have been inserted where appropriate, and it should be fairly easy to find, for example, all the required material on conversation or interactional analysis, even though this is spread over several chapters.

Different sections of the book have rather different aims which attempt to balance the reasonable ambitions of students against the complexity of the subject matter or special training required. Some sections give an introduction to a general area of linguistic description and others give more detailed instructions and exercises which should allow students to make an analysis of data they have collected themselves. Most sections include 'activities' as is customary in Open University materials. These help practise certain skills, or help review a particular argument in the text. Where a section is just intended as a quick overview of research traditions in an area, then we have avoided activities, judging that they would interfere, rather than help, with study. Each section has associated with it an annotated reference list showing where students should go for more detailed treatment of particular topics and listing any standard reference works in that area.

There is a cassette which accompanies this book. It is not essential listening for readers other than Open University students but it is a useful companion to *Describing Language*. See Appendix 1 for details of its contents and availability.

1 The nature of language

1.1 INTRODUCTION

It has been suggested (Harris, 1980, pp. 1–3) that anyone who asks 'What is a language?'

> must expect to be treated with the same suspicion as the traveller who inquires of the other passengers waiting on platform 1 whether they can tell him the way to the station. ... The language user already has the only concept of a language worth having.

Harris raises several important points with this colourful metaphor. It cannot be assumed, of course, that those who 'know' how to use language can readily tell us what language is. They can *show* us instances of language; we can *observe* them using language; but if they are able to explain articulately and usefully what the nature of language is, then they are demonstrating a special *metalinguistic skill* brought about by an extensive consideration of language as an object of knowledge.

This chapter discusses some of the basic issues facing any serious student of language. A distinction is first made between *a language* (e.g. French as opposed to Japanese) and *language* (i.e. the general faculty of speech). The main issues which arise from attempts at description are discussed in sections 1.2 and 1.3. Section 1.4 shows how certain theoretical assumptions as to the nature of language and languages affect how scholars set about their investigations.

1.2 THE NOTION OF 'A LANGUAGE'

The English language has a special place in the world today. It has become an international language, both in the sense that it is now the native language of people from several continents and in the sense that many others have learnt to speak it as a second language. People who live in Britain and speak English as their mother tongue constitute very much a minority of English speakers. Since the status of their own language is a most unusual one and they are insulated to a considerable degree from the multilingual nature of most populations, their perception of the number and status of other languages may easily be distorted. Activity 1.1 is intended to make you reflect on this point.

Activity 1.1

Make a list of the languages you know of. Do not attempt to look anything up—just jot down names as they come to you.

Mark those six languages which you think are most widely spoken in the world. Hazard a *very rough* guess at how many million people speak each of them.

If you managed to get more than 20 or so languages on your list, then you did well. But even if you had prepared a much longer list, writing fluently and rapidly for a full five minutes, you would not have made much impression on the stock of world languages. It has been estimated that there are between 3000 and 4000 languages spoken in the world today. If we take into account known dialects, the number is even more staggering. In the index of the world's languages prepared by Voegelin and Voegelin (1977) there are over 20,000 entries.

Approaches to language classification

The existence of so many languages means that, for practical purposes, some method of classifying and grouping is needed. Two approaches to classification are common. The first is *typological* — which groups languages according to their similarities and differences in linguistic structure. The second is *genealogical* — which groups languages according to supposed historical relationships. The first approach is concerned only with linguistic comparisons, the second uses as a basis only those similarities between languages for which a historical explanation can be provided.

Typological classification

One way of classifying languages is in terms of their characteristic patterns of *word order*. For example, the English language uses a word order in which the subject appears in the sentence before the verb, which in turn is followed by the object. Thus: '*Jill caught the mouse*'. English is sometimes referred to as an *SVO* language, for this reason. Other languages, such as Welsh, are known as *VSO* languages, since they place the verb first. This provides a rough and ready method of classifying languages, and it leads to certain interesting insights — it turns out, for example, that certain word orders, such as *OVS*, are extremely uncommon.

Another, and much older, typological classification divides the world's languages into three groups:

Analytic (or *isolating*) — languages like Chinese in which words are usually simple units without any word endings or affixes.

Synthetic (or *inflectional*) — languages like Latin which have elaborate systems of suffixes indicating things like the tense of verbs or whether a noun is the subject or object.

Agglutinative (or *affixing*) — languages like Turkish or Swahili in which words contain a series of 'slots' into which are placed small elements corresponding to pronouns, tense and so on.

Typological approaches have been subject to many refinements over the years and for some specific purposes have proved very useful. On the whole, however, they have met with less acceptance than genealogical classifications.

Genealogical classifications

A genealogical classification attempts to show the historical relationships between languages. All languages tend to change through time, and if a language changes in form faster in one community than another, or if some changes occur in one place and not another, then linguistic differences will arise. One important consequence of such historical processes is that the resultant language varieties will be related, and the extent to which they are related will depend on how long ago they began to diverge from each other.

All languages which have evolved from a single *parent language* are regarded as belonging to the same *language family*. Many of the European and Indian languages are thought to be derived from a single prehistoric language, which has been called *Proto-Indo-European*. This means that modern English and, say, Gujerati are linguistic relatives; whereas English and Turkish are not. Linguists have tried to represent the relationships between the Indo-European languages by means of a *family tree*. One version of this tree is shown in Figure 1.1. The actual historical and present-day relationships between languages are far more complex than the family tree suggests, but it is nevertheless a useful way of drawing attention to similarities and differences between modern languages.

There are, however, two important limitations with family trees. The first is that the model seems to work particularly well for the Indo-European languages (which were most intensively studied during

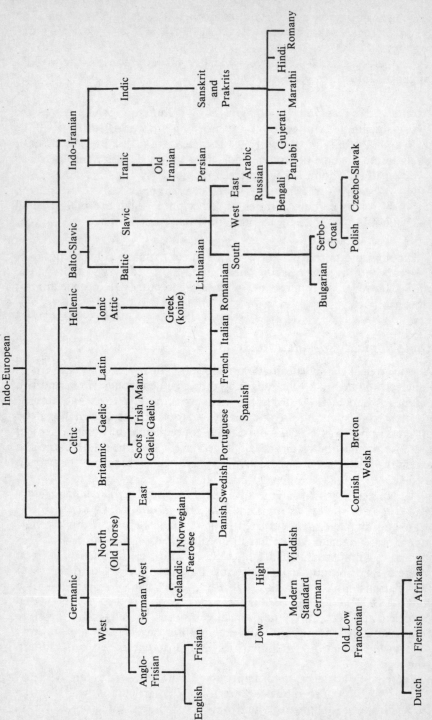

Figure 1.1.   The Indo-European family of languages

the nineteenth century when genealogical theory was developed). Genealogical models are much less able to give a satisfactory account of the relationships within other language families such as Bantu. This may be in part because of the lack of documentary and historical evidence from such languages, but it is also likely that different patterns of population movement, of contact between communities, and of size of community have led to a less clearly structured family tree.

The second limitation is that the genealogical model fails to take into account any contact between languages after the supposed historical divergence. Just as ideas, customs and objects tend to spread from one culture to another, so also do words get introduced into one language from another. English has many such loan words, and has, in turn, been the source of many in other languages. This borrowing from language to language may give rise to similarities between languages which do not share a common ancestor. Borrowings may occasionally extend beyond vocabulary to include pronunciation or grammatical features.

Social and political criteria

We have discussed the question of classification as if it were merely a linguistic issue in which different languages, at least, were easy to identify and name. This is far from being the case. Languages have a social and political identity as much as a linguistic one.

This may become clearer if you return to the list of languages which you made in Activity 1.1. What may be more interesting than the number of languages which you managed to list is the mental strategy you used to get them. Did you, for instance, write down the names of languages as they came to you, or did you go through a mental list of countries and mark down the language spoken in each? Either way, you probably ended up mainly with European languages on your list and about one language for each country. Certainly, the experience of most people in Britain is largely a monolingual one — you may have come to think it natural that one language should serve a whole population. If your list contains such spurious languages as 'Swiss' or 'Belgian', then you have been misled by this experience. If not, did you get the four officially recognised languages of Switzerland: German, French, Italian and Romansch? Or the three of Belgium: Flemish, French and German? The existence of more than one language in a country is by no means unusual. In New Guinea there are literally hundreds of languages.

Let us now turn to the number of speakers. Table 1.1 shows which are the top 13 languages according to one author (column A), and it also shows how other sources rate these languages (column B and C).

Activity 1.2

Study Table 1.1 carefully. Compare your own results from Activity 1.1 with the table, then compare each source with the others.

Table 1.1. *The major languages of the world*

Language	Number of speakers (*in millions*)		
	A	B	C
Chinese	750(1)	780( )	541 ( )
English	300(2)	300( )	300 ( )
Hindi	175(3)	180( )	90 ( )
Russian	160(4)	190( )	150 ( )
Spanish	115(5)	225( )	150 ( )
Japanese	100(6)	100( )	100 ( )
German	95(7)	100( )	95 ( )
French	85(8)	75( )	64 ( )
Arabic	75(9)	120( )	50–80 ( )
Bengali	65(10)	125( )	76 ( )
Italian	65(10)	60( )	56 ( )
Malay	65(10)	7( )	10 ( )
Portuguese	60(13)	105( )	76 ( )

Source: *A* Parlett (1967): *B* Katzner (1977); *C* Voegelin and Voegelin (1977).

Column A is ordered by rank, according to the number of speakers. Work out the rank orders suggested by columns B and C, writing the numbers in the brackets after the number of speakers.

On which languages is there most agreement and on which the most disagreement?

Table 1.1 shows considerable variation among estimates of a language's status. Why should there be this kind of disagreement between authorities? How, for instance, can we account for the discrepancy between the 65,000,000 speakers of 'Malay' in column A and the 7,000,000 in column B? How is it that one authority can claim 105,000,000 speakers for Portuguese when Portugal's total population is only 10,000,000?

The answers to these questions tell us something about the nature of languages and their use in the world. For instance, Portuguese is used extensively in South America. In Brazil alone there are 85,000,000 people or more who speak Portuguese. Then there is the practical problem of how one arrives at any specific figure for Chinese, which is spoken in many areas where census information may be hard to come by, and how one finds out, in some isolated part of the world, what language or languages each and every person speaks. This then, may explain why all three sources agree on the number of English speakers — the relevant information may be easier to find and be more reliable.

These are straightforward answers, but they hardly explain the major discrepancies which exist between some estimates. These discrepancies are more likely to reflect disagreement about how languages are to be classified and about what 'counts' as a given language. Such titles as 'Chinese' or 'Malay' may be little better than our spurious languages 'Swiss' and 'Belgian' — there are at least eight Chinese languages (according to Voegelin and Voegelin, 1977) and hundreds of dialects. So although there may be doubt about the size of the Chinese population, this may not be the major problem. There may be disagreement about what should be included in the blanket term 'Chinese'. Again, some sources may be including Javanese and other Indonesian languages under 'Malay', while others may not. Problems of classification arise out of the nature of languages themselves. And the fact that languages have political and social identities as well as linguistic ones can complicate both classification and the collection of accurate information.

The use of a language varies a great deal from one speaker to another. Much of this variation, however, is not haphazard, but correlates with socially significant facts, such as the region of origin and the social class of the speaker. Such non-random variation within a language is often referred to as *dialect variation*, but this does not indicate that sharp divisions exist between one dialect and another. Distinctions of this kind are an attempt to divide up a linguistic continuum into discrete entities. Although such divisions may be useful, they will necessarily reflect social and political facts rather than linguistic ones. The same problem arises with the term 'language'. The decision to call certain language varieties distinct languages will often depend on a number of political and cultural factors affecting the autonomy of the language variety in question, rather than on linguistic criteria or a criterion based on mutual intelligibility. The Scandinavian languages are an example. Although Danes, Swedes and Norwegians often find they can understand one another, they each speak a language which has its own agreed standards and which is symbolic of the political and cultural integrity of their native countries.

Minority languages

There are many more languages used in Britain today than most people appreciate. In addition to the old indigenous Celtic languages (Welsh and Gaelic) there are now many languages used in multilingual urban communities throughout Britain. Recent estimates of the languages spoken by schoolchildren in London, for example, put the number at around 150. The Linguistic Minorities Project (LMP) (1983) found that which languages were most used varied from town to town. Figure 1.2 shows data collected from five local authorities in 1980–1. The notes

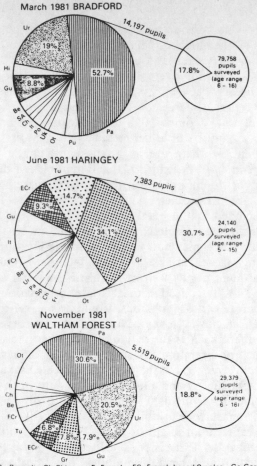

March 1981 BRADFORD

14,197 pupils

79,758 pupils surveyed (age range 6 – 16)

June 1981 HARINGEY

7,383 pupils

24,140 pupils surveyed (age range 5 – 15)

November 1981
WALTHAM FOREST

5,519 pupils

29,379 pupils surveyed (age range 6 – 16)

Be Bengali   Ch-Chinese   Fr-French   FCr-French-based Creoles   Ge-German
Hi-Hindi   Ot-Other   Po-Polish   Pu-Pushtu   SA-other S. Asian languages   Sp-Spanish   Uk-Ukrainian

Notes on the Schools Language Survey Findings
Based on the SLS data collection

The data of this Schools Language Survey are based on pupils' self-report, mediated through teachers and inevitably collected in a range of differing classroom situations. Readers should bear in mind that:
1 The survey questions were designed to elicit reporting of even modest language skills and, therefore, make it impossible to comment on the level of language ability of the pupils, either in oral or in literacy skills.
2 The process of recording the data inevitably involved some element of interpretation by the teacher of what the pupil reported speaking, reading or writing.

Naming of languages

The level of detail in a pupil's answer or teacher's reporting of it may be affected by very local factors (even to the level of what other pupils in the class have said, or the kind of relationship between teacher and pupil). One tendency is for some teachers in classes where there is a large number of pupils of one language group to give detailed information about

Figure 1.2.   The main languages reported as spoken in 5 LEAs

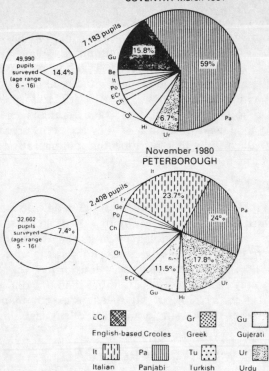

COVENTRY March 1981

49,990 pupils surveyed (age range 6 – 16) — 14.4%

7,183 pupils

Gu
Be
It
Po
ECr
Ch
Ot
Hi
Ur

15.8%

59%

6.7%

Pa

November 1980
PETERBOROUGH

32,662 pupils surveyed (age range 5 – 16) — 7.4%

2,408 pupils

It
Fr
Ge
Po
Ch
Ot
ECr
Gu
Hi

23.7%

24%

17.8%

11.5%

Ur

Pa

ECr ▨ English-based Creoles   Gr ▦ Greek   Gu ☐ Gujerati

It ⊞ Italian   Pa ▥ Panjabi   Tu ⋮ Turkish   Ur ⣿ Urdu

dialects and places of origin, while in classes with fewer pupils answering 'yes' to the first SLS question ('Do you yourself ever speak any language at home apart from English?'), or where there is a wide range of languages, little more than the language name is given.

The method by which pupils and teachers (neither of whom may have a detailed knowledge of the linguistic background) were asked to record answers to a single question meant that some answers referred to the local spoken dialect used at home, some to the regional standard spoken language and others to the language of community loyalty or even the language of literacy.

Thus, for example, a number of pupils with a Pakistani background may have reported speaking Urdu when in fact it is likely that their first spoken language is a regional variety of Panjabi, and that Urdu for them is a language of literacy which may also be a second spoken language. Other children of similar language background may have reported speaking Panjabi.

The term used to refer to a language or dialect also varied according to the pupil's or teacher's perception of the status of this language or dialect in the wider community, either in the country of origin (e.g. Urdu given for Panjabi), or in England (e.g. 'Pakistan' given for Panjabi, 'Italian' for Sicilian, 'Indian' for Hindi, Panjabi or Gujerati).

'Creoles' refers to a large group of diverse languages which we divided into two main categories: 'French-based' and 'English-based and all other Creoles'.

'Chinese' is a group including all language labels referring to one of the regional Chinese languages, e.g. Cantonese, Hakka, and the general label 'Chinese'.

In other categories simple language labels, and those which give more detailed geographical or dialect specifications, were all grouped together under the name of the national or regional official language, e.g. Kutchi is subsumed in the Gujerati group and Sicilian in the Italian group.

Literacy is to be interpreted in the broadest sense, i.e. 'Pupils have reported that they can read and/or write one or more of the spoken languages given, or have reported one or more separate languages of literacy'.

supplied by the LMP indicate clearly some of the practical problems involved in carrying out such surveys. It will be clear that languages have very different kinds of status within a community. What makes a language a *minority language* has nothing to do with how many speakers it has. Faeroese is the native language of only around 40,000 people — about equal to the population of the British towns of Hereford or Scarborough — but has official status within the islands. Languages such as Chinese are minority languages in Britain — they are poorly recognised for the purposes of education and governmental administration.

Classifying speakers

Another difficulty in making linguistic surveys is that people do not speak a single language variety invariantly. Multilingual speakers will use a variety of languages, but they may not have equal fluency in them all. Even monolingual speakers will usually command a range of styles of speaking, reserving some for more formal occasions or just for writing, for instance, or they may be able to speak in more than one dialect. For these reasons it is better to think of all speakers as commanding a *language repertoire* rather than a single monolithic language.

1.3   LANGUAGE AS A HIERARCHICAL SYSTEM

The components of language

Language is a highly complex system of communication, and an important task of linguistics is to describe this system, analysing the contrasts and relationships that obtain between different components. To make this task somewhat easier it has been conventional to regard language as if it was composed of a series of 'boxes', each containing a distinct kind of machinery. While the number and nature of the boxes identified vary in different linguistic theories, the most commonly recognised ones are:

| SOUND | GRAMMAR | MEANING |

Further subdivisions are often made. For instance, in the box marked 'sound' it is common to distinguish *phonetics*, the study of the sounds produced by speakers, and *phonology*, the study of the sound system of a language. In the 'grammar' box a distinction between *morphology* (word structure) and *syntax* (sentence structure) is also usual.

We have followed the convention of distinguishing different components of analysis in the organisation of this book: the sounds of language are discussed in Chapter 2, grammar in Chapter 3 and meaning in Chapter 4.

'DUALITY' OR 'DOUBLE ARTICULATION'

However many components one recognises for the purposes of analysis, it is clear that some of them, at least, are arranged on a series of *levels*. Furthermore, these levels do not operate independently but only in relation to other levels: 'the units on the "lower" level of phonology (the sounds of a language) have no function other than that of combining with one another to form the "higher" units of grammar (words)' (Lyons, 1968, p. 54).

According to views such as this, language is seen as having a dual structure (sometimes also referred to as *double articulation*). Units of sound, meaningless in themselves, combine to form larger units of meaning. This leads to considerable economy in the system: it is possible to construct an enormous number of words, or meaningful parts of words, from a relatively small number of sound units. This property of language has been seen as a defining characteristic, distinguishing it from other systems of communication.

The autonomy of language

The way we have described language so far, as an autonomous system that can be analysed in terms of internal relationships and contrasts, represents a highly abstract view. It is conventional, in linguistics, to make a distinction between such an abstract *system*, and language *in use* (what people actually say or write on any occasion). This distinction is differently expressed in different theories. The linguist Saussure, for example, distinguishes *langue* (often translated 'language') from *parole* (translated as 'speech' or 'speaking'). *Langue* is a social product (Saussure, 1974, pp. 13–14):

> It is a storehouse filled by the members of a given community through their active use of speaking, a grammatical system that has a potential existence in each brain, or, more specifically, in the brains of a group of individuals. For language is not complete in any speaker; it exists perfectly only within a collectivity.

Parole is the individual act of speaking (or, presumably, writing).

Chomsky made a similar distinction between *competence* and *performance*. Competence here refers to a speaker's knowledge of what constitutes a well-formed sentence in his or her language; performance is language use, complete with 'numerous false starts, deviations from rules, changes of plan in mid-course, and so on' (Chomsky, 1965, p. 4). Chomsky regarded competence as the proper, or at least the prior, object of study for linguistics — recognising that language in this sense is an idealisation (Chomsky, 1965, p. 3):

> Linguistic theory is concerned primarily with an ideal speaker-listener, in a completely homogeneous speech-community, who knows its language perfectly and is unaffected by such grammatically irrelevant conditions as

memory limitations, distractions, shifts of attention and interest, and errors (random or characteristic) in applying his knowledge of the language in actual performance.

An alternative approach is to give full recognition to 'performance', to recognise actual *utterances* produced by real speakers in specific contexts (as opposed to *sentences* which are the products of a grammar) as legitimate objects of study. Rather than disregarding utterances as simply imperfect realisations of competence (subject to errors, memory limitations, etc.), researchers have been able to discern interesting patterns and regularities in language in use. There has been a rapid growth of interest in this area in recent years but earlier scholars also saw the dangers of regarding language as an autonomous system. Sapir (1949, pp. 578–9) wrote in 1939:

> In linguistics, abstracted speech sounds, words, and the arrangement of words have come to have so authentic a vitality that one can speak of 'regular sound change' and 'loss of genders' without knowing or caring who opened their mouths, at what time, to communicate what to whom.

It is precisely these aspects of language that interested, more recently, the linguist Dell Hymes, who established the notion of the *ethnography of speaking*, the study of the interaction between language and social life. Hymes coined the term *communicative competence* (by analogy with Chomsky's 'competence'). 'Communicative competence' is, however, far more extensive, encompassing the knowledge a speaker needs in order to use language appropriately — depending upon the person being spoken to, the context in which an utterance is produced, the communicative goals of the speaker, etc. Interest in this area has come from a branch of linguistics known as *sociolinguistics* (which studies the relationship between language and society; see Trudgill (1983) for a discussion of the discipline) and from other disciplines outside linguistics such as *anthropology* and *social psychology*. The area has also engendered a proliferation of descriptive terms. In addition to those mentioned above, the term *pragmatics* will be found in the literature to refer to certain aspects of the study of language in its communicative context.

You will find the 'autonomous system' versus 'language in use' dichotomy represented in various chapters in this book. We have already mentioned the distinction between 'phonology' and 'phonetics' — which will be considered in Chapter 2. Chapter 4 will make a similar distinction between 'sentence meaning' and 'utterance meaning', and Chapter 5 between 'text' and 'discourse'. You should remember, however, that the study of language use is not concerned with idiosyncratic utterances, but with patterns of use and how they may be interpreted. Language here is not considered an abstract, autonomous system but the use of language in context may nevertheless be quite systematic.

The sentence and beyond

According to Palmer (1984, pp. 66–8), 'it is the function of syntax to state what words can be combined with others to form sentences and in what order ... The sentence is, then, the largest unit to which we can assign a grammatical structure'. Traditional linguistic analyses of the language system have tended to regard the *sentence* as the largest unit of analysis (you will see this in Chapters 3 and 4 below). When regarded as a theoretical unit in this way, sentences form part of a speaker's competence — they can be contrasted with *utterances*, which are sequences actually produced by speakers.

Some researchers have tried to identify larger units of analysis, or to specify systematic patterns and relationships between components that operate beyond the level of the sentence. Chapter 7 discusses such notions in approaches to text and discourse analysis.

Analyses of utterances, of necessity, do not restrict themselves to sentence-like structures. Chapter 7 also discusses approaches such as *conversation analysis*, which has identified patterns in talk which has been collaboratively produced and interpreted by speakers and listeners.

1.4 INVESTIGATING LANGUAGE

In section 1.3 we discussed two rather conflicting views of language. On the one hand, it could be regarded as an autonomous system; on the other, as inextricably bound up with social and contextual factors. Which view is taken by linguists will clearly affect the methods they select as appropriate to its study.

Intuition

According to Chomsky (1957, p. 15), 'the set of grammatical sentences cannot be identified with any particular corpus of utterances obtained by the linguist in his fieldwork'. Chomsky took as his object of study not just the body of observed utterances (as earlier linguists had done) but the whole potential stock of sentences which were, in principle, allowed by the grammatical rules of a language. The only means of gaining access to such a store of unused, unspoken sentences was through introspection, and the use of the speaker's intuitive judgements concerning the acceptability of grammatical structures. Such judgements gained something of a special status in Chomsky's theory of *transformational-generative grammar*, but native speaker intuitions provide important evidence for linguistic descriptions emanating from other traditions. One could go further and say that the description and explanation of socially organised behaviour of all kinds relies, explicitly or implicitly, on a belief in the possibility of tapping the tacit understandings of members of a given community.

When linguists are investigating their own language, they may consult their intuitions as members of the speech community. Some concern has been expressed, however, about the validity of linguists' intuitions. Labov (1975) suggested that 'experimenter' effects might cause a researcher to perceive linguistic facts that accord with his or her theoretical expectations, and to see points of doubt as clear-cut.

Spencer (1973) demonstrated that a consensus judgement made by disinterested subjects did not match those which linguists had promulgated in the name of the speech community. One hundred and fifty illustrative sentences were culled from half a dozen influential articles and presented to a population of naive and non-naive native speakers. Although some 80 per cent of these subjects agreed amongst themselves on acceptability judgements, little more than half of their judgements agreed with the linguists'. The implication to be drawn is that a linguist who has a particular theoretical motivation in judging an example may fail to arrive at the consensus judgement of uncommitted parties. Spencer suggests that, merely by virtue of getting too close to the data, a linguist's perceptions may become distorted. If Spencer's explanation is correct, then the linguist is advised not to consult an intuition too often, lest it be worn away and replaced by some unauthentic perception. Right or wrong, Spencer's results indicate that professional linguists' intuitions may not be shared by the rest of the speech community.

An alternative approach is to consult the intuitions of other (linguistically untrained) native speakers of a language.

Activity 1.3

How well do you know your own language?

Answer the following questions. Consider, in each case, how sure you are about your answer, and what kind of justification you might give to another person.

Do you say:

1 (a) Put out the light.
    or
    (b) Put the light out.
2 Do you pronounce the *t* in the word *postman*?
3 At school we are taught that sentences can be active or passive. According to this distinction, sentence (a) is active; sentence (b) is passive. What are the others?:
    (a) This bus carries forty people.
    (b) This elephant is frightened by helter-skelters.
    (c) This banana will feed the whole family.
    (d) This cottage sleeps the whole family.
    (e) This angel cake eats well with Madeira.

4 Are any of the following sentences ungrammatical?
   (a) A person may need to blow their nose.
   (b) Brian set out to boldly go where no snail had been before.
   (c) Walking down the garden path, the daffodils were very
        striking.

You are probably familiar with both versions of the sentence in Question 1, so much so that you may find it difficult to decide which expression you yourself use. The placement of the object varies to a certain extent in different parts of the UK but also seems to depend on the particular verb phrase used, the length of the noun phrase which contains the object, and numerous other factors. These make it very difficult for individual speakers to decide exactly what they would say, even though it is highly likely that in each context only one of the two orderings would be used. For example, one might say *At midnight, I put the cat out*, but not *At midnight, I put six milk bottles, a note for the newspaper boy, and the cat out*.

Question 2 again requires an accurate knowledge of your own speech habits. You may have convinced yourself that you pronounce the *t*, since the spelling makes this seem like the 'proper' pronunciation. In fact, the usual and accepted standard pronunciation of this word in English is *posman*.

Question 3 is much more complex. It should illustrate, though, that our ability to describe and analyse sentences depends almost entirely on formal training. The traditional categories and classifications which have been used for many years in the English classroom cannot cope with the syntactic relationships which hold between the nouns in some of these sentences. Sentences (d) and (e) look 'active', but is *the family* really the object of a transitive verb *sleep*, and is *angel cake* really the subject of *eat*? The semantic relationships in these sentences seem at odds with the syntactic descriptions we are led to give them.

The last question contains a number of traditional solecisms, which are mostly frowned upon by etiquette books, such as Fowler (1926). Had they appeared in the text of this book or in a school essay, they would probably have been hastily corrected by the editor or teacher. If you thought they were ungrammatical, then you are prepared to accept criteria that have more to do with social acceptability, than with the linguistic fact that these kinds of expression are governed by grammatical rules and are regularly used.

A final point is that the form of the question asked of a native speaker is likely to affect their judgement. If you give a speaker an example of a sentence and ask whether they would say it, if they find it acceptable, or if it is grammatical in their language you may well get three different answers.

A dramatic example of the unreliability of native speaker intuitions about their own usage was discovered by the American sociolinguist William Labov. Labov (1975) asked members of the Philadelphia speech community about their use of the word *anymore* in a positive sense which was peculiar to the district — that is, said of something which 'was not true at some previous time and is true at this time':

> We now have ample evidence that introspective reports about positive anymore have a very weak relation to what speakers actually say. Since 1972 we have collected twelve cases of speakers who used positive *anymore* quite freely though their introspective judgements were entirely negative ... Faced with a sentence like *John is smoking a lot anymore* they said they had never heard it before, did not recognize it as English, thought it might mean 'not smoking' and showed the same signs of bewilderment that we get from Northern speakers outside the dialect area (Labov, 1975, p. 34).

Nor are native speaker intuitions about 'acceptability' or 'grammaticality' infallible, as Chomsky (1965, p. 38) concedes:

> Obviously, every speaker of a language has mastered and internalized a generative grammar that expresses his knowledge of his language. This is not to say that he is aware of the rules of the grammar or even that he can become aware of them, or that his statements about intuitive knowledge of the language are necessarily accurate. Any interesting generative grammar will be dealing, for the most part, with mental processes that are far beyond the level of actual or even potential consciousness; furthermore, it is quite apparent that a speaker's self-reports and viewpoints about his behaviour and his competence may be in error.

Linguists are thus faced with a methodological problem. If competence is the object of study then one needs access to speakers' tacit understanding of the 'rules' of their language. But neither linguists themselves nor naive native speakers can produce reliable reports of what they understand, presumably at a subconscious level. Competence cannot be tapped by reflecting on sentences, or potential sentences, out of context. Paradoxically, at least as a check on intuition, we need some means of eliciting, or observing, situated utterances — in other words, performance — from which we may make inferences about competence.

What is a speech community?

We mentiond above (section 1.3) that the traditional, Chomskyan notion of *competence* relied on an (idealised) homogeneous *speech community*. However, the use of intuition in any tradition implies homogeneity among a group of speakers — for it to be valid, others must share the intuition. In practice speech communities are likely to be far from homogeneous.

Activity 1.4

Consider the following questions (much as you did for Activity 1.3).
1 Are any of the following sentences ungrammatical?
  (a) My hair needs washing.
  (b) My hair needs to be washed.
  (c) My hair needs washed.
2 Which of the following expressions do you use?
  (a) Do you have any money?
  (b) Have you any money?
  (c) Have you got any money?

If one or two of the sentences in Question 1 were ungrammatical for you, then you probably speak a southern variety of British English. All constructions are used perfectly regularly in one part of the UK or another. Type (c) is associated particularly with Scots. This example draws attention to the fact that, like other languages, English is not a single monolithic entity — different speakers use different, grammatically regular varieties of English. Such variation is probably more extensive than most speakers realise.

In Question 2, variants (a) and (b) seem rarely to be used by the same speaker. If you think you use both, you are probably wrong. All three variants are likely to be familiar to you, and you may have found it difficult deciding which you actually use. Which you do use will depend partly on your regional background, but also on your age and education.

Within any community there is likely to be considerable variation in language. In the UK the region a speaker comes from, their age, sex, ethnic background, social class, and other social factors will affect the varieties of language they use and also (though perhaps to a lesser extent) the varieties they find acceptable.

Up to now, we have been using the term 'speech community' as though this were unproblematical, but it has been variously defined in the literature. Consider the following definitions:

(a) Speech community: all the people who use a given language or dialect (Lyons, 1970, p. 326).
(b) A speech community is a group of people who interact by means of speech (Bloomfield, 1933, p. 42).
(c) ... a speech community cannot be conceived as a group of speakers who all use the same forms; it is best defined as a group of speakers who share the same norms in regard to language (Labov, 1972, p. 158).
(d) To the extent that speakers share knowledge of the communicative constraints and options governing a significant number of

social situations, they can be said to be members of the same *speech community* ... since such shared knowledge depends on intensity of contact and on communicative networks, speech boundaries tend to coincide with wider social units, such as countries, tribes, religions or ethnic groupings (Gumperz, 1972, p. 16).

Lyons' definition is inadequate as it stands — it makes no allowance for bilingual — or bidialectal — communities. Nor does 'community' here suggest geographical or cultural proximity: English speakers in Delhi, in New York and in Devon could, according to the definition, be in the same speech community by virtue of speaking English. Bloomfield's definition emphasises communication between speakers — and allows that this need not involve use of the same language. Labov allows for linguistic variation but stresses shared linguistic norms (e.g., that speakers would agree on which variety of language was the most prestigious). This would be inadequate for Gumperz, who argues that speakers would also need to agree on a variety of communicative 'rules' (including when to speak and when to be silent, for instance) — or to share *communicative competence* (see section 1.3). Hudson (1980) discusses several definitions of 'speech community' (including some of those mentioned above). See also Romaine (1982) for a detailed consideration of variation in speech communities.

In considering where one draws the boundaries of a speech community, it is likely that the more culturally diverse one allows this to be the more linguistically heterogeneous it will also be. By definition, members of the same speech community will have various linguistic and communicative features in common, but absolute linguistic homogeneity may well not be found even within an *idiolect* (the variety of language spoken by one individual). This makes more problematical the notion of native speaker intuitions: while many of these may be shared with a larger group of speakers (the majority of speakers in Norwich, for instance) some will be more restricted (children from a particular housing estate) and some idiosyncratic.

Investigating language in use

It is this very diversity in language that has been a key interest of socio-linguists, who are concerned to investigate social patterns in language use. Earlier *dialectologists* had examined regional variation. For instance, the Survey of English Dialects began in the 1940s to investigate different words, grammatical structures and pronunciations in use in rural areas of England, plotting the distribution of variants on maps (see Orton *et al.*, 1978). To measure social variation, however, different techniques were needed. In the mid-1960s the sociolinguist Labov developed a technique that involved the use of *sociolinguistic variables*. Rather than attempting a comprehensive description of the language variety of a particular social group, Labov selected one or two linguistic features and recorded their distribution across social groups and in different contexts. These features were taken as indicators of different varieties of language in use in the speech community. In principle a variable can be any feature of language that is variably used by different social groups but in practice sociolinguists most often have recourse to phonological variables (i.e. differences in pronunciation). These occur relatively frequently in small amounts of data and speakers also tend to be less conscious about their use.

The sociolinguistic variable has been used to investigate large-scale patterns of variation (differences between women and men, between speakers from different social classes and from different age groups, for instance). There has also been an increasing interest in more specific aspects of a speaker's lifestyle and patterns of interaction that might lead him or her to adopt a particular variety of language. See Trudgill (1983) and Hudson (1980) for a discussion of sociolinguistics and sociolinguistic methodology; Milroy (1980) for an interesting example of a recent study carried out in a Belfast community; Gal (1979) and Le Page and Tabouret-Keller (1985) for studies in a bi- and multilingual community.

We have mentioned here one approach to the study of language in use; however, methods vary considerably in different research traditions and depending on the purposes of the investigation. You will find examples of other methods in the chapters that follow.

2 The sounds of language

2.1 INTRODUCTION

Phonetics is one of the oldest traditions of linguistic analysis, being well developed in ancient India. In Europe it was regarded throughout the nineteenth century, and well into this century, as the prime basis for any scientific study of language. The principles of description, therefore, which are laid out in sections 2.2 and 2.3 are very well-established ones, and have served as a practical framework of description for scholars over many decades.

Section 2.4 ventures onto less well-trodden ground. The linguistically important characteristics of speech delivery — particularly stress and intonation — have been studied for a somewhat shorter time than have consonant and vowel sounds, and with less clear results. The section attempts to pick out some basic features of stress and intonation on which there seems to be some agreement among scholars.

This chapter contains some rather technical and complex material, and it may seem that our decision to give it so much space in an introductory book is a mere hangover of the Victorian tradition. A solid grasp of phonetics is, however, still very important when attempting to understand a wide variety of research in language. In historical linguistics, for example, it helps explain why some changes in pronunciation occur and not others; in sociolinguistics it is necessary in order to understand the principles of social variation in pronunciation. There is still a sound argument for insisting that basic phonetic and phonological description should be one of the first areas to be studied.

Nevertheless, this chapter is no more than an introduction to the subject and makes no attempt to give training in *phonetic transcription*. The ability to transcribe accurately requires much ear-training and practice and cannot be successfully acquired from a text book.

2.2 PHONETIC DESCRIPTION OF SOUNDS

Phonetics is the name given to the scientific study of the sounds of language. Phoneticians set about the task of describing and analysing sounds in a variety of ways. One approach, known as *articulatory phonetics*, has been particularly important, and it is this which is introduced here.

The organs of speech

When we make the sounds of our language we modify the flow of breath through the mouth and nose by moving the tongue and other organs in and around the mouth. This modification gives each sound its characteristic quality. For thousands of years it has been realised that a

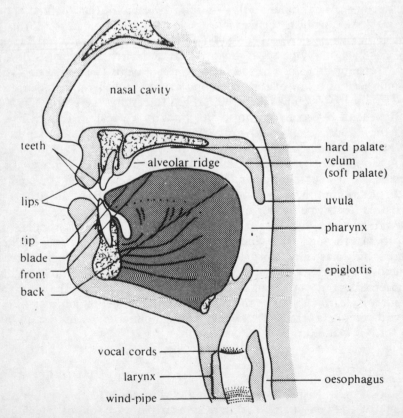

Figure 2.1. The vocal tract

study of what we do with these organs of speech affords a useful way of classifying and describing sounds.

Let us start by looking at which muscles and organs are particularly important in producing sounds. Figure 2.1 shows a cross-section of what is known as the *vocal tract*. What is interesting about the organs used in speech production is that none of them are used exclusively for this purpose. In fact, they all seem to have more basic functions. The tongue and teeth, for example, are used for eating, and the vocal cords are folds of muscle, rather like a pair of lips, which form a valve at the top of the windpipe. These lips are what enable us to close off the windpipe, which we do when we cough or hold our breath under pressure. Although none of the speech organs are used exclusively for language, they seem to have evolved in humans in ways which aid their dual function.

VOICING

To make any sounds we first need to set air in motion. We normally do this naturally by letting air escape from the lungs. If we follow this airstream from the lungs up the windpipe, we can see that the first point at which we can do anything to interfere with it is where it passes through the gap between the vocal cords. Of course, if the cords are fully open, then the air simply passes through. Breathe out forcefully — as if you were breathing on a pair of spectacles to clean them. The only sound you should hear is a sort of rushing sound caused by general turbulence in the airstream. If you had breathed out less forcefully, there would be less turbulence and scarcely any noise. But what if the vocal cords were firmly closed, so that no air could escape? Take a deep breath and then hold it. Make sure you maintain lung pressure while you do this. Now let go. You should have been able to feel the vocal cords release as you let your breath go. The sensation is similar, but more forceful, when you cough.

In addition to these two states — fully open and firmly closed — the vocal cords can be loosely closed in a way which allows the air to be forced through. When this happens the cords vibrate and allow pulses of air to pass through. This vibration or buzz resonates in the oral cavities and is known as voice. Voice is an important constituent in many speech sounds. Try saying the word 'her'. Do not whisper it — declaim it boldly and prolong the vowel sound. You should be able to hear the resonant vibration clearly. Compare the sound with the 'breathing on spectacles' sound you made earlier. That was made without voice; the vowel sound in 'her' is made with voice.

Consonants

By no means all speech sounds require vibration of the vocal cords. Many of the consonants of English form pairs of sounds which are distinguished only by the presence or absence of voice. Activity 2.1 deals with some of them. To do it, you will need to find a quiet corner where you can hum and make noises to yourself. Do not feel foolish when you do this — trying out the sounds for yourself is the only way of learning how they are made.

Activity 2.1

Below is a list containing ten different consonantal sounds. They all share one feature — they are *continuants*, i.e. you can indefinitely lengthen them or continue them until you run out of breath. These sounds are all illustrated on Band 1 of the cassette (see the cassette contents in Appendix 1). Do not refer to the cassette until completing this activity unless you get into difficulty.

1	rum	mmmm...	6	bus	sss...
2	buzzing	zzzz...	7	vision	zhzh...
3	rush	shsh...	8	buff	ffff...
4	love	vvvv...	9	this	thth...
5	run	nnnn...	10	thistle	thth...

(a) Go through the list, making sure you know which sounds are represented. Pronounce each sound in turn, both in the word given and then on its own, and prolong the sound for a second or two.

(b) Try singing each sound, i.e. try to produce a pitched note (it doesn't matter what note or whether it's steady) as if you were humming or buzzing. Again, it is important to do this boldly, not hesitantly. You should find that only some sounds can be sung like this. The others can't be sung without their turning into one of the sounds that can. Draw a line down the middle of a piece of paper. In the first column make a list of the sounds which can be sung; in the second column list the sounds which can't be sung.

(c) Lastly, mark against each sound in the second column which of the sounds in the first it turns into if you attempt to sing it.

What you have just done is identify some of the voiced and voiceless continuants of English. Since, in order to sing a note, the vocal cords must vibrate, those consonants which could be sung must be voiced ones. You should have the following sounds in your first column: *m*, *z*, *v*, *n*, *zh*, *th* (as in *this*). The remaining four sounds belong in the second column. Each of the four voiceless consonants has a voiced counterpart, i.e. there are voiced consonants which are formed in exactly the same way, except for the fact that they are uttered with the vocal cords vibrating. You should have found that the letters *th* can signify either a voiced sound (as in *th*is) or a voiceless one (as in *th*istle). Indeed, if there were no difference between these two sounds, we would not be able to distinguish between the words *thy* (which begins with a voiced consonant) and *thigh* (in which the initial consonant is voiceless) or between the verb *mouth* (voiced) and the noun *mouth* (voiceless). Although these are distinct sounds, the English alphabet does not distinguish between them. These two, then, should be one of the pairs you found. The other pairs are *v* and *f*, *z* and *s* and *zh* and *sh*.

MANNER OF ARTICULATION

What, then, distinguishes each pair of these sounds from other pairs? The answer lies in what you do to the airstream after it has passed through the vocal cords, but before it finally escapes from the mouth. There are a number of ways of interfering with the airstream and thus affecting the quality of the sound, but most involve manipulating the tongue. Of all the organs of speech, the tongue is the most flexible. This, no doubt, is why the word 'tongue' is used figuratively in many languages for language itself. Indeed, our own word 'language' derives from the Latin word for tongue, *lingua*. Besides using the tongue, we can do more limited things by moving the lips, the lower jaw and some of the soft parts at the back of the mouth.

Make the *f* sound again. Notice what happens to your lips as you make this sound. The lower lip touches the upper teeth and air is forced through the constriction, creating friction (Figure 2.2). Exactly the same happens when you utter the voiced counterpart *v*, except that now the vocal cords are vibrating in addition.

Make the *s* sound again. Feel what happens to your tongue. The air is forced between the tongue and the roof of the mouth (Figure 2.3). The

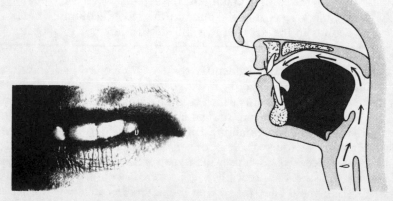

Figure 2.2.   Articulation of [f]

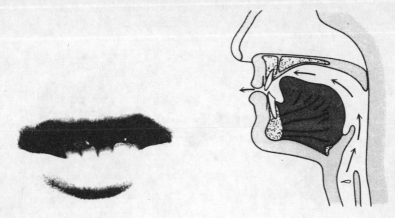

Figure 2.3. Articulation of [s]

action is happening out of sight now, but the principle involved in making the sound is similar. Both these sounds, *f* and *s*, are called *fricatives*, because of the way the airstream is forced through a constriction.

It is also possible to make a sound by blocking the airstream completely and then letting it go. Make a *p* sound. Notice what happens to your lips. Here, both lips start by being firmly pressed together, preventing any escape of air (Figure 2.4). If there is a complete blockage like this, there can be no sound, of course. The sound comes when the lips are opened again and the sudden release of the airstream causes a small explosion of air.

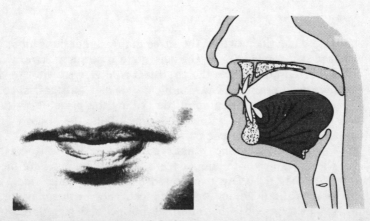

Figure 2.4. Articulation of [p]

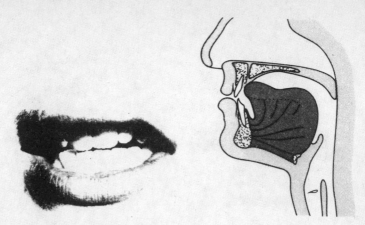

Figure 2.5.   Articulation of [t]

Make a *t* sound. Feel what happens to your tongue. Again, a complete blockage is formed, but out of sight in the mouth (Figure 2.5). When the blockage is released, a characteristic *t* sound is produced. Sounds like *p* and *t* which are made in this way are called *plosives*.

The *manner of articulation*, as it is technically called, is one of the important dimensions along which sounds are classified. Unlike voicing, which is largely a two-way distinction, manner of articulation is more variable. There are half a dozen or so different categories, but the categories of fricative and plosive are two of the most important.

PLACE OF ARTICULATION

We have now identified two of the three major dimensions along which consonants are classified. The third is quite a straightforward one. It describes where in the mouth the airstream is interfered with, regardless of whether the interference is a complete blockage or a partial constriction. The only difficult thing about describing the place of articulation is that it requires you to know something about the anatomy of the mouth and what the different parts are called.

The *f* sound and *v* sound which you made earlier were created by placing the lower lip on the upper teeth. This, then, is where the place of articulation is for these two sounds. They are called *labio-dental* sounds after the Latin names for lip and teeth. So, we now have the three elements which provide the minimal phonetic description of these sounds:

Sound	Voicing	Place of articulation	Manner of articulation
f	voiceless	labio-dental	fricative
v	voiced	labio-dental	fricative

The *p* sound was made by placing both lips together. This place of articulation is called *bilabial*. Although *p* is a voiceless sound, it too has a voiced counterpart. This is *b*. So we can give this pair of sounds their three-part description:

Sound	Voicing	Place of articulation	Manner of articulation
p	voiceless	bilabial	plosive
b	voiced	bilabial	plosive

THE PHONETIC ALBHABET

In an ideal world we would be able to represent each distinct sound with a separate letter of the alphabet. We have already seen, however, that the English alphabet is not ideal in this way. Two separate sounds were represented by *th*, for example, which is in any case two letters put together. We can get around this problem by devising a special alphabet, with special regular rules for its use, in which we reserve one letter for each sound. We can then avoid the confusion which is sometimes caused by the spelling system of English. Many such phonetic alphabets have been devised, but one of the most widely used today is the *International Phonetic Alphabet* (IPA). As far as possible, familiar letters are used and you will find this is true of many of the consonant symbols. But because there are far more sounds than there are letters, special symbols are also employed. The two sounds which th represents in English, for instance, are written as θ (voiceless) and ð (voiced). The first symbol comes from the Greek alphabet and is known as 'theta'; the second was once used in the English alphabet, but originated in Scandinavia, where it was called 'eth' pronounced as in l*eath*er. It is still used in modern Icelandic and in Faeroese writing.

The consonant symbols of IPA are usually laid out in a table which lists the place of articulation horizontally and the manner of articulation vertically. In each cell of this table, symbols are given for both voiceless and voiced sounds. Table 2.1 shows some of the IPA consonant symbols. By reference to the table you can work out which is the correct symbol for a particular sound or, conversely, what sound is represented by a particular symbol.

By convention, phonetic symbols are enclosed within square brackets [ ] to indicate that it is the sound of some utterance which is being described and that a phonetic alphabet and not the ordinary one is being

Table 2.1. Some IPA consonant symbols

	Bilabial		Labio-dental		Dental or interdental		Alveolar		Retroflex		Palato-alveolar		Palatal		Velar		Uvular		Labio-velar		Glottal
Manner of articulation / Place of articulation	voiceless	voiced	voiceless	voiced	voiceless	voiced	voiceless	voiced	voiceless	voiced	voiceless	voiced	voiceless	voiced	voiceless	voiced	voiceless	voiced	voiceless	voiced	voiceless
Nasal		m						n						ɲ		ŋ					
Plosive	p	b			t̪	d̪	t	d	ʈ	ɖ					k	g					ʔ
Fricative	ɸ	β	f	v	θ	ð	s	z	ʂ	ʐ	ʃ	ʒ			x	ɣ	χ	ʁ	ʍ		h
Approximant								ɹ		ɻ				j						w	
Lateral fricative							ɬ														
Lateral approximant								l													
Trill								r									ʀ	ʀ			
Tap or flap								ɾ		ɽ											

Note: affricates contain both a plosive and a fricative element and can be written as digraphs, e.g. ʤ ʧ.

used. If you know the value of the symbols, then you will be able to read off not just the word or words used in the original utterance, but also how the utterance was pronounced.

The next activity is intended to help you try out what you have learned so far. You will need to refer to the labelled diagram of the vocal tract (Figure 2.1) and to the table of IPA consonant symbols (Table 2.1).

Activity 2.2

Figure 2.6 shows a cross-section of the vocal tract. It differs from Figure 2.1 in that the soft palate (or velum) is raised so that the nasal cavity is sealed off. This position is the usual position for sounds which are not *nasal*. (Nasal sounds are those in which the air in the nasal cavities is allowed to resonate with air in the oral cavities.) The sounds referred to

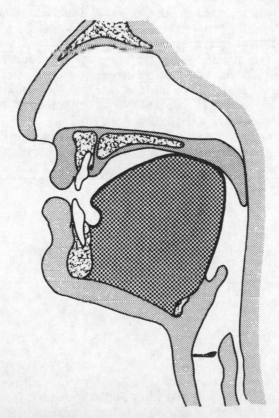

Figure 2.6   Tongue position for a consonant

in this activity are all illustrated on Band 2 of the cassette (see the cassette contents in Appendix 1). Do not refer to the cassette until you have completed this activity, unless you get into difficulty.

Work through the following questions.

(a)   State whether the sound is voiced or voiceless. (Note: The vocal cords are not shown as vibrating.)

(b)   Where does the tongue make contact with the roof of the mouth? Refer back to Figure 2.1 if you are not sure what the part is called and look across the top of the IPA chart for the place of articulation term which seems appropriate. (This term will be the adjectival form of the noun shown on Figure 2.1.)

(c)   If the tongue created a complete blockage in the airstream at this point and then released it, what manner of articulation would this be? Look down the left-hand side of the IPA chart and select the appropriate term.

(d)   You should now have the necessary three-part description of the sound. Look at the IPA chart and decide which symbol is appropriate for this sound.

(e)   In (a) you recorded whether or not the sound was voiced. What sound would result if the opposite had been true? Use the appropriate symbol.

(f)   What if the tongue did not create a complete closure at this point, but, instead, air were forced between the tongue and the roof of the mouth? Give the manner of articulation that would result.

(g)   Look at the IPA chart again. What symbol would now be used for this sound if it were (i) voiced, (ii) voiceless?

(h)   Try making these sounds. Are they normally used in English?

The answers to this activity can be found in Appendix 2.

Activity 2.3

Listen now to the section on consonant sounds on Band 3 of the cassette.

Vowels

In this section we consider how vowel sounds are made, how they can be described and classified, and what symbols are used for them in the IPA alphabet. Most of the section consists of activities. Work through these carefully.

Activity 2.4

When doctors or dentists want to examine your mouth, they ask you to say 'aahh'. Why should he choose that vowel sound? Why, for example, do they never ask you to say 'eee' instead?

(a) Figure 2.7 shows the tongue position for four vowels. First find the tongue position marked [ɑ] (this is the IPA symbol for the sound dentists ask for, as in English Received Pronunciation (RP) *part* [pɑːt] and [i] (this is the IPA symbol for the 'eee' sound, rather like that in RP *peat* [piːt]). Compare the position of the two tongues carefully. Answer the following questions.

    (i)   Is the tongue generally higher in the mouth for [ɑ] or [i]? State which is higher.

    (ii)   Mark the highest point of the tongue on each of the two diagrams with a cross. Is the highest point of the tongue nearer the front or nearer the back of the mouth? For which sound is the tongue highest nearest the front?

    (iii)   Try saying each of these two sounds [ɑ] and [i] to yourself. Does your tongue feel to be in the position shown for these vowels?

(b) Now find the tongue positions marked [a] (as in *pat* — particularly the northern British English pronunciation [pat]) and [u] (as in *boot* [buːt]). Again compare the position of the tongues and answer the following questions:

    (i)   Is the tongue generally higher in the mouth for [a] or for [u]? State which is higher.

    (ii)   Mark the highest point of each tongue with a cross. Is the highest point of the tongue nearer the front or nearer the back of the mouth? For which sound is the tongue highest near the front?

    (iii)   Try saying each of these two sounds [a] and [u] to yourself. Does your tongue feel to be in the position shown for these vowels?

(c) You should now have four crosses marked on the diagrams. The last diagram shows a vocal tract without a tongue. Mark the position of each of the four crosses on this last figure. Identify each cross with its appropriate IPA symbol. Draw a line from one point to another, forming a rough rectangle. This shows the outermost limits of the space swept by the highest point of the tongue during the articulation of vowel sounds. At no point is the airstream completely constricted, but the available space is modified and this gives a characteristic resonance to each of the vowels.

(d) The four vowels given do not, of course, exhaust the possible number of distinct vowel sounds. Others are made by putting the

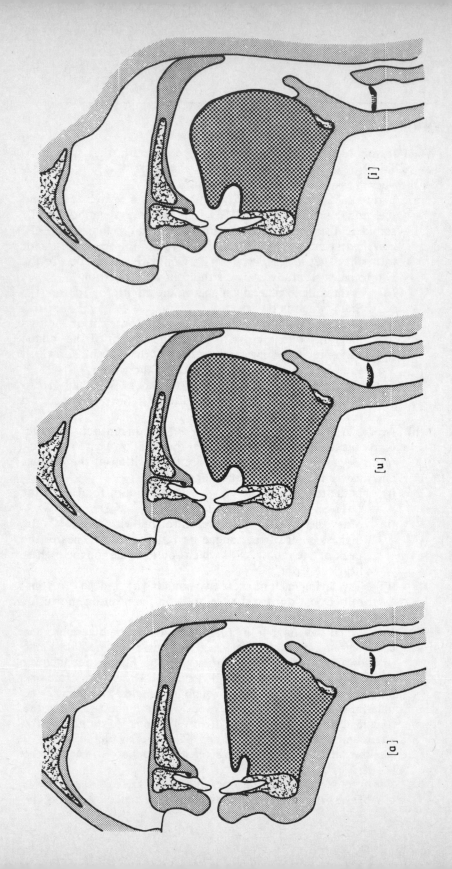

[i]

[u]

[a]

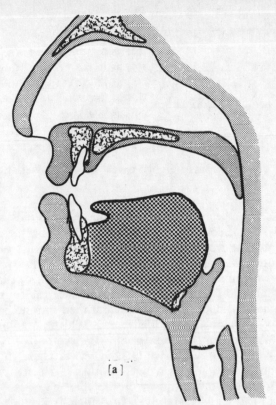

[a]

Figure 2.7. Tongue position for four vowels

tongue in intermediate positions. We can describe these positions by stating where the highest part of the tongue falls on a 'high–low' and 'front–back' dimension. These positions are commonly plotted on a diagram resembling the shape you arrived at by marking the location of the tongues. Thus, the vowel [e] (heard in northern British English pronunciations of *date* [det]) is a front vowel like [i] but is a little lower. [ɛ] (the sound in *pet* [pɛt] — particularly northern British English pronunciations) is likewise a front vowel, but is distinguished from [i] and [e] by being lower still, but not quite as low as [a]. A similar range of tongue heights separates the back vowels. Thus many of the vowels of English can be represented on a standard *vowel chart*. The four degrees of tongue height are often described as being on a *close* (or *high*) to *open* (or *low*) dimension, the two mid-way points being *half-close* and *half-open*. For example, [i] is a close vowel and [a] is an open vowel (see Figure 2.8).

(e)   The position of the tongue does not tell us everything we need to know about the quality of a vowel, however. Just as we needed

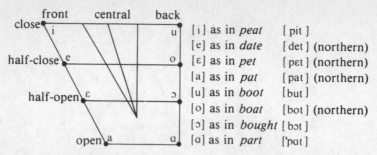

Figure 2.8. The position of eight vowels on the vowel chart

at least a three-way description of consonant sounds, so we do for vowels. What could such a third dimension be?

(i)   Say the words *keep* [kip] and *coop* [kup] one after the other. Observe what happens to your lips as you make the two sounds. Use a mirror, if this helps, or place a finger lightly on your lips as you pronounce the sounds. One of these is made with the lips bunched up and rounded; the other made with the lips spread. Which is a rounded vowel? Write down the appropriate IPA symbol.

(ii) Work your way around the vowel chart in Figure 2.8 pronouncing each vowel in turn. Which are the other rounded vowels shown on the chart?

The answers to this activity are given in Appendix 2.

CENTRAL AND PERIPHERAL VOWELS

Vowel sounds are classified according to tongue height and where the tongue comes closest to the roof of the mouth. In addition, the degree of lip rounding affects the quality of the vowel. In principle, it is possible to produce an infinite variety of vowel sounds, each subtly differing from one another according to tongue height, where they fall on the front–back dimension, and lip rounding. Vowels which fall somewhere in between front and back vowels are known as *central* vowels. Central vowels often have a less distinct quality than *peripheral* vowels, but one central vowel [ə], sometimes known as *schwa*, is one of the commonest English vowels, occurring frequently in unstressed syllables, as in *about* [əbaut].

CARDINAL VOWELS

Since vowel sounds are infinitely variable, both in principle and practice, it may take a great deal of ear-training before some can be reliably

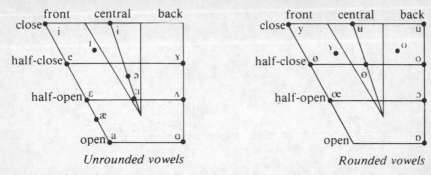

Figure 2.9. IPA symbols for unrounded and rounded vowels on the vowel chart.

differentiated. One technique used by phoneticians to describe subtle differences in tongue position is to compare the sound they wish to describe with a set of 'reference' vowels which they have been trained to remember. These *cardinal vowels*, as they are called, are situated at well-spaced intervals around the vowel chart. Thus cardinal [i] represents the highest front vowel and [a] the lowest. The continuum from [i] to [a] is then divided into equal auditory intervals by [e] and [ɛ]. Similarly, cardinals [u], [o], [ɔ] and [ɑ] are chosen on the high-low continuum for back vowels. By agreeing on the quality of these eight vowels (more or less the ones used in Activity 2.4), phoneticians can say, for example, when they meet with a particular vowel in someone's speech, that 'it is slightly lower than cardinal [e]' or that 'it is halfway between [ɛ] and [a]'.

DIPHTHONGS

All the vowels so far described are single or 'pure' vowels. You will have noticed though, that in many instances we have had to specify 'northern British English' pronunciation when giving examples. This is because many vowels in English, and especially in southern English, are not pure, but begin with one quality and move towards another. Such 'double' vowels are known as *diphthongs*. The RP pronunciation of *date*, for instance, begins at a point somewhere between cardinal [e] and [ɛ], but ends with a vowel slightly higher and more central. We can show diphthongs on the same kind of vowel chart as we use to show 'pure' vowels, albeit a little more clumsily, indicating where the starting and finishing points lie in relation to the cardinal vowels. RP *date*, which could be transcribed as [deɪt], is shown in Figure 2.10. All diphthongs can be described in terms of their initial and final vowel qualities, and thus do not require special symbols. You will be able to work out the values of diphthongs by referring to the same chart as used for 'pure' vowels (see Figure 2.9).

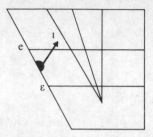

Figure 2.10.   The diphthong [eɪ] in RP *date*

VOWEL LENGTH

In the course of this section and the section on consonants we have discussed all the major dimensions by which the qualities of language sounds are described. Both vowels and consonants can vary in *quantity* as well as *quality*, however. Fortunately, although English consonants do vary in length, it is rarely necessary to describe this. Variation in the length of vowels in English is often more important, as we shall see, but it is rarely necessary to classify vowels more finely than into the two categories of long vowels and short vowels. A number of ways of symbolising long vowels exist, some of which may be familiar to you: a length-mark may be placed above a symbol, for example *ā*, or a letter may be doubled, for example *aa*. The method used by the IPA alphabet, however, will be adopted here. A mark ':' after a symbol indicates that the sound is long, for example [ɑ:].

Activity 2.5

Band 4 of the cassette contains an illustrated talk on English vowel sounds. Listen to this band now.

2.3   SEGMENTAL PHONOLOGY

We have now looked at the production of both consonants and vowels, but only as isolated sounds. Usually, of course, these sounds are pronounced in words or utterances, where one sound follows closely on the next. In such 'joined-up speech' there are many transitional effects as one sound merges into the next, and we find that many sounds are modified in systematic ways according to what other sounds surround them. This means that there is considerable variation in the articulation of what might have appeared as instances of the same sound — far more so than is apparent when we study sounds in isolation. But, as we shall show, underneath the complex patterns of phonetic variation lie much simpler functional patterns. In this section we shall discuss the respects in which continuous speech displays complex variation and the ways in which the simpler functional patterns can be discerned within this.

The composite nature of sounds

In connected speech there is a continuous movement of the vocal organs from one position to another, not an abrupt cut-off after one sound followed by a short silence as the muscles move to take up the position required to articulate another pure sound. If we examine the transition from one sound to another, we can find some rather strange sounds which are not normally regarded as occurring in English. For example, the voiced bilabial fricative [ß] does not normally occur in English, but, if we examine continuous speech very carefully, it is possible to find examples of this as a transitional sound. In pronouncing the word *obvious*, for instance, a speaker must make the transition from a voiced bilabial plosive [b] to a voiced labio-dental fricative [v]. As tension on the lips is relaxed, preparatory to making the fricative sound of [v] but before taking up the necessary lip position, a bilabial fricative sound occurs: [ɒbßviəs]. Try pronouncing *obvious* slowly and see if you can detect this happening in your own speech.

Transitional sounds of this kind appear frequently in everyday speech. Figure 2.11 is a profile diagram which shows the movement of the tongue and the action of the vocal cords during the articulation of the word *cleaned*. It shows that, as one would expect, the back of the tongue starts with a complete closure (i.e. a plosive position) but that before this velar plosive is released, the tip of the tongue rises to touch the alveolar ridge — time (a) — in anticipation of the [l] sound. Thus, when the plosive is released, the tongue is already positioned for [l] — the two articulations [k] and [l] overlap to some extent.

In spite of this state of readiness, what we might regard as a proper [l] is a voiced sound, yet there is a delay between releasing the voiceless plosive [k] and beginning the voicing for [l]. Thus, a voiceless variant of [l] occurs between times (b) and (c). But this is not all that is going on at this point. There is more to an isolated [l] than the fact that the tongue tip touches the alveolar ridge and the fact that it is voiced. [l] is said to be a lateral sound, which means simply that the sides of the tongue are not sealed against the upper teeth (as they are for the alveolar plosive [d], for instance) but instead allow air to escape. We can see from Figure 2.11, however, that in the pronunciation of *cleaned* the sides of the tongue, in moving from an airtight to an open position, create a brief intermediate 'leaky', or fricative, position between times: [kɬliːnd]. In this way, what we might regard as a proper [l] does not

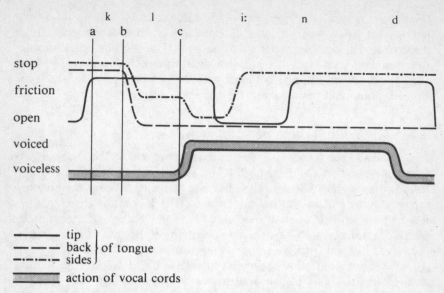

Figure 2.11. Transitional sounds in the pronounciation of *cleaned* (adapted from O'Connor, 1973).

begin until time (c) and it is preceded by a voiceless fricative sound not unlike that found in Welsh in words like *llyn* [ɬin] (lake).

We could go through the profile diagram (Figure 2.11) and find other transitional phenomena (such as the fact that [d] starts voiced, as expected, but finishes voiceless), but the point is probably sufficiently illustrated by looking at one example in detail. We have found that we cannot strictly think of sounds as discrete units joined together like beads on a necklace. They are non-unitary, both in the sense that the articulation of one sound may overlap with that of the next, so that we cannot easily define the boundaries of a sound, and in the sense that what we hear as a single sound may actually consist of several phonetically distinct sounds flowing one into another.

The influence of surrounding sounds

These two phenomena mean that a far greater variety of sounds occurs in ordinary speech than might at first be apparent. In particular, the overlapping of one sound with the next is a source of considerable variation. One of the consequences of the overlap between [k] and [1] in *cleaned*, for example, is that the [k] itself will be given a characteristic quality which is heard only in those [k] sounds which precede an [1]. We can see, in fact, that the [k] in *cleaned* is not exactly the same as the [k] in *keen* or *cow*. If we examined every sound which we heard in someone's speech and identified as a [k], we should find that a surprising variety of sounds was included.

The [k] in *cool* [kuːl] is different from that in *keel* [kiːl] in at least two respects. In [kuːl] the lips are already rounded in anticipation of the rounded vowel [uː] which follows, and the point of articulation of the [k] is further back in the mouth than for [kiːl], anticipating the fact that [uː] is a back vowel. What is happening is that the lips and tongue are preparing to make the vowel sound when the [k] is articulated, and so some of the features of the vowel are imposed on the preceding consonant. Try saying *cool* and *keel* to see if you can feel the difference between the two [k] sounds.

ASSIMILATION

So far, we have identified at least three phonetically distinct [k] sounds. The differences are, admittedly, subtle ones — too subtle, in fact, for us to distinguish them easily with symbols. For many purposes, as we will show, it is unnecessary to distinguish them. Indeed, it is notable that our problem has not been to try and persuade you that several easily distinguished sounds are really the same thing. On the contrary, we have had to take pains to demonstrate that what appeared to be the same sound was in reality a very variable phenomenon. For the moment, though, we want to concentrate on the fact that it is entirely predictable where each kind of [k] will be used. The predictability arises because of the way that the special qualities of each sound derive from its juxtaposition with certain other sounds in connected speech. But if we continued studying [k] sounds, we would soon find that we had by no means discovered all the possible variants. There would be many more which resulted from [k] sounds overlapping with other sounds and acquiring a characteristic colouration. This phenomenon of adjacent sounds becoming more like each other is called *assimilation*.

A certain degree of assimilation is more or less inevitable in connected speech, but it is not always possible to draw the line between what is unavoidable and what is not. An unmodified sequence of sounds might, in some cases, be physically possible, just a little awkward to produce, or there may be some alternative modification which might equally ease an awkward articulation. So, when we say that one [k] sound rather than another is predictable in a particular position, this is not the same as saying that it is inevitable. This is demonstrated by the fact that there are some modifications which occur predictably in one person's speech but do not occur in another's.

ASPIRATION

When [k] occurs at the beginning of a stressed syllable in RP and precedes a vowel (as in *kip* but not *skip*), it is usually followed by a puff of air as the plosive is released. This puff of air, called *aspiration*, does not occur when [k] appears in other positions in a word (for brevity's sake we will refer to these as non-initial positions). This is quite an interesting modification. In RP its occurrence is quite predictable — it only occurs when the [k] is initial — but it is not explained nearly so easily in articulatory terms as the modifications we have already looked at. Aspiration, then, is predictable but avoidable. Although characteristic of RP, it does not occur in many British regional varieties of British English (so you may have difficulty in detecting it in your own speech) and it does not apply to [g] in RP, even though this shares both place and manner of articulation with [k]. For RP speakers, then, this modification, at least, must be regarded as a characteristic part of their language, rather than a simple necessity of speech production.

Phonetic redundancy

This example shows that it would be wrong to think of these systematic modifications merely as lazy articulations. It is probably true that assimilatory phenomena are greater in casual than in precise formal speech, but even very precise speech contains many systematic modifications which are a proper and important part of the sound pattern of the language. They aid communicational efficiency, which may be one reason why they appear everywhere in natural language. By overlapping sounds and inserting additional systematic variation, we distribute the information required to identify sounds. Even if we fail to hear a segment of sound — perhaps because it was masked by noise — it may be possible to reconstruct the missing sound by listening to the clues in adjacent sounds. So, for example, that puff of air in RP gives us an additional clue that the preceding sound was voiceless and, indeed, in some instances this clue may be more important than the lack of vibration of the vocal cords itself. We know from experimental evidence that clues such as this are of great importance to listeners. *Phonetic redundancy* of this kind aids efficiency in communication.

Predictability

All these variants of [k] are, of course, phonetically very similar, and you may be tempted to think that we could classify them more easily as variants of a single sound unit on the basis of their phonetic similarity than on the predictable way in which they alternate with each other. Phonetic similarity is, however, by no means a reliable guide, as we shall see, and it is the predictable way in which these sounds are distributed in speech which is the important criterion in linguistic analysis. A very similar phenomenon occurs in written language, and it may be easier to grasp the argument if we use writing as an analogy.

Activity 2.6

As to a publick *Academy*, invefted with authority to afcertain the ufe of words, which is a project that fome perfons are very fanguine in their expectations from, I think it not only unfuitable to the genius of a *free nation*, but in itfelf ill calculated to reform and fix a language. We need make no doubt but that the beft forms of fpeech will, in time, eftablifh themfelves by their own fuperior excellence : and, in all controverfies, it is better to wait the decifions of *Time*, which are flow and fure, than to take thofe of *Synods*, which are often hafty and injudicious. A *manufacture* for which there is a great demand, and a *language* that many perfons have leifure to read and write, are both fure to be brought, in time, to all the perfection of which they are capable. As to the little varieties which the interpofition of an academy might prevent, they appear to me very far from having a difagreeable effect in the ftyle of different perfons writing upon different fubjects. What would *Academies* have contributed to the perfection of the *Greek* and *Latin* languages? Or who, in thofe free ftates, would have fubmitted to them ?

The propriety of introducing the *Englifh grammar* into *Englifh fchools*, cannot be difputed ; a competent knowledge of our own language being both ufeful and ornamental in every profeffion, and a critical knowledge of it abfolutely neceffary to all perfons of a liberal education. The little difficulty there is apprehended to be in the ftudy of it, is the chief reafon, I believe, why it hath been fo much neglected. The *Latin* tongue was fo complex a language that it made of neceffity (notwithftanding the *Greek* was the learned tongue at Rome) a confiderable branch of Roman fchool education : whereas ours, by being more fimple, is perhaps lefs generally underftood. And though the *Grammar-fchool* be on all accounts the moft proper place for learning it, how many Grammar-fchools have we, and of no fmall reputation, which are deftitute of all provifion for the regular teaching it ? All the fkill that our youth at fchool have in it, being acquired in an indirect manner ; *viz.* by the mere practice of ufing it in verbal tranflations.

Indeed it is not much above a century ago, that our native tongue feemed to be looked upon as below the notice of a claffical fcholar ; and men of learning made very little ufe of it, either in converfation or in writing : and even fince it hath been made the vehicle of knowledge of all kinds, it hath not found its way into the fchools appropriated to language, in proportion to its growing importance ; moft of my cotemporaries, I believe, being fenfible, that their knowledge of the grammar of their mother tongue hath been acquired by their own ftudy and obfervation, fince they have paffed the rudiments of the fchools.

Up to the close of the eighteenth century, many printed books used the 'old-fashioned' letter shapes 'ʃ' and 'f' for 's'. If you study texts printed at this time, you will find that not all 's's were printed in this way, though. Sometimes an ordinary 's' appears. In addition, a capital 'S' was used. In these books, then, four distinct letter shapes were employed, but their distribution in text was never random. Study the piece of text above (from Priestley, *The Rudiments of English Grammar*, 1761, pp. vii–ix, published in a facsimile edition by Scolar Press, Menston, 1969) and try to establish what rules the typesetter must have been following when he decided which symbol was appropriate in each case.

You should have found that the large capital 'S' was used in the same way as in present times. In fact, only one example appears in this piece of text, at the beginning of the word *Synods*. Capital 'S' was used at the beginning of sentences, and as the initial letter of proper names and other important words, particularly nouns. This latter use was much more frequent than is the case today. The other three letter shapes are used in a less obvious way. The 'ʃ' is only used in italicised words where it replaces the 'f''. The small 's' is used only at the end of a word. Hence 's' alternates with 'S' and 'f' according to the position of the letter in a word.

Here, then, we have an example of various letter shapes being used in predictable ways, rather as the various [k] sounds were used in speech. Handwriting is a closer analogy to speech than printing, however, in that there is greater variation in the shape of letters and in that handwriting is accomplished by means of a series of flowing muscular movements. It is not surprising, therefore, that we can find regularity in the distribution of handwritten letter shapes and see that the form of a letter is affected by the shape of adjacent letters. In the following example, for instance, four shapes are used for 's':

ʂ ʃ ʃ ʃ.

These different shapes are used in a systematic way, according to the preceding and following letters.

A surprise awaits you on the sands, for the shells which you sorted into heaps have all been scattered by the sea and smashed to bits.

The term *graph* is applied to any written or printed letter shape. We can summarise the analysis of the examples above by saying that certain graphs seem to alternate with other graphs in a predictable way. This means that we can consider a given set of graphs as being variable tokens of a single functional letter. This functional unit is called *grapheme*. In the example of printed text given in Activity 2.6 the graphs 'S' 's' 'ſ' 'ʃ' could be regarded as all representing an 's' grapheme. These variants are known as *allographs*. So 'S' 's' 'ſ' 'ʃ' are allographs of a single grapheme.

Phonemic analysis

Exactly the same is true of speech, except that in speech the tokens are known as *phones* rather than graphs. If we studied continuous speech for long enough, we could identify a vast number of phonetically different phones. But we could also work out how the distribution of these phones could be predicted in any one speaker's speech. This would enable us to identify how many significant sound units, or *phonemes*, were used by that speaker and what tokens, or *allophones*, were used to represent them.

So, we can say that in RP [k] and [kʰ] — the [ʰ] indicates that the [k] is aspirated — are allophones of a single /k/ phoneme. This will not surprise you, so familiar will you be with the fact that these sounds are functionally the same. But this functional equivalence is by no means inevitable. Just as a new printer might decide to use the 'ſ' symbol as an allographic variant of some other grapheme, for example 'f', so the way sounds are organised and assigned to functional units — phonemes — varies from language to language, or from dialect to dialect. For instance, in some languages the difference between aspirated and non-aspirated 'k' is most important. In Basque, Lappish and Hindi, for example, the two sounds [k] and [kʰ] are not variants of the same unit. If you substituted one sound for the other, you would not be heard to pronounce a word curiously, rather to utter a different word. *Kana* means 'one-eyed' in Hindi, but if you were an RP speaker and assumed you could aspirate the initial *k* with impunity, you would be mistaken. *Khana* means 'to eat'. So we can say not only that in RP [k] and [kʰ] are allophonic variants of a single /k/ phoneme, but that in Hindi they represent different phonemes.

Phonemic analysis is a useful way of reducing the very large number of sounds which actually occur in a language or are used by a speaker to a manageable set of items which are functionally distinct. We can test for the phonemic status of sounds in any language or dialect by looking for *minimal pairs* of words. A minimal pair is the term given to two words that are differentiated — 'kept apart' — solely by one sound, for example *gap* and *cap*, which differ only in the initial sound. Since the difference between [g] and [k] leads to a difference in word meaning, these two sounds must represent different phonemes. A number of minimal pairs can be found to establish the phonemic distinction between [g] and [k] in English, for example: *got* and *cot*; *bag* and *back*; *granny* and *cranny*. But we can find no minimal pair for [k] and [kʰ] in English: [kap] and [kʰap] would be heard as different pronunciations of the same word.

Phonemic transcriptions are distinguished from phonetic ones by the use of oblique strokes rather than square brackets: /kap/. This indicates that a transcription is not intended as a faithful indication of pronunciation, rather as an analysis showing the phonemic structure of an utterance.

It will be obvious that the ordinary alphabet in which we write English is partially phonemic. But English dialects contain more phonemes than there are letters in the alphabet. Those letters which we do have are not always used in a consistently phonemic way. Written English has developed a regularity and system of its own (as is discussed in section 5.3); the alphabet and the phoneme inventory make a different set of distinctions. Table 2.2 is the phoneme inventory for the speech of many RP speakers. You will see that it contains 44 phonemes — many more than the 26 letters of the alphabet.

A phonemic account is a structural one, i.e. it allows us to characterise the sound system of a dialect or language in terms of the internal system of contrasts and relationships between sounds without regard to the

Table 2.2. RP phoneme inventory

Consonants

/p/ poppy	/f/ fife	/h/ ha-ha
/b/ bible	/v/ verve	/m/ mimic
/t/ totter	/θ/ thigh	/n/ nine
/d/ dad	/ð/ they	/ŋ/ singing
/k/ kick	/s/ sea-sick	/l/ loyal
/g/ gag	/z/ zoos	/r/ rarer
/ʧ/ church	/ʃ/ shush	/j/ yo-yo
/ʤ/ judge	/ʒ/ azure	/w/ wayward

Vowels

/iː/ peat	/ʊ/ put	/ɪə/ pier
/ɪ/ pit	/uː/ pool	/eə/ pear
/e/ pet	/ɜː/ pearl	/ʊə/ poor
/a/ pat	/eɪ/ pail	/ə/ banana
/ʌ/ putt	/əʊ/ pole	
/ɑː/ part	/aɪ/ pile	
/ɒ/ pot	/aʊ/ foul	
/ɔː/ port	/ɔɪ/ foil	

phonetic quality of the sounds themselves. You may find it easier to grasp this idea if you think of this analogy. The British monetary system consists of units — such as pence and pounds — which are defined in relationship to each other, not in terms of their individual physical properties. Indeed, physical appearance, although not highly variable, is little more than a practical clue which helps us identify instances of the different units. A good example of this was the one pound note, which, for a while, co-existed with the new pound coin. Both represented the same functional unit, but it is clear that there was nothing in their physical shape which defined them as being of the same value. Rather, it was their common transactional value.

Phonology versus phonetics

Just as the value of a unit in a monetary system is defined in terms of its relationships with other units in that system and not by its physical appearance, so a phoneme is defined in terms of its contrast with other phonemes and not by its phonetic properties. The phoneme system is thus an abstract system, but this should not worry you. It is largely at this abstract level, as we have seen, that you are aware of your own language. Furthermore, the description of regularities in language is much simpler at this abstract level than at the superficial level of phonetics. This abstract level of description is called *phonology* and is regarded by most linguists as a branch of grammar. If phonetics is concerned with the physical properties of speech sounds, then phonology is concerned rather with the way these sounds are functionally organised and distributed in a particular language or dialect.

Phonemes are by no means the only units in phonological analysis. Although we have assumed that features such as voicing are entirely phonetic (to do with the fact that the vocal cords are vibrating or not), it appears on closer inspection that such features have a phonological rather than a phonetic status. The profile diagram for *cleaned* (see Figure 2.11), for example, showed that although we would regard /d/ as a voiced phoneme, it was partially unvoiced if pronounced at the end of a word. Might not such devoicing — which is a regular phenomenon — cause confusion between pairs of words such as *bead* and *beat*? Fortunately, other phenomena occur at the phonetic level which keep these words apart. We described above how aspiration in RP of the voiceless plosive /k/ helped to indicate that the sound was voiceless. Likewise we have another clue in words such as *bead* and *beat* which indicates the voicing of the last phoneme. The sound before a voiced phoneme is characteristically longer than that before a voiceless one. So, the length of the /iː/ in beat and bead may be more important to us in distinguishing the /d/ from the /t/ in these words than any vibration of the vocal cords. In this way we can see that the feature of 'voicing' is an abstract one — in actual speech it is signalled in a number of regular but complex ways.

Phonological rules

Although there are complex and regular patterns at the phonetic level, it is necessary to operate at a more abstract analytical level — that of phonology — before we can see clearly the structural and functional properties of sounds. It makes sense to describe the sounds in terms of straightforward phonological features — such as voiced, plosive, velar, etc. — and leave as a separate exercise the description of how such abstract features, or abstract units, are realised in actual speech.

One succinct way of making the link between phonological and phonetic levels is by devising 'rules'. Such phonological rules are no more than a description of the way different sounds are systematically distributed in speech. Another way of looking at rules is to think of them as characterising the knowledge that speakers must have about how phonemes are to be realized in speech. Take the aspiration of /k/ in RP, for example. We noticed that the /k/ in *skip* is not aspirated, but that the /k/ in *kip* is. After looking at many such words, we can formulate the rule as follows:

> Aspirate /k/ whenever it occurs in an initial position before a stressed vowel.

Since RP speakers must know this rule in the same way as they know the rules of English grammar, let us coin the term *sound-grammar*. We can now say that this rule is contained in the sound-grammar of RP.

The aspiration rule in RP does not just affect /k/ — it applies also to /p/ and /t/. Rather than make three different rules for the sound-grammar — one for each of these consonants — it would be much more succinct to capture this regularity in a single, more general rule. What we need is a means of describing the sounds /k/ /p/ /t/ as a single but exclusive group. This we can do by using the (phonological) features *plosive* and *voiceless*. We can state that the rule applies to all voiceless plosives in an initial position.

We can also describe in terms of a rule the modification of /k/ which depends on the quality of the following vowel. In fact, wherever there is systematic variation of this kind, we can devise a rule which captures the regularity. Such a rule will contain two parts:

(a) A description of what is to happen, for example:
    (i)   voiceless plosives are to be aspirated;
    (ii) velar plosives are to be rounded.
(b) A description of the context or conditions in which the rule is to be applied, for example:
    (i)   when the voiceless plosive occurs in an initial position;
    (ii) when the velar plosive precedes a rounded vowel.

Each rule should be as succinct as possible, yet as broad as possible in application. The art — and point — of devising rules is to make occurrences of apparently quite different things appear as instances of a single, more general phenomenon. Employing phonological features in a rule of this kind has allowed us to make a useful generalisation. It should, of course, be clear that rules such as these describe what we observe happens; they are far from being instructions from linguists to speakers about the 'correct' way to talk.

Activity 2.7

Now listen to the section on phonemes and allophonic variation on Band 5 of the cassette.

2.4 PROSODY

The term *prosody* is used to describe a variety of phenomena connected with the pitch, loudness and duration of speech sounds. All three features operate in a domain which is longer than individual phonemic segments. For this reason they are often also called *suprasegmental* features.

The description of prosody, despite the familiarity of the basic ingredients, is extremely complex and difficult. There is probably less agreement among linguists about prosody than in any other area of descriptive linguistics and, as Lieberman (1986, p. 239) put it: 'Although these aspects of speech [intonation, stress and general "melody" of speech] are among the first that develop in human infants, we still have much to learn concerning the biological bases, the development and the linguistic function of these aspects of human speech.'

On one thing, at least, however, there is some agreement. This is that the three features we have described above are not in themselves of great interest. In order to analyse how utterances are organised at a prosodic level, we have to appeal to a more abstract level of description, and in this respect, prosody is no different from other aspects of phonological description. Two phenomena are usually identified at this abstract level: *rhythm* and *intonation*.

Rhythm

THE DIFFERENCE BETWEEN SYLLABLE STRESS AND
SENTENCE FOCUS

A sense of rhythm in speech comes about from a regular pattern of *stressed* and *unstressed* syllables. The term *stress*, like those of pitch and loudness, is a familiar one, but there are various sources of possible confusion in the way the term is used in linguistic description. The word is used to describe two different phenomena. It is used to refer to the way individual syllables are heard to be more prominent than others, as in the phrase

(1) syllabic prominence /sɪ'labɪk 'prɒmənəns/

(The IPA marker of stress ['] is placed before the stressed syllable.) Here one syllable of each word is stressed compared with the others.

The term 'stress', however, is also sometimes used to refer to the way one part of an utterance is given emphasis or focus for contextual or semantic reasons:

(2) I bought potatoes

can be said with any one of the three words emphasised, and each version would be appropriate according to what question had been asked or implied:

(3) *I* bought potatoes (as opposed to *you* or *Jane*)
(4) I *bought* potatoes (as opposed to *stole* or *found*)
(5) I bought *potatoes* (as opposed to *carrots* or *asparagus*)

Since it is confusing to use the same term for these rather different phenomena, we will refer to this kind of sentence emphasis as *sentence focus* and reserve the term 'stress' for syllable prominence. Sentence focus will be discussed below in the section on intonation.

There are two interesting problems attached to stress phenomena. The first is the phonetic problem of what stress consists of, and hence how it might be recognised. The second is what determines which syllables in an utterance get stressed.

THE PHONETIC NATURE OF STRESS

It might be thought that a stressed syllable is simply one which is louder than others, but in fact variation in intensity has been found to be only one, and perhaps a not important, aspect of stress. The intuition that stressed syllables arc articulated more forcefully is probably correct, but higher pitch and longer duration seem to be more important indicators of this forcefulness (to listeners) than increased intensity (see Fry, 1955 and 1958, for reports of the classic experiments on listeners' perceptions of stress).

These features of pitch, duration and intensity combine to mark stressed syllables. In addition, unstressed syllables in English may be marked. Unstressed vowels may be reduced in quality to schwa [ə] or may be centralised in quality. Thus an alternation of vowel qualities may be associated with an alternation in stress and help support the perceived sense of rhythm.

ALLOCATION OF STRESS

Lexical stress   Some languages have a strict system of fixed stress on a particular syllable of every word. Polish, for example, stresses the penultimate syllable of every word, whilst Czech places the stress on the first syllable. English is, by comparison, a language with free stress. A speaker of English cannot predict easily which syllable of a word should be stressed — it must be learned and must be given as part of the pronunciation details in dictionaries.

Free stress means that occasionally it is possible for two different words to contrast only in stress. (e.g., *billow* /'bɪləʊ/ and *below* /bə'ləʊ/), and such contrasts are quite frequent with noun-verb pairs ('*contrast* and *cont'rast*). Some longer or compound words may have more than one stressed syllable ('*civilis'ation*, '*co-oper'ation*).

Although the allocation of stress in simple words seems unsystematic, when words are given affixes (see section 3.4 for a fuller discussion of word division) or are put together to form compound words, certain regular patterns do emerge.

Stress in connected utterances   When words are strung together in connected speech, the resulting stress pattern is not, as might be supposed, a simple stringing together of the stress pattern of individual words. There are at least two phenomena which need to be explained. First, it seems to be the case that some words in an utterance get more stress than others and in a way which cannot be explained by sentence focus. In the phrase *white elephants*, the word *white* seems more lightly stressed than the stressed syllable in *elephants*. There are, therefore, differences in degree of stress which need explaining. Second, expected stress patterns seem to rearrange themselves on occasion. A well-known example is the word *thirteen*, where the stress migrates to the first syllable from the last in phrases such as *thirteen men*. Phonologists have directed much effort to describing the patterns of such shifting.

It might be thought that all such variation in stress patterns takes place for reasons of ease of articulation. Since word stress may fall on any syllable, it is often the case that two stressed syllables may occur one after the other, and such sequences seem more difficult to articulate fluently. This can be experienced by comparing a sentence with monosyllabic words (excluding words like *of* or *the* which are usually unstressed) with one which contains a mixture of stressed and unstressed syllables.

(6)   No cat caught mice
(7)   A second animal was caught

There is indeed a difference between the sentences, but it is difficult to say whether or not it is a matter of ease of articulation. There is, however, a sense of impeded progress when one tries to utter the first sentence, as if each syllable refuses to be hurried. In the second sentence, the intervention of unstressed syllables seems to allow a more satisfying rhythm. This, of course, is a highly subjective way of looking at things. The very existence of sentences which consist of stressed monosyllables demonstrates that they can be articulated and hence that 'ease of articulation' is not sufficient explanation for stress patterns.

It is noticeable that English speakers tend to impose a fairly regular rhythm on their speech. English has been called a *stress-timed* language, in that the timing from one stressed syllable to another is roughly equivalent, regardless of how many unstressed syllables may intervene. French, by contrast, is *syllable timed*, in that roughly equal time is given to each syllable.

(8)   No cat caught a mouse
(9)   No cat caught any mice

In (8) there is an extra unstressed syllable between *caught* and the next stressed syllable as compared to (6) but the duration of the articulation of *caught* is reduced. The result is that roughly the same amount of time elapses between the two stressed syllables (*caught/mice* and *caught/mouse*) in each case, despite the existence of an extra syllable. In (9) yet another syllable is introduced, and the duration of *caught* seems to reduce again.

Such a principle is known as *isochrony* and demonstrates that there are language-specific rhythmic patterns, but it is still insufficient to explain why some syllables are stressed and others unstressed.

Many linguists have observed that stress assignment is closely related to the syntactic structure of a sentence. Probably the best developed theory of this kind is the *metrical theory* proposed by Liberman and Prince (1977). They note that relative syllable prominence tends to be assigned one way in compound words and another way in phrases. To see this, we have to imagine we are in a situation which is not yet confused by the addition of sentence focus (which might alter the neutral rhythm to give special emphasis or meaning). Take the pair of words 'white house'. This might be a phrase *white house* (which describes the colour of the house) or it might be a compound noun *White House* (the building in Washington, USA). The stress is different in the two cases. In the phrase, it is the right-hand word which seems to be more prominent, in the compound it is the left-hand one. This can be represented diagramatically:

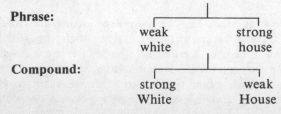

Phrase:

weak   strong
white   house

Compound:

strong   weak
White   House

These relationships of relative prominence hold true even when each pair (a constituent) is embedded into a larger structure. A phrase such as *White House Official* has a syntactic structure which can be represented as follows:

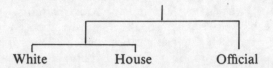

(for a more detailed discussion of syntactic structure and phrase diagrams see Chapter 3.)

We can use exactly the same simple rules to assign relative prominence between the higher-order constituents:

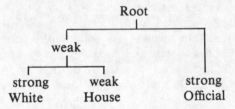

This suggests that the constituent 'official' will be relatively stronger than that of 'White House' whilst 'White' retains its prominence as compared to 'House'.

Such a process generates a pattern of relative prominences and allows us to predict which items are stressed and how. It also predicts, however, that there is a range of stress levels, some items being more highly stressed than others. The hierarchical range of stress strengths assigned to different items will reflect the way those items are embedded through strong and weak branches in the structure.

Liberman and Prince do not claim that syntactic structure is entirely sufficient to predict where stress will fall. The two rules described above, for example, assume that relative prominences assigned within a constituent will be retained, even if that constituent has been embedded in larger structures. Yet the example we started with of *thirteen men* indicates that this is not always true. Here the relative prominence assigned to the syllables in *thirteen* have changed as a result of embedding the word into the phrase.

Liberman and Prince suggested that the pattern of strong and weak items generated by the above rules may contain clashes of rhythm which require readjustment. Such clashes were not to be seen as an ease-of-articulation requirement since what exactly counts as a clash varies from language to language. Rather, certain kinds of scansion seem to be avoided in English. Liberman and Prince proposed a *metrical grid* as a device for readjusting rhythm so that it fits into an appropriate and permissable pattern. Whether something counts as a clash, however, may depend on the constituent structure of the sentence and not just the final outward rhythmic pattern. In this sense, it would be wrong to think of the grid arrangement as simply being a list of possible metric patterns, like those available to a poet writing in a particular metre.

Metrical theory describes the rhythm of a sentence in terms of a hierarchical pattern of stress levels, but it is important to realise that these levels — and indeed the notions of strong and weak — are abstract categories. The theory provides for an indefinite range of stress levels which are unlikely to be identifiable in an acoustic analysis. Nevertheless, metrical theorists claim that there is a psychological justification for positing so many differential levels of stress. We may perceive a more subtle gradation in stress levels than acoustic cues warrant since we are, they claim, aware of the abstract syntactic structure and hence abstract metrical structure of the utterance.

Intonation

People do not usually talk in a complete monotone. Indeed, monotonous speech is not only difficult to listen to, but also difficult to understand. Speakers give many clues to the syntactic structure of their utterances, as well as to how what they say is to be taken, by altering the pitch of their voice. What is important, though, is not the absolute level of pitch — the natural pitch range of different speakers varies greatly — but rather the relative changes in pitch. Hence, in RP we can pronounce a word such as *sure* with rising intonation and indicate that it is to be taken as a question:

sure

Or we can give it a falling intonation and imply, perhaps, a reassuring reply to a question:

sure

INTONATIONAL GROUPS

In longer utterances, intonation patterns work with stress patterns to organise the delivery and meaning of utterances. Rhythm, for example, helps divide utterances into separate intonational groups. We can distinguish *I don't know* from *I don't, no* by giving separate intonational groups to *I don't* and *no* and showing the unity of structure by a single intonational group for *I don't know*.

The length of intonational groups is generally restricted by the fact that they are usually said in one breath, so that they rarely exceed seven words or so. Here is a passage divided up into possible intonational groups:

[When I go to London] [I like to make a day of it] [and go to a museum] [John] [on the other hand] [likes to rush there and back as soon as possible]

The boundaries between groups usually come at points where there is a major break in grammatical structure, so that such groups often correspond with a clause (*When I go to London*), sometimes with the subject only (*John*), or the predicate only (*likes to rush there and back as soon as possible*), and sometimes with an adverbial phrase (*on the other hand*). (These syntactic descriptions are more fully explained in Chapter 3.)

The intonational group itself has been analysed in a number of ways. The pattern of pitch movement over the whole intonational group is often referred to as the *pitch contour*. An early British tradition, not entirely superseded in some American analyses, treated the whole contour as carrying a particular meaning. This approach, which may be termed an *intonational lexicon*, suggests that an intonation contour cannot profitably be broken up into smaller units. Instead, the whole prosodic envelope of the intonational group must be regarded as a single entity.

In most current analyses of intonation, however, a number of distinct subdivisions are recognised. An intonational group must consist of at least one syllable (which will necessarily be stressed) which will carry a major pitch movement. In longer utterances the last stressed syllable of the intonational group will carry the main pitch movement. This part of the pitch contour is known as the *nuclear tone* or simply the *nucleus*. Exactly which syllable is given this stress will depend on *sentence focus*, that is, the word which is picked out for special emphasis by the speaker.

The kinds of pitch movement which form the nuclear tone vary slightly from dialect to dialect. Different linguists also come to different conclusions about how many basic pitch movements exist. Ladd (1978) has identified four basic types in RP: a fall, a fall-rise, a high rise, and a low-rise.

All utterances must contain a nucleus, but there may be (and usually is) other material in the intonational group which precedes the nuclear tone. The stretch from the first stressed syllable up to (but not including) the last stressed syllable is known as the *head* and any preceding unstressed syllables form the *pre-head*. If there are any syllables after the nucleus, then these are known as the *tail*. The following utterance, for example, has a tripartite structure:

pre-head	head	nucleus
I	'wanted to 'go to the	'zoo

This analysis assumes that the sentence focus, and hence the nuclear tone, falls on *zoo*. If the speaker placed the focus on *go* then the organisation would be as follows:

pre-head	head	nucleus	tail
I	'wanted to	'go	to the zoo

The pitch patterns in the head are regarded as acting independently of those in the nucleus. Furthermore, unlike the nucleus, the head may vary in length. The actual organisation of head and nucleus will depend not just on the syntax of the utterance, but crucially on where the speaker places the sentence focus. This in turn depends on a variety of contextual and semantic factors.

PARAGRAPHING

There are various intonation-like phenomena which occur over longer passages than the intonation group itself. We recognise syllable prominence and pitch movement by identifying deviations from the general pitch level of the utterance. The general pitch level may itself decline gradually over the length of an utterance. Some researchers have suggested that such effects are to be regarded as a part of intonation, in that the speaker plans their execution to help segment the utterance into various clausal groups. In support of this claim they have shown that although the general pattern is a decline in the level which pitch peaks reach throughout the utterance, there appears to be a mild resetting of the level on clause boundaries. The following tracing of a pitch contour shows the pattern:

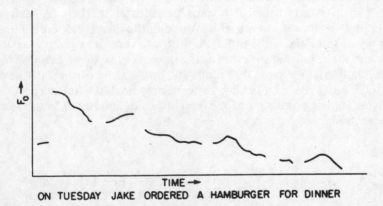

Figure 2.12.
Source: Cooper and Sorensen (1981).

Such patterns are referred to as *declination patterns*. There is, however, a certain controversy as to whether such patterns should be regarded as a part of the intonational system, or whether, indeed, they exist at all. Lieberman (1986) has argued that the declinations observed are merely reflections of breath control, and, while listeners must take them into account in some way when picking out local prominences and significant deviations from the baseline, the declination pattern itself does not carry intonational information. Umeda (1982) has queried whether declinations exist outside experiments in which long sentences are read aloud. Short spontaneous and conversational utterances do not seem to show declination behaviour at all.

Even if declination is still a controversial issue, there are other well-attested intonational effects which range over longer stretches of talk. If you listen to BBC newsreaders, for instance, you will hear that the intonation groups at the beginning of a new subject are relatively high, whereas by the end of a subject the overall height of the intonation group will be very much lower. With the introduction of a new topic, the overall pitch goes back to relatively high again. Such pitch movement is rather different from declination, since it regularly occurs over several sentences and breath groups. Furthermore, the ending of such passages is also prosodically marked, not just by a special lowering of pitch, but by a regular lengthening of segments and slower rhythm. It has been shown that listeners can tell whether brief tape-recorded clauses have been taken from the beginning or end of such paragraphs.

Transcription of prosody

There is no single transcription method for prosody which has widespread currency, though this is scarcely surprising in view of the disagreement about the basic phenomena themselves. The International Phonetic Alphabet provides a stress marker ['] and a half stress marker [ˌ], but offers no further help apart from length markers. A variety of notations for intonation are to be found in the literature, representing a variety of solutions to the problem of how to show how pitch movement fits with the segmental structure of the utterance (as shown in a phonemic transcription). Perhaps the simplest, but also most unsatisfactory, method has been adopted by conversation analysts (see section 7.3). Arrows showing direction of movement can be inserted into the textual transcription:

↓ ↑   Thatcher: I am however (0.2) very ↓fortunate
                  (0.4) in having (0.6) a ↑mar:vlous
                  dep↓uty

Source: Atkinson and Heritage (1984)

This is unsatisfactory from the point of view of an intonational analysis because it fails to distinguish between a generally high or low level of pitch and actual pitch movement. It fails also to cope with compound movement, such as fall-rise. It is useful, however, when no sophisticated analysis of intonation is intended, and only a general impression of pitch behaviour is needed.

A better method but much disliked by publishers, involves the physical rearrangement of words on the line:

                    that
        What does
                have to do with it?

Source: Bolinger (1985)

Another, less clumsy, method is to show the direction of pitch movement by means of lines and arrows above the words (as in our own examples above). This has the benefit of being immediately interpretable, but shares with Bolinger's method the disadvantage that the relationship between pitch movement and stress cannot be easily shown. This problem has been overcome elegantly by some British linguists, who use a system of blobs on an imaginary stave below the orthographic representation. A large blob shows stress:

‖ I *want* to be *absolutely sure* about it. ‖

Source: O'Connor and Arnold (1973)

This system is also used in a more refined version by Crystal (1969), who adds lines which show the precise relationship between pitch movement and location of stress:

the |ninety NÍNE [|point *l*NÎNE [per |cÈNT]]|

'no refe↑rendum of [↑ÂLL] "↑JÛDGES|

the ap↑PĒAL [ma|chinery in the cÕURTS]|

Source: Crystal (1969)

These by no means exhaust the variety of notations used, particularly in American writing, but it demonstrates the range of problems which all methods must face.

It must be admitted that transcription of intonation is a somewhat arcane skill. Newcomers will find it sometimes difficult to decide exactly where the main pitch movement is and where it is heading, and two different listeners are quite likely to disagree. This is partly a reflection of the complexity and speed of the phenomena, and the need for a keen and trained ear. It may also be in part, however, an indication that the analytical frameworks within which the various transcriptions are made do not entirely capture the kinds of thing which are salient to ordinary listeners.

Some researchers, particularly psychologists and some conversation analysts, prefer to work directly with analyses of pitch made by machines (as in Figure 2.12). This certainly lends a more objective appearance to analyses but it is notable that such researchers rarely invoke any well-developed intonational framework. Such tracings are not, in fact, sufficient and are often not helpful in making intonational analyses. Intonational analyses require such tracings to be mapped on to the actual syllables and patterns of stress in the utterance, for example. In addition, the use of instrumental tracings raises various new methodological and analytical questions. Since they contain various incidental perturbations, due to breath control and segmental articulation, and contain gaps due to voiceless segments, they require a theory (as yet even more poorly developed than intonational theories) which relates the abstract categories of nuclear movement to the actual phonetic characteristics of a pitch contour. For these reasons, linguists tend to be rather sceptical about the usefulness of instrumental tracings, as this typical comment from a recent research paper by Gussenhoven (1986, p. 77) shows:

The analysis was carried out by the author on an auditory basis. This was not out of a cavalier attitude towards instrumental registrations of periodicity, but because the recognition of nuclear tones on the basis of periodicity tracings is still beyond the power of man or machine.

The functions of prosody

The fact that the internal workings of intonation and rhythm have proved difficult to describe does not seem surprising when one considers the different functions they serve.

The first and foremost is a segmenting function. In written language we use punctuation, capital letters, paragraphing and other visual means of dividing language up into smaller units and showing significant structural boundaries. Prosody carries out this function in speech.

Prosody also serves several pragmatic functions. Sentence focus, in particular, is used to mark out the given (old) information from the new. Such marking depends on speakers' and listeners' knowledge of prior discourse or prior information and it can be used to signal what is to be regarded as mutual knowledge. Since the use of sentence focus implies certain presuppositions (these are discussed more fully in section 4.3), it can be used to communicate information indirectly. If someone says *I didn't do it*, this it carries a presupposition that someone else did do it and that there is agreement about the fact that an action was actually carried out. If Fred utters this as Aunt Edith comes into the room, but before she could be expected to have noticed anything wrong, it might be heard as an indirect way of telling her that her favourite vase has been broken.

Prosody, particularly intonation, can be used to establish the *illocutionary force* (see section 4.3 for a fuller discussion of speech acts) of an utterance, where this is not clear from the syntax. *Has John gone to London?* may be said as easily with a falling intonation as with a rising, questioning one. If word order does not show that this is a question, however, the fact can be shown by the use of a questioning intonation: *John's in London*?

Another function of prosody is the signalling of attitude. Exactly how this is done is not very clear, but the fact that it is done is familiar to us all. The area is one of greater interest to psychologists, perhaps, than to linguists. One issue has been the question of whether there is a set of intonational categories through which attitude can be conventionally signalled. A second issue is the way in which the intonational system for marking linguistic categories fits in with that of attitude.

Prosody plays yet another important function in conversational interaction. It helps speakers indicate that they are coming to the end of a turn, and is used to mark interruptions and other competitive situations. These *management* functions are described in section 6.3.

3 Sentence and word structure

3.1 INTRODUCTION

The great expansion of linguistics as a discipline in the 1960s and 1970s was associated with advances then being made in theories of grammar. The work of Noam Chomsky and others not only generated great excitement within linguistics, but also had considerable impact in other fields as diverse as psychology and architecture. Today, there is perhaps a more even balance in the prominence of major areas of linguistic research, but theories of grammar are still regarded by many as the essential basis for any theory of language.

In view of the revolutionary nature of the new approaches to the analysis of sentence structure, it may seem surprising that they still incorporate many traditional and familiar concepts and categories. Nouns, subjects and phrases, to name just a few, still appear in modern accounts of grammar. At the level of rudimentary description, less has changed than might be supposed. In this chapter, we discuss some of the basic characteristics of sentence and word structure which any grammar, of whatever theoretical persuasion, must take into account. We also provide an introduction to an important descriptive framework for English — the grammar of Quirk *et al.* (1972) — which is supported by several comprehensive reference works.

3.2 NOTIONS OF GRAMMAR

Intuitive knowledge

The term *syntax* refers to the organisation of words into longer sequences. Speakers of a language know the principles that govern this organisation, though they may not necessarily be consciously aware of their linguistic knowledge. For example, we can judge whether the following sentences are grammatically acceptable or not:

(1) The broke her leg woman
(2) They heard to what was said

To decide that these are ungrammatical implies that we know what rules govern the order of words and what word combinations are allowed. Our familiarity with the rules also allows us to make judgements about the relationship between sentences. Compare:

(3) My brother drove the car into a wall
(4) The car was driven into a wall by my brother

Although the order of the words is different, we know that these sentences are related, and that the meaning is the same (though the emphasis is slightly different). In a similar way, we can judge whether the following sentences have the same grammatical organisation:

(5) The fireman phoned up the station
(6) The fireman rushed up the road

Although they look similar, if we think about it we intuitively know that the syntactic organisation is different. For (5) we can say

(7) The fireman phoned the station up

but we cannot say

*(8) The fireman rushed the road up (*Note*: the asterisk denotes an anomalous example)

Up in (5) 'belongs' with the verb *phoned*, but can nevertheless be moved to come after *the station*, but *up* in (6) 'belongs' with *the road* and cannot be moved. As a final example of our syntactic knowledge, we can recognise that

(9) The chicken is ready to eat

can mean either

(10) The chicken is about to eat

or

(11) The chicken is about to be eaten

In the first sense, the chicken is the subject of the verb *eat* (it is the chicken that will do the eating) whereas in the second sense the chicken is the object of the verb *eat* (someone will eat the chicken).

The linguistic knowledge that we have about our language is often termed our *linguistic competence*. The 'rules' mentioned above are part of this competence and are constantly being applied in daily life whenever we read or listen to speech. They are abstract rules that govern the organisation of words into sentences, and the organisation of

sentences into longer stretches of discourse. We do not need to be consciously aware of the rules in order to use our language, but we can
become aware of them by analysing our own language and the language
of others. Syntactic analysis tries to formalise the rules that are part of
a native speaker's linguistic competence, (see also section 1.4 for a
discussion of problems associated with the use of speaker intuitions.)

Descriptive grammar versus prescriptive grammar

The descriptive rules of a syntactic analysis are quite different from the
prescriptive rules that are set out in traditional grammar books. These
prescriptive rules attempt to prescribe what individual grammarians consider to be good usage. There is sometimes disagreement between
traditional grammarians about which features of language are good
usage and which are not. An example of a prescriptive rule is the statement that sentences should not end with a preposition, such as *to*: many
traditional grammars tell us that we should say, for instance, *to which
shop are you going*? rather than *which shop are you going to*? Modern
syntactic analysis does not prescribe how people should speak. Instead,
it attempts to describe how people actually do speak. This enables us to
discover a great deal about the organising principles of syntax.

Frameworks of analysis

There are several different frameworks used by linguists to analyse
syntactic structure. Since the knowledge that people have about their
language is very complex, it is difficult to devise a single framework that
can satisfactorily account for everything that they know. Different
frameworks tend to vary in the relative prominence that they give to the
different aspects of our linguistic competence. Some of the frameworks
that are most widely used have been developed as part of a theory of
language in general, rather than simply as a framework for analysing
syntax. Their approaches to the analysis of syntax, therefore, reflect their
overall orientation to the study of language. *Transformational-
generative grammar*, for example, which is best known, perhaps,
through the work of Chomsky, aims not only to describe and to explain
language structure, but also to investigate the nature of the mind.
Systemic grammar, on the other hand, focuses more on the social aspect
of language, aiming to account for the various linguistic choices that are
available to us in different social situations (such as, to give a simple
example, the use of the word *nick* rather than *steal*). Within these broad
general approaches, different frameworks have been developed that give
more prominence to one aspect of syntactic structure than to others.
Case grammar, for example, is a type of generative grammar that em-

phasises the functions of the units of syntax, such as the two alternative functions of *chicken* in example (9) above. Case grammar would label *chicken* in sentence (10) as the 'agentive' case and *chicken* in sentence (11) as the 'objective' case. Some suggestions for further reading on these different approaches to the analysis of syntax are given at the end of this book.

Grammar and grammars

When the word 'grammar' is used in phrases such as 'case grammar' or 'systemic grammar' it has a broad sense, referring to a theory of language. It is also commonly used in a more restricted sense, to refer to syntactic structure (it is used in this way in the title of this section) or to descriptions of the syntactic structure of a particular language. Sometimes these descriptions use the framework that has been developed as part of a theory of language, so that we may have, for example, a transformational grammar of English. These descriptions differ considerably in the terminology that they use, which can naturally be very confusing at times. Despite this, however, and despite the different approaches that these frameworks may adopt for the analysis of syntax, there are some general features of syntactic structure that all analytical frameworks take into account, whatever their preferred emphasis. We will discuss some of these general features in the next section, before giving an outline of a particular framework that can be used for the analysis of English sentence structure. We have chosen to outline the framework of analysis that was used by Quirk *et al*. (1972) and subsequently developed by Crystal *et al*. (1976). Their framework of analysis draws on the insights of several different schools of linguistics and is not tied to one particular theory of language. In what follows we will therefore use their terminology.

3.3   SENTENCE STRUCTURE

Word order

We can see the importance of word order in the syntactic structure of a language by comparing different languages. In English, it is usual for adjectives to come before their noun. English word order therefore requires *the round table* and not *the table round*. In French, on the other hand, adjectives often follow their nouns. It would be usual in French to say *la table ronde* rather than *la ronde table*. Similarly, in English it is usual for the subject to come before the verb in a simple declarative sentence, such as *my cat loves fish*. This is not necessarily the case for other languages: in Classical Arabic, for example, the subject usually comes after the verb.

Word classes

Word classes can be thought of as the units of syntax. We will discuss word classes in some detail, since they illustrate clearly some of the important differences between the modern linguistic approach to syntactic analysis, and traditional grammar.

If you have studied traditional grammar at school, you will probably be familiar with terms like noun, verb, adjective and adverb. You may have known them as 'parts of speech'. In traditional grammar these were defined in 'notional' terms, such as:

noun: name of a person, place or thing
verb: doing word

or in functional terms, such as:

adjective: qualifies a noun
adverb: modifies a verb

There are many problems with these definitions, however. For example, it is not at all clear what the verb *feel* is 'doing' in *I feel hot*: and *gold* in *a gold watch* is surely a 'thing' in the same way that *gold* in *gold is expensive* is a 'thing', although the first *gold* would be labelled an adjective rather than a noun.

A more scientific approach is to set up word classes in a language in terms of what are called the *syntagmatic* and *paradigmatic* relations that words have with each other in sentences. A *syntagm* is a sequential pattern which reflects the restrictions on word order in a language, created by syntax. A *paradigm* is the set of alternative words which could be used equally legitimately in a particular position in the syntagm. Words can be regarded as belonging to the same word class if they may occur at the same point in a specific sequence.

```
              p
              a
              r
s y n t a g m a t i c          the    green   grass
              d
              i                the    fat     cat
              g
              m                the    slow    train
              a
              t
              i
              c
```

We can get a good idea of our unconscious knowledge of syntagmatic and paradigmatic relations by analysing nonsense poetry. For example, Edward Lear's nonsense is very much 'English' nonsense, since it conforms to English patterns of syntactic structure.

Activity 3.1

Using the traditional labels 'noun' and 'adjective', identify the words belonging to these two word classes (or 'parts of speech') in the Jabberwocky verse below. Then try to explain how you knew that the word belonged to that class.

'Twas brillig, and the slithy toves
   Did gyre and gimble in the wabe:
All mimsy were the borogoves,
   And the mome raths outgrabe.

We would expect you to identify the nouns and adjectives either like this:

nouns	adjectives
toves	brillig
wabe	slithy
borogoves	mimsy
raths	mome

or like this:

nouns	adjectives
toves	brillig
wabe	slithy
borogoves	mimsy
mome	

(In this second analysis *raths* is a verb and *outgrabe* an adverb.)

The -s on *toves*, *borogoves* and *raths* may have helped you to decide that these words were nouns (though the -s ending also functions as a present tense marker on third person verbs, which is how the alternative interpretation of the last line of the verse becomes possible). Similarly, you may have taken the -y ending on *slithy* and *mimsy* as an indication that these words were adjectives (though by no means all English adjectives end in -y). However, these clues would not have been enough on their own. In addition to your knowledge of English word structure, you must have drawn on your knowledge of the syntagmatic patterns of sequence and the paradigmatic relations of choice that are part of the syntactic structure of English — though you may not have explained it in these terms.

For example, all four of the nouns occur after the word *the* — though two of them (*toves* and *raths*, in the first analysis) have an adjective between *the* and the noun. In English the word *the* has to be followed by a noun: we can say *the wave*, *the cake*, *the crowd*, for example, but we cannot say *the has*, *the quickly* or *the to*. We can use this pattern of occurrence to identify a word class. One of the defining characteristics of a noun, then, is that it can occur after *the*. It is perfectly acceptable to insert another word between *the* and its noun, but again there are restrictions on the words that can occur. We can say:

the big white wave
the tidal wave

but not:

*the quickly wave
*the go wave
*the from wave

As speakers of English, then, we know that there is a syntagmatic sequence:

the   adjective(s)   noun

and since we are given the word *the* in the Jabberwocky verse we can use our knowledge to identify the word class of the nonsense words in the verse.

Paradigmatic relationships are equally important: if you labelled *toves*, *wabe*, *borogoves* and *raths* as nouns you did so because of your knowledge of other words that could have occurred in this pattern, that you already know as nouns, such as *house*, *wave*, *crowd* or *crumb*. Similarly, you will have labelled *brillig*, *slithy* and *mimsy* as adjectives because of your knowledge of other English words that you know as adjectives, and that could also occur in this position, such as *red*, *tall*, or *wonderful*.

Classifying words into parts of speech on the basis of their syntagmatic and paradigmatic relations uses *distributional criteria*. It is important to use distributional criteria to set up word classes, rather than trying to fit the language into pre-existing categories that may not necessarily be suitable.

Activity 3.2

The extract below is an example of the problems that occur when distributional criteria are not used to set up word classes. The extract is from a traditional grammar book designed for learners of English as a foreign language (Eckersley, C. E., *A Concise English Grammar for Foreign Students*, London, Longman, 1958).

THE ADJECTIVE

AN ADJECTIVE is a word that qualifies a noun; it adds to its meaning, but limits its application, e.g. the *new* book; the *black* sheep.

An adjective may be used (i) to qualify a noun, i.e. as an EPITHET as in the examples above, or (2) to form PART OF THE PREDICATE and say what the person or thing denoted by the subject is declared to be, e.g. The book is *new*; the sheep is *black*. It is then said to be used PREDICATIVELY.

Kinds of Adjectives

(1) ADJECTIVES OF QUALITY: which show WHAT KIND, e.g. a *brave* boy; a *German* student.

(2) ADJECTIVES OF QUANTITY: which tell *how many* or *how much*. These may be:

    (i) *Definite* e.g. one, two, etc.

    (ii) *Indefinite*, e.g. all, some, several, half, no.

(3) POSSESSIVE ADJECTIVES: which show possession, e.g. *my*, *her*, *its*, *our*, *their*, etc.

(4) DISTRIBUTIVE ADJECTIVES: which show that the persons or things denoted by the noun are taken singly or in separate lots, e.g. *each*, *every*, *either*, *neither*.

(5) INTERROGATIVE ADJECTIVES: which are used in questions, e.g. *Which* man did you see? *What* time is it?

(6) DEMONSTRATIVE ADJECTIVES: which point out, e.g. *this*, *that*, *these*, *those*, *a*, *an*, *the*.

The definition of an adjective that is given in the first two paragraphs works well for the words *new* and *black*, which are given as the examples, but does it work so well for the six different types of adjective that are listed in the rest of the extract?

Only the first type of adjective (adjectives of quality) can occur both attributively (i.e. before a noun, as an epithet) and predicatively (in the sequence *the + noun + is + ——*). Types 2–6 all occur before a noun (for example, *one book*, *all books*, *my book*, *each book*, *which book*, *this book*) but they do not normally occur in the sequence *the book is ——*. We cannot say, for example, **the book is each*, or **the book is my*, and although it is conceivable that we may say, *the book is this* or *the book is which*? we would only do this if we wanted particularly to emphasise the word *this* or *which*.

Traditional grammarians classified these words as adjectives because they were using categories that described the syntax of Latin to try to describe the syntax of English. English and Latin, however, are very different in their syntactic structure. In Latin the equivalent words to most of the kinds of adjective listed in the extract agree with their noun in gender and in case; but this does not apply in English. Modern grammars of English have a separate word class for the 'adjectives' of types 2–6, which have similar patterns of distribution in English (though not necessarily in other languages). This word class is termed *determiner* in the Quirk *et al.* (1972) framework.

The need to let the language that we are analysing determine the word classes to be used can be seen very clearly when analysing children's language. For example, some typical sentences from two-year-old children are:

> Dadda run
> Mummy car
> Give doggy paper

Children of this age typically speak in utterances that contain two, three or four words. Their utterances are not organised according to the same syntactic principles as those ordering the words in an adult's utterance, and it would be pointless to try to use the same categories to analyse their speech. It is worth pointing out, too, that the words that belong to a particular word class may not necessarily be the same in all varieties of a language. Consider, for example, *pass me them books*. In standard English *them* occurs as a personal pronoun (for example, in the phrase *I know them*). In many non-standard regional varieties, particularly in the South of England, *them* also belongs to the class of determiners, together with words like *the*, *which* and *each*.

Like all human behaviour, language does not always fit neatly into clear-cut categories. Although it is very useful to set up word classes as part of a syntactic analysis, we often need to recognise that the categories that we use have 'fuzzy' edges. For example, using distributional criteria we could class the words *rich* and *poor* as adjectives, since they occur in sequences such as *the rich people* or *the poor people*. But we can also say *the rich should give to the poor*. Do these words now belong to the category of noun (in the same way that a word like *round* can be both an adjective — as in *the round table* — and a noun — as in *let's sing a round*)? Or are they still members of the 'adjective' category? We undoubtedly understand the sentence above as meaning *the rich people should give to the poor people*.

There is no right or wrong answer to questions like this. We set up word classes to help analyse syntactic structure, but they are not necessarily watertight categories. There is vagueness in syntax, just as there is vagueness in semantics (see section 4.2).

Word classes can be divided into *open classes* and *closed systems*. The words that belong to a closed system are relatively small in number and if we use one member of the system the rules of syntax usually prevent us from using another. An example of a closed system is the class of personal pronouns. We can say *my book* or *your book*, but we cannot say *my your book*.

The members of an open class, on the other hand, are usually very numerous. The class is open in the sense that new members are continually being added. For example, the verbs *breakdance* and *bodypop* are fairly recent additions to English. It is often possible to use two or more members of an open system together, or conjoined with *but*, as in the phrase *this is naughty but nice* (*naughty* and *nice* are both adjectives).

Nouns, verbs, adjectives and adverbs are examples of open classes; pronouns, prepositions, and conjunctions are examples of closed classes.

As with many distinctions that we try to make when we are analysing language, the distinction is not absolutely clear-cut, but it can be a useful one. For example, it suggests one reason why attempts to introduce a new third person 'sex-indefinite' pronoun have been unsuccessful: the pronoun system is a closed system, and it is more difficult to add to a closed system than to an open class.

Hierarchical structure

We have discussed word classes at some length, but this has taken account of only one level of syntactic organisation. Words are not simply strung together to form sentences; they combine to make up *phrases* which themselves combine to make up *clauses* within a sentence. Consider, for example, the paradigmatic choices that could be made in the sequence:

   ——   loves   sugar.

We could insert in the sequence a noun or a pronoun: *Maud* or *She*. But we could also insert a longer phrase, such as *My friend*, *The old man*, or *The old grey mare*. There are restrictions on the phrases that can occur at this point in the sentence, just as there are restrictions on the word classes that can occur within the phrase. We cannot insert, for example:

*By the old mill stream   loves   sugar
*Was going   loves   sugar

The level of analysis at which we group together words is called the *phrase level*. The level at which we group phrases together is the *clause level*. Clause level constructions are themselves constituents of the sentence. We can divide the sentence *the old grey mare loves sugar* into three clause-level constructions, using the syntagmatic relations of sequence and the paradigmatic relations of choice as a guide:

   the old grey mare   loves   sugar

Different choices can be made at each point in the sequence, as follows:

the old man	might love	it
my friend	may have loved	the sea
Maud	will see	the new baby
she	sells	seashells

The words *might*, *may*, *have* and *will* can be classified as members of a word class termed *auxiliary*, still using distributional criteria.

There are sentences that have only two clause-level constituents. Consider, for example, the following:

Pigs	snort
Birds	sing
The old man	snores

Different frameworks of analysis label the constructions differently, though they would all divide the sentence in the same places. For example, Quirk *et al.* (1972) would label the first construction of our example sentence *the old grey mare loves sugar* the *subject*, the second the *verb* and the third the *object*:

clause level	subject	verb	object
phrase level	det. adj. adj. noun	verb	noun
	the old grey mare	loves	sugar

The sentences given above that have only two constituents would contain a subject and a verb:

clause level	subject	verb
phrase level	det. adj. noun	verb
	the old man	snores

Activity 3.3

Divide the sentences below into their clause-level constituents (you need not try to name the constituents).

Example:	Aunt Mary loves green beans		
	Aunt Mary	loves	green beans

a) This bag of potatoes weighs twenty-eight pounds
b) All the nice girls love a sailor
c) Cats have been walking in the sandpit
d) The winner is the lady in the pink hat
e) This bad egg stinks

Using syntagmatic patterns of sequence and paradigmatic patterns of choice, the sentences can be divided as follows:

This bag of potatoes	weighs	twenty-eight pounds
All the nice girls	love	a sailor
Cats	have been walking	in the sandpit
The winner	is	the lady in the pink hat
This bad egg	stinks	

There are other frameworks of analysis that use instead the terms *noun phrase* (abbreviated to NP) and *verb phrase* (abbreviated to VP) where Quirk *et al* (1972) use the terms *subject* and *verb*.

noun phrase	verb phrase
the old man	snores
the old grey mare	loves sugar

The hierarchical structure of sentences such as these is sometimes represented diagrammatically, in a *phrase marker* or *tree diagram*. Such a diagram shows that a *verb phrase* can consist of a *verb* and a *noun phrase*:

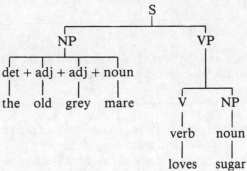

Sentence relations

It is part of our linguistic competence to know when sentences are related. We saw earlier, for example, that we intuitively know that the following sentences are related:

My brother drove the car into a wall
The car was driven into a wall by my brother

A somewhat different example is that of negative sentences. We intuitively know that the sentences:

I do not like cheese
I like cheese

are related and that the first sentence is a negative version of the second. A syntactic analysis has to make this relationship explicit. We can say, for example, that the first sentence is formed from the second by a rule which adds the auxiliary verb *do* and the negative word *not* between the subject and the verb. In other words, the structure of the negative sentence is:

subject + *do* + *not* + rest of sentence

As with all aspects of syntactic analysis, it is important to describe sentence relations in terms of the language material that we are analysing, rather than in terms of pre-existing ideas that we may have.

Activity 3.4

Consider these negative sentences used by a child aged between about 18 months to two years:

no wipe finger
not a teddy bear!
wear mitten no
no sit there
no the sun shining

(based on Klima and Bellugi, 1966, adapted from Clark and Clark, 1977). How would you describe the rule governing negation in these sentences?

The rule is clearly different from the one that we used to describe negation in adult sentences. The negative word can be *no* as well as *not* and it can be inserted either at the beginning of the sentence or (in one case) at the end, rather than between clause elements. The structure of the negative sentences can be described as:

$$\left.\begin{array}{l} no \\ not \end{array}\right\} + \text{sentence}$$

or

sentence + *no*

Creativity

There are some sentences that we use over and over again in our lives. Many people, for example, use these sentences fairly regularly:

It's a nice day today
How's your mother?
Where are my keys?
We're late

However, many of our sentences are sentences that we have never spoken before. We can produce an infinite number of new sentences, and we can understand sentences that we hear although we may never have heard them before. For example, as far as I am aware I have never spoken or written this sentence before, and I would think it unlikely that you have ever heard it:

This pink-eyed walrus does not enjoy king-size shrimps

Although you may never have come across this sentence before, it is very likely indeed that you can understand it. You can do so partly because you can draw on your knowledge of the syntactic structure of English. My sentence has the clause elements subject, verb and object that we identified earlier, and it conforms to the rule of sentence negation that we have already discussed. The rules that we set up to describe syntactic structure can account for the sentences that it is possible to say in a language, as well as those that have actually been said. Some grammatical frameworks (notably generative grammars) give particular prominence to this aspect of syntax.

3.4 THE QUIRK GRAMMAR

The Quirk *et al.* (1972) descriptive framework for English was based on the analysis of a large corpus of spoken and written English, and it has been used extensively in a modified form to analyse further samples of spoken and written English. It is very helpful to have a specific analytical framework as a starting point in any analysis, though as we have stressed in previous sections one needs to be careful not to try to fit data into a rigid framework that may not be suitable. We have chosen the Quirk grammar as a framework to use in analysing the hierarchical structure of English sentences since this is a method of analysis that has proved its practical usefulness, particularly in the *Language Analysis, Remediation and Screening Procedure* (LARSP) described in Crystal *et al.* (1976). However, we should bear in mind that the framework is based on standard English and that it may need to be modified somewhat if we want to analyse a non-standard variety.

The outline that follows is very brief. If you want to follow up the description provided here, you are recommended to refer to Quirk *et al.* (1972) and Crystal *et al.* (1976) for fuller details.

A framework for analysing English

The modified Quirk grammar uses the terms *sentence*, *clause* and *phrase* for the different levels in the syntactic hierarchy (see section 3.3). It is possible to analyse sentence structure at the level of the word also, as we will see in section 3.5.

SENTENCE STRUCTURE

As in most modern grammars, the sentence is taken as the largest unit of analysis. The sentences that we have considered so far have all been simple sentences, in that they consisted of only one clause. Sentences may also be complex: that is, consisting of more than one clause. The sentences:

Spring is in the air and the days are getting longer
I can feel that spring is in the air

are both complex sentences consisting of two clauses. The first sentence consists of two clauses co-ordinated by *and*. The second sentence also consists of two clauses, but here the second clause *spring is in the air* is subordinate to, or dependent on, the main clause *I can feel*: the clause *that spring is in the air* cannot occur on its own. The difference between the two types of complex sentence can be shown diagrammatically. In the first sentence, the two clauses are of equal status and each could occur on its own as an independent sentence:

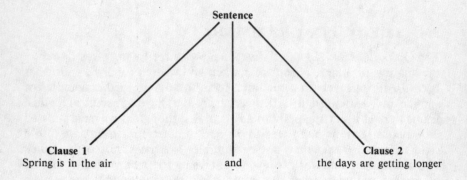

Clause 1   and   **Clause 2**
Spring is in the air   the days are getting longer

The clauses in the second sentence are not of equal status. Clause 1(a) is subordinate to Clause 1:

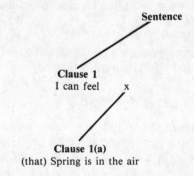

Clause 1(a)
(that) Spring is in the air

We can go on increasing the number of subordinate clauses almost indefinitely:

   I can feel that spring is in the air because the days are getting longer

and we can have complex sentences consisting of two or more co-ordinated clauses each of which contains one or more subordinate clauses such as 'because' clauses:

   I'm late because the car broke down and he's late because I'm late

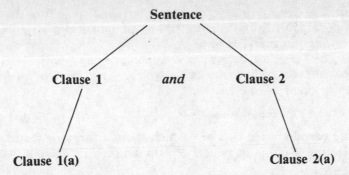

Subordination and *co-ordination* are often indicated by words which have the grammatical function of linking clauses: *subordinators* and *co-ordinators*.

Subordinators
I know *that* Spring is in the air
While you were out, the gasman called
Although still young, she produced a masterpiece
He will turn up *when* he feels like it

Co-ordinators
He needs money *but* he refuses to work
She ate no fat *and* he ate no lean *or* is it the other way round?

The indicators of co-ordination and subordination may be absent:

Always willing to help, she offered to work late

In our grammatical description, subordinators and co-ordinators are marked with a lower case *s* and *c*, respectively.

The simple and complex sentences referred to above are termed *major* sentences. This term distinguishes them from *minor* sentences, such as:

Hi!
Good morning.
Thank you.
No.
Martha!

Unlike major sentences, these minor sentences are of fixed structure. Compare the greeting *Good morning* with the same words in:

It's a good morning for fishing

You can substitute a word in the phrase, add extra words or change the word order:

It's a very bad morning for fishing
The morning is good for fishing

The greeting *Good morning*, on the other hand, is a formula which cannot undergo structural change. In our grammatical description such sentences are just marked *minor*.

One other sentence construction should be mentioned here. This includes sentences such as *you know, you see, you know what I mean*, which may occur as comments:

He was an athlete, you know

They are best described in a way which shows their parenthetic nature and therefore in our grammatical description their structure is placed in parentheses.

CLAUSE STRUCTURE

The structure of a clause can be described in terms of a number of slots or sites, such as a site for a subject, an object or a verb — terms which are probably familiar. The *clause sites* identified in this description are:

subject   S
verb   V
object   O $\longleftarrow$ direct object, O_d
                      indirect object O_i
complement   C
adverbial   A

Most sentences have a subject and a verb and may or may not have other clause sites occupied. The sentence:

              Pigs   fly
Clause level   S   V

has the clause pattern SV and no other elements are required.

It is the nature of the verb which determines whether other clause sites will be occupied. If the verb *fly* is used, we need no other items apart from the subject to form an acceptable sentence. If the verb *wear* is used then other sites must be filled.

*Pigs wear

is unacceptable and an object, such as *rubber wings*, is needed to provide an acceptable sentence.

Pigs wear rubber wings
 S   V   O

A verb such as *gave* usually requires two objects:

He gave the pigs flying lessons
 S   V O_i O_d

The pigs is the indirect object, O_i, and *flying lessons* is the direct object, O_d.

Some verbs require a site known as a *complement* to be occupied

A pig is not a flying animal
S   V   C

The complement here provides further information about the subject. *A flying animal* is thus known as a subject complement, C_{sub}. In:

They elected her president
S   V   O   C

the complement provides further information about the object. *President* is therefore known as an object complement, C_{obj}.

The final clause site is the *adverbial*. This site is required to be occupied by a small class of verbs.

He leaned against the wall
S   V   A
They lived near the river
S   V   A

The adverbial category is slightly different from the others. While it is an obligatory element for a few verbs, it can occur as an optional element in most sentences, with relative feeedom of position.

(This morning) I felt tired
      A   S V C
I was feeling tired (this morning)
S   V   C   A

The parentheses indicate the optional nature of this constituent. Furthermore, in any one clause there can be more than one adverbial whereas there can only be one of each of the other types of clause element.

(At lunch time) (on Mondays) (after a long meeting) I feel tired
      A   A   A   S V C

Combinations of these categories of clause structures: S, V, C, O and A provide us with seven basic types of sentence (Table 3.1). Some of the main characteristics of each of these elements of clause structure are looked at below.

The subject   A subject usually precedes the verb in statements.

My plants died
S   V

In interrogative sentences the subject will follow the auxiliary verb

Did my plants die?
     S   V

Table 3.1.   Basic sentence structures

Clause structure	Examples
S V	Crocodiles cry
S V O	Sam bought some eggs
S V O_i O_d	I knitted my wife woolly socks
S V C	Jerome is intelligent
S V O C	They have proved me wrong
S V A	Kirby lives in New York
S V O A	I put the tablets in the bathroom

The subject site is usually occupied. The main exception to this is the case of certain imperatives such as *Fly*!, *Go away*!, though there is often an implied subject with such sentences.

The subject agrees with, or is in concord with, the present tense form of the verb. When the present tense third person singular form of the verb is used a singular subject is required.

> The child laughs
> S   V

The object   An object usually follows the verb.

> He broke the eggs
> S   V   O

Occasionally, for a particular effect, the object can be placed before the subject.

> The floor, he cleaned
> O   S   V

Where there is both a direct and an indirect object, the indirect object usually comes first:

> I gave him a dozen eggs
> S V O_i O_d

The indirect object can, however, be freed from its position before the direct object by the addition of an item such as *to* or *for*.

> I gave a dozen eggs to him
> S V O_d O_i

> To him I gave a dozen eggs
> O_i S V O_d

The object does not have to be in concord with the verb:

He drives a car
He drives cars

The complement   The subject complement occurs after certain verbs (such as *appear*, *seem*, *feel*, *become*) which allow one to say more about the subject.

He appeared happy
S   V   C

She felt tired
S   V   C

The verb *be* is the most commonly used verb to take a complement. In our grammatical description it is termed the copula (cop), from a Latin word meaning 'linking'.

I am happy
S V   C

It is important to distinguish the copular verb *be*, which is used to say something about the subject, from the form of *be* which is used to mark the verb tense and aspect (see below). Compare:

(1) He is happy
    S   V   C

(2) He is laughing
    S   V

In (1), you can ask:

What is he? Happy

but in (2) you would need to ask:

What is he doing? Laughing

The complement may occur in a sentence with an object, in which case it follows the object it complements.

They thought her a genius
S   V   O   C

The complement does not have to be in concord with the verb (cf. subject). It does, of course, have to agree with the subject or object that it complements.

He is a horse-thief

is acceptable, but:

*He is horse-thieves

is not.

The complement differs from an object in that the complement provides additional information about the subject or object. Compare:

(1) He grew sulky
   S   V   C
(2) He grew sugar
   S   V   O

(2) does not imply that he was sugar!

The adverbial   The adverbial is a compulsory element with a small number of verbs. It usually occurs after the verb, but may occur in the initial position.

She lay on the bed
 S V   A
On the bed she lay
   A   S V

The adverbial may occur as an optional element in any sentence and, as has been noted, more than one adverbial may occur.

On Monday, after lunch, we caught a train
   A   A   S   V   O

Negatively defined, the adverbial is any element which is not the subject, verb, complement or object.

Distinctions can be drawn between different types of adverbial. Some adverbials modify part of a sentence (e.g. He *almost* broke his finger). In Quirk *et al.*, (1972), these adverbials are termed *adjuncts*. Other adverbials modify the whole sentence (e.g. *Frankly*, I was disappointed). These are termed *disjuncts*. A third type of adverbial is used to connect two sentences (e.g. He broke his leg on Monday. *The next day* he caught pneumonia). These adverbials can be termed *conjuncts* or *connectives*. In the descriptive procedure adopted here all adverbials are marked A. Those used for connecting sentences are marked A_{conn}. (Note that this use of A_{conn} differs a little from that of Crystal *et al.* (1976).) The exception to this is the use of *and* to link clauses in children's writing and speech. *And* often appears to be a 'filler' between clauses and it is difficult to determine whether it is a true connective. In the description used here *and* is simply marked as a co-ordinator.

The verb   The verb is the compulsory element. It determines what other sites will be occupied.

In statement sentences it occurs after the subject and precedes the object and complement.

The verb is the easiest category of clause structure to recognise as it is occupied by the part of speech which may be marked for tense, number, aspect, voice and mood. These characteristics will be explained when we turn to the internal structure of each clause category (i.e. phrase structure).

The examples used to illustrate the elements of clause structure have all been simple sentences (i.e. consisting of one clause). When there are subordinate clauses you need to show more than one level of clause structure. The sentence *I can feel that spring is in the air* has the clause structure S V O.

	I can feel that spring is in the air
Clause level	S V O

The object *that spring is in the air* is itself a clause and its clause structure needs to be shown:

	I can feel that spring is in the air
Clause level 1	S V O
Clause level 2	s S V A

Here the object is shown to have its own S V A clause structure.

The other clause sites, except the verb, may themselves be clauses.

Clause as subject What I earn is my own business
                          s   S   V   C

Clause as object I know what you mean
                        S V   O
                           s   S   V

Clause as complement I am what I am
                            S V   C
                               s S V

Clause as adverbial They left because they were hungry
                           S   V   A
                              s   S   V   C

In these examples one clause element (S, O, C or A) is itself a clause. You may also find subordinate clauses that are only part of one clause element: that is, they are dependent on elements within the *same* clause part. In traditional grammar these are referred to as relative clauses. For example:

The man who lives next door is a miser
     S   V   C

has the clause structures S V C, but there is a clause *who lives next door* which is subordinate to *the man*. We can show this type of subordinate clause using two levels of clause analysis:

	The man	who	lives	next door	is	a miser
Clause level 1	S				V	C
Clause level 2		s	V	A		

The relative clause subordinators such as *who*, *that* or *which* may be absent.

	The man	I	like	lives	next door
Clause level 1	S			V	A
Clause level 2		S	V		

PHRASE STRUCTURE

We need now to look at the phrase structure of elements which can occupy subject, verb, complement, object and adverbial sites.

Subject, object and complement can be occupied by noun phrases: pronouns or nouns which may be modified by articles, adjectivals and a few other elements.

My best game is *wonder woman*

noun phrase as S   noun phrase as C

She catches *criminals*

noun phrase as S   noun phrase as O

Complement sites may also be occupied by adjectivals, adjectival phrases and certain other constructions such as the comparative.

She is *good*

adjective as C

She is *better than Batman*

comparative as C

Adverbial sites may be occupied by noun phrases and also by adverbs or prepositional phrases (i.e. phrases introduced by a preposition, pr).

The police put them *in a cellar*

prepositional phrase as A

We nearly play it every day

Adverb as A   noun phrase as A

The verb site can only be occupied by a verb phrase: a main verb along with any necessary auxiliaries, negative particles and other particles.

She *was not putting up with* his behaviour

The noun phrase and verb phrase are examined further below.

The noun phrase As with clause structure, one can talk about phrase structure in terms of sites. The compulsory site of the noun phrase is that occupied by the head noun, N, or pronoun, (pron).

> *Unicorns* live
>   N
> *Nobody* writes to me
>   pron

The head word is the compulsory element in the noun phrase. It may be modified by preceding or following items.

> The three plastic unicorns in the shop   are broken
> pre-modification   N   post-modification

Pre-modification Before the head noun we can identify different categories of words. Following the LARSP classification, the three categories identified are *initiators* (I) *determiners* (D), and *adjectivals* (adj). Examples of these are given in Table 3.2.

Table 3.2 Examples of pre-modifiers

Initiators(I)	Determiners(D)	Adjectivals (adj)		
		ordinals	cardinals	adjectives
half (of)	*the*	*first*	*one*	*old*
both (of)	*some*	*second*	*two*	*young*
all (of)	*many*	*third*	*few*	*English*
only	*an*	*last*	*many*	*sharp*

Note. For convenience the ordinal, cardinal and adjective classes have been grouped together as adj. However, if a closer study of noun-phrase modification is felt necessary, the description can be refined accordingly.

The fifth column of words (adjectives) differs from the other four in that more than one of the words may occur in a noun phrase.

> both the dirty white plastic unicorns
> I D adj adj adj   N

With the other classes, only one item from each may occur. For example

> *The some young children

is unacceptable.

Some words may have a different classification depending on their position in the noun phrase. The word *few* provides some good examples:

Few of the children behaved
   I   D   N

A *few* people will come
D adj   N

Few trains run on Sunday
 D N

Few came to the meeting
pron

Where names are used in the noun phrase (e.g. *John* lived in *Bexhill*), they are not further classified at phrase level as they have no internal structure (this applies even to two-part names like *Mr Jones*).

Post-modification   In the post-modification position in the noun phrase there may be a range of items such as prepositional or adverbial phrases, adjectivals or adverbs, or relative clauses.

Prepositional phrase	The bull *in the china shop* pr D adj N
Adverbial phrase	Those sick *a week later* D N adv
Relative clause **Clause level 1**	The sailor *who saw an albatross* S
Clause level 2	s V O
Phrase level	pron v D N

The verb phrase   The head of the verb phrase is the verb, v. This is the compulsory element which may be marked for such characteristics as tense, aspect, mood, voice and number.

The main verb may occur on its own and be marked for past pre-sent. The third person of the present tense is marked for number as well.

Present The cat *washes* its foot
Present The cats *wash* their feet
Past   The cats *washed* their feet

The main verb may be accompanied by one or more auxiliary verbs (aux), which indicate the mood, aspect, voice and tense of the verbs:

The cats *may have been washing* their feet

The mood of the verb may be marked by the use of modal auxiliaries such as *may*, *can*, *will*, *ought to*, *could*, etc., indicating such things as intention, possibility, ability and obligation. The modal auxiliaries *will* and *shall* are one means of indicating future time.

They *will* attack

Aspect is concerned with the way an action is viewed. Perfective aspect is represented by a form of the auxiliary *have* plus the past participle form of the verb.

He has/had written the letter

Progressive aspect is represented by a form of the auxiliary *be* plus the present participle form of the verb.

He is/was writing a letter

These two aspects can be combined, as in:

He had been writing a letter.

Lastly, we can mark the verb for the passive voice by the use of a form of the auxiliary *be* plus the past participle of the verb.

The letter was written.

Combining all the auxiliaries you have a verb phrase for tense, mood, perfective and progressive aspect and for passive voice.

	The letter may have been being written
Phrase level	aux aux aux aux v

Here, the different auxiliaries are all marked 'aux' at phrase level. A more refined analysis, differentiating the different auxiliaries, could be used if necessary.

Other major features of the verb phrase are summarised below.

In the verb phrase one may also find the negative particle *not* or *n't* which is notated as 'neg' at phrase level.

Some verbs consist of more than one word:

Turn off the light
Come up with a solution

These are notated as v + part (+ part)

	turn off the light
Phrase level	v part

	come up with a solution
Phrase level	v part part

It is important to distinguish multi-word verbs from verbs plus prepositional phrases. Compare

He turned off the light (verb + part)
He turned off the road (verb + prepositional phrase)

(see Quirk *et al.*, 1972, para 12.19–28).

Sometimes a clause has more than one verb

I like playing the fool
I wanted to go shopping

Following the analysis used by Crystal *et al*. in LARSP, these are all classified as verbs (v), at the phrase level.

	I	like	playing	acrobats
Phrase level		v	v	

The copular use of the verb *be* (see above) is indicated at the phrase level in our description by the use of the notation, cop.

	I	am	happy
Phrase level		cop	

SENTENCE TYPES

Four different major sentence types are usually recognised on the basis of their grammatical characteristics: *interrogatives*, for example *Who wants to leave?*; *imperatives*, for example *Leave!*; *exclamations*, for example *What a good idea!*, and *statements*, for example *You will have to go*. These correlate with, but do not exactly correspond to, the semantic functions of sentences: asking questions; giving orders; exclaiming; providing information. A statement can be used to give orders:

You need to wear gloves (i.e. put your gloves on)

or as a question:

There's a draught (i.e. is the door open?)

and so on. To decide which sentences belong to each sentence type involves an analysis of clausal and phrasal structure.

Statements The grammatical structure of simple and complex sentences that are statements have been our major concern. The seven basic types of sentence (Table 3.1) are all statements.

Interrogatives Interrogatives are formed by the inversion of the subject and the auxiliary verb. When there is no auxiliary in the verb phrase, an appropriate form of the verb *do* is used.

	He	is	laughing
Clause level	S		V
Phrase level	pron	aux	v

	Is	he	laughing?
Clause level		S	V
Phrase level	aux	pron	v

```
               Did they laugh?
Clause level    S      V
Phrase level    aux pron   v
```

They are also formed by the use of *wh*-question words, Q.

```
               Who  is  laughing?
Clause level    Q       V
Phrase level         aux    v
```

Tag questions are also used to form interrogatives.

```
               She  is  leaving, isn 't  she?
Clause level    S       V      V      S
Phrase level   pron aux   v    aux neg pron
```

Imperatives   Three types of imperative structures are identified here. Imperative sentences may be formed with the subject omitted (though usually implied).

```
Get out!
  V
```

They may also have the subject included.

```
Nobody move!
  S    V_imp
```

(The V is marked V_{imp} to differentiate this structure from the SV statement type *Nobody moved*). The items *let* or *do* may be used. In the LARSP notation, they are written in full.

```
Let go!      Do hurry up!
let V        do  V
```

Exclamations   Exclamatory sentences are major sentences introduced by the *wh*-question words *what* and *how*.

```
               What a ridiculous idea that is
Clause level    Q         C        S V
               How smartly he dressed
Clause level    Q     A    S   V
```

Other exclamatory expressions such as *Gosh*! *Bless you*! are classified as minor sentences.

3.5.   WORD STRUCTURE

Our analysis of syntax has so far used words as the smallest units of language. However, it is often helpful to examine the structure of words themselves. The analysis of word formation is termed *morphology*.

We can identify elements that are smaller than words, that occur over and over again in a language with the same meaning. These elements are termed *morphemes*. Consider, for example, these words:

jumped	walked	laughed	reached
unfair	unhappy	untrue	undo

The words can be divided into smaller units, as follows:

jump + ed	walk + ed	laugh + ed	reach + ed
un + fair	un + happy	un + true	un + do

These units are morphemes.

There is a difference between the *ed* and the *un* morphemes and many of the others in the examples above. Both the *ed* morpheme and the *un* morpheme recur with the same meaning in English, but they appear only in combination with another morpheme. Morphemes of this type are termed *bound morphemes*. The way in which they are bound to other morphemes can be shown by a hyphen, like this:

-ed (the morpheme comes after another morpheme, as in jump*ed*)
un- (the morpheme comes in front of another morpheme, as in *un*lucky)

Morphemes that can occur alone are termed *free morphemes*. Examples are *jump*, *walk*, *laugh*, *reach*, *fair*, *happy*, *true*, and *do*.

Words can be made up of free morphemes, such as *jump* or *fair*, or of a combination of bound and free morphemes:

free + free: black-bird, hat-trick
free + bound: black-ness, black-er
bound + free: dis-please, be-friend
bound + bound: con-clude, re-sist

We can identify within one morpheme a number of *allomorphs*, or *morpheme variants*, in a similar way to the identification of allophones and phonemes (see section 2.3). The *-ed* form, for example, expresses past tense in English, but it is not the only form that does this. There are irregular verb forms such as *took* and *saw* that can be considered as allomorphs of the past-tense morpheme. In addition, the pronunciation of the *-ed* morpheme is affected by the sound that comes before it. Consider, for example, the pronunciation of:

lifted
descended

jumped
pushed

pulled
died

After /t/ and /d/ (termed alveolar plosives, see section 2.2), such as in the first pair, the morpheme is pronounced /əd/; after other voiceless consonants, such as in the second pair, it is pronounced /t/; and elsewhere (after all other voiced sounds) it is pronounced /d/.

A further distinction can be made between morphemes such as *-ed* and morphemes such as *un-*. Both are used to form words in English, but the processes of word formation are of a different kind. The *-ed* morpheme expresses the grammatical relationship of past tense in a sentence in which it occurs. This process of word formation is termed an *inflectional* process. Verbs are said to *inflect* for tense. The verb *jump*, for example, has the inflectional forms *jumped*, *jumping* and *jumps*. Another example of an inflectional process in English is the formation of plural nouns by the addition of the *-s* morpheme. The noun *cat*, for example, has the inflected form *cats* in a phrase like *these two cats*.

Un-, on the other hand, is used in the *derivational* process of word formation. The morpheme *un-* does not express a grammatical relationship but forms a new word from an existing word. *Unlucky* means the opposite of *lucky* and *unexciting* means the opposite of *exciting*.

An analysis of syntactic structure can include the syntactic information expressed by bound, inflectional morphemes by analysing the sentence at word level as well as at phrase level and at clause level. Some of the morphemes that can be included at this level of analysis are:

in noun phrases

plural (pl)	the three bear*s*
genitive (gen)	the little bear'*s* porridge
comparative (*-er*)	the bigg*er* bear's chair
superlative (*-est*)	the bigg*est* bear's bed

in verb phrases

third person present singular (3s)	he mend*s* toys
present participle form (*-ing*)	she is laugh*ing*
past participle form (*-en*)	he was tak*en* home
past tense forms (*-ed*)	she laugh*ed*

contracted forms of

the auxiliary (aux)	she'*d* like to come
the copula (cop)	she'*s* clever
the negative (n't)	it is*n't* fair

the adverb marker

(-ly)	he nearly won

Note that *-en* and *-ed* are also used in the Crystal *et al.* (1976) framework to indicate past participle and past tense forms of irregular verbs which do not have the morphemes *-en* and *-ed*. The example sentence below would be analysed as shown:

	she	brought	him	flowers
Clause level	S	V	O_i	O_d
Phrase level	pron	v	pron	N
Word level		*-ed*		*-s*

Similarly, irregular plurals, such as *children*, *women* or *sheep* are also marked plural (pl.).

4 Meaning

4.1 INTRODUCTION

The branch of linguistics that is concerned with how meaning is expressed in language is called *semantics*. The analysis of meaning has proved one of the most difficult and elusive tasks in linguistic description. This is hardly surprising, since it involves investigating the relationship between language and everything that we use language to talk about: and this amounts to the entire world! Yet an understanding of how we use language to talk about the world is fundamental to appreciating how communication works. We shall start by outlining some of the ways in which the meaning of individual words in a language can be analysed, then turn to the analysis of words in context and finally to an analysis that tries to take account of the knowledge that we have to use in order to interpret words in context.

4.2 WORD MEANING

Words as symbols

Words can be regarded as symbols. For example, the word *cat* in English, or *chat* in French, or *Katze* in German, functions as a symbol of the real-world animal; or rather, it might be more prudent to say, as a symbol of the mental concept that we have of a cat. It can do this because there are agreed conventions amongst language users about the interpretation of the word, though we may not necessarily be conscious of these conventions unless we stop and think about them. Without these agreed conventions, communication could not take place.

The relationship between a word and the entity that it symbolises, however, is much more complex than for other symbols. Words may well be symbols, but they are very flexible symbols, whose meaning shifts in different contexts — sometimes a considerable distance from what we might think of as their 'usual' meaning. This is particularly true of poetry, to give an extreme example. Yet it is because of their flexibility that we are able to use the words in the vocabulary of a language to talk about anything in the world, and to do so in all kinds of different ways — jokingly or sarcastically, for instance, as well as straightforwardly. Semantic analysis has to try to account for the way that we can do this.

REFERENCE, DENOTATION AND CONNOTATION

A very simple approach to the analysis of word meaning sees words as 'naming' or 'labelling' things in the world. A distinction can then be drawn between *denotation* and *reference*. Denotation is used for the class of things indicated by a word, whereas reference is used for a particular thing that is indicated when the word is used. For example, the word *cat* denotes the class of all cats in the sentence *a cat makes a good pet*, but it refers to a particular cat in the sentence *a cat scratched her arm*.

This approach, however, takes no account of the flexibility of word meaning. *Cat* in the (admittedly rather dated) phrase *cool for cats* denotes a different class of things from *cat* in the two examples above, and a different class of things again in *that girl's a real cat* (meaning that she's spiteful). It is difficult, too, to see how this approach can apply to all the words in the vocabulary: what, for example, could the words *until, is* or *thus* denote? Abstract words are also harder to deal with in terms of denotation. We undoubtedly have a concept of *power, love* or *job*, but this is less easy to specify than for concrete entities such as *cat* and *gatepost*. The approach does, however, allow a useful distinction to be made between these 'naming' types of meaning (which together can be termed referential meaning) and a second type of meaning referred to as *connotation*.

Connotation refers to the associations that words have for us. Psychologists have long been aware that there is more to words than referential meaning. In addition to 'naming things', words carry overtones of meaning which colour our reaction to them. Even the most innocent of words can conjure up associations that may affect our attitude and our response to an utterance which contains them. Table 4.1 shows the words which first came to mind to 1,000 people who were given the stimulus word *chair* in an early word-association experiment (Kent and Rosenoff, 1910). The stimulus word seemed to tap a cultural, experiential and contextual knowledge of the object. Perhaps, in view of the (by and large) shared functional and cultural significance of the object, it is not surprising that there is a consensus among speakers in their first associations: nearly 60 per cent of the sample answered with *table, seat, furniture, sit,* or *sitting*.

It may seem that all this kind of study shows is what speakers know about chairs and how they are used, but at least one interesting, and

Table 4.1. First responses in a word-association test for the stimulus word chair.

Frequency of response	Response	Frequency of response	Response
191	table	2	broken, hickory,
127	seat		home, necessity,
108	sit		oak, rounds,
83	furniture		seating, use
56	sitting	1	back, beauty,
49	wood		bed, book,
45	rest		boy, bureau,
38	stool		caning, careful
21	comfort		carpet, cart,
17	rocker		color,
15	rocking		crooked,
13	bench		cushions, feet,
12	cushion		foot,
11	legs		footstool, form,
10	floor		Governor Winthrop,
9	desk, room		hair, implement,
8	comfortable		joiner, lunch,
7	ease, leg		massive, mission,
6	easy, sofa, wooden		myself, object,
5	couch, hard, Morris, seated, soft		occupy, office, people, place,
4	arm, article, brown, high		placed, plant, idleness, platform,
3	cane, convenience, house, large, low, lounge, mahogany, person, resting, rug, settee, useful		pleasant, pleasure, posture, reading, rubber, size, spooning, stand, stoop, study, support, tables, talk, teacher, timber, tool, upholstered, upholstery, white

Source: Kent and Rosenoff (1910)

perhaps surprising, thing comes to light. Of the subjects 107 gave as their *first* response words which seem to indicate some evaluatory association. *Comfort, convenience, rest* and *idle pleasure* were evoked for some subjects, whereas others responded with *hard*. The number of respondents who associated pleasant sensations with the stimulus word outnumbered those who found the chair *hard* by 102 to 5. We find that there is some degree of agreement within the sample over *connotative meaning*.

If people react to lexical items in this way, with value judgements, sensations of like and dislike and so on, then it is important to know both in what ways they respond to words and the degree to which it may influence them in their reaction to speakers who use them. A much more direct way of getting at such connotative or associative meaning is to ask speakers to rate words on scales such as good–bad, pleasant–unpleasant, strong–weak, fast–slow, etc. Even where such evaluations appear bizarre or in appropriate, subjects manage to perform this task remarkably well, and find it possible to indicate how 'rough', 'tasty', or 'hot' they perceive a word such as *sin*.

Activity 4.1

You can try out this technique yourself. Think of the word *natural* and mark it on the scales below, indicating how close or far from each polar extreme you judge the word to be:

<pre>
         good————————bad
         hard————————soft
        happy————————wretched
        light————————dark
    worthless————————valuable
       strong————————weak
    beautiful————————ugly
      sincere————————insincere
    masculine————————feminine
      violent————————gentle
</pre>

Although subjects' responses are in some ways idiosyncratic and may tell us more about their backgrounds, anxieties and personalities than about the word itself — indeed, the technique has been used in diagnosing psychiatric disorders — yet there are areas of consensus which reflect, minimally, culture-wide reactions. Those who have a sensitivity for such things may use it with effect. Such are the professional persuaders — skilled orators, politicians, advertisers — but the art is also found in the best novelists and prose writers. Indeed, at times words may be chosen entirely for their connotative value—whether political or emotive — apparently without regard to their referential meanings. An advertisement in the *New York Times* reads: '100 per cent sudsable *natural* acrylic'.

DICTIONARY ENTRIES

In highly literate societies such as the UK, dictionaries are produced as part of the process of language standardization. Besides giving syntactic, phonetic and (sometimes) historical information, dictionary makers, or *lexicographers*, try to make explicit the conventions that language users share about the meanings of the words in the language. They do not normally try to deal with connotative meaning, for although there may be a high consensus among language users about the associations that individual words have for them, there are also differences, which reflect the different life experiences that individual language users have had. It is denotative meaning that dictionaries try to describe; but since the meaning that individual words can have is very flexible, it can be surprisingly difficult to describe word meaning in the form of a dictionary entry. It is instructive to see how compilers of dictionaries have tried to capture the flexibility of word meanings, and to see how different lexicographers have often made different decisions about their organisation of entries for the same word.

Activity 4.2

Taking the noun *mug* as an example, consult two different dictionaries to see how the entries are set out (ignore the verb *mug* for the purposes of this activity). Try to specify the principles that have been used to classify the different meanings.

The two dictionaries that I consulted were *Collins English Dictionary* and the *Shorter Oxford English Dictionary* (*SOED*). *Collins English Dictionary* has two main entries for *mug*, with the second entry subdivided into three further entries, as follows:

mug 1. a drinking vessel with a handle, usually cylindrical and made of earthenware.
mug 2. 1. *slang*. A person's face or mouth. 2. *slang*. A grimace. 3. *slang*. A gullible person, especially one who is swindled easily.

The *Shorter Oxford English Dictionary*, on the other hand, has four main entries for the noun *mug*, with the first entry subdivided into three further entries and the fourth into two further entries:

mug 1. *dialect*. Any (large) earthenware vessel or bowl; also a pot, jug, or ewer. **2.** A drinking-vessel, usually cyclindrical, with or without a handle. **3.** A cooling drink.
mug *slang*. the face or mouth.
mug *slang*. a stupid person: a muff, duffer; a card-sharper's dupe.
mug *slang*. 1. An examination. 2. One who mugs or reads hard

There is a difference in the actual meanings that are given in the two dictionaries: the *SOED* gives the meaning 'examination' or 'someone who reads hard', whereas *Collins* does not. It is the organisation of the entries that is interesting, though, rather than the actual meanings that are given. Both dictionaries have decided that *mug* with the sense of 'drinking vessel' is a different word from *mug* with the sense of 'face or mouth' or 'a gullible or stupid person'. They both give *mug* as a 'drinking vessel' as a separate entry; and they both give this meaning first, perhaps because they take into account the history of the word. They differ, however, in the way that they organise the other meanings of *mug*.

To simplify, we shall look at just the entries for *mug* = 'a person's face or mouth' and *mug* = 'a gullible person' (*Collins*) or 'a stupid person' (*SOED*). (We shall ignore the possible different nuances of meaning between ' a stupid person' and 'a gullible person'!) *Collins* has decided that these are two different meanings of a single word, and lists them as two of the three meanings of *mug* 2:

The *SOED*, on the other hand, has decided that these are two separate words, and gives them as separate entries:

We can say that *Collins* treats the relationship of meaning to word form as an example of *polysemy* (where a single word has two or more separate meanings), whereas the *SOED* treats it as an example of *homonymy* (where two or more separate words, with separate meanings, have the same form). Neither dictionary is necessarily more correct than the other: they have simply chosen different ways of representing the meanings that *mug* can have — which, like all words, is flexible and not easy to pin down. If you consulted a different dictionary from my two, it will be interesting to see which aspects of the meaning of *mug* your dictionary considers important, and to see how it organises its entries.

Sometimes, as Palmer (1981) points out, looking for a 'central' or 'core' meaning among the different meanings that we might want to include in a dictionary entry can help in deciding whether to treat these meanings as belonging to a single word or as belonging to different words. For example, the compilers of *Collins English Dictionary* may have decided that *mug*2 meaning 'face' and *mug*2 meaning 'a gullible person' both have the central meaning of referring to a person, whereas *mug*1 has the central meaning of referring to a drinking vessel. These central meanings may reflect the shared conventions of language users (amongst whom we can, of course, include lexicographers!) However, if these are the 'core' meanings, then it seems from the dictionary entries given above that these core meanings are decidedly fuzzy. Take, for example, the 'drinking vessel' meaning. Both dictionaries consider that the purpose of the vessel is important ('drinking') and so is its shape ('cylindrical'), but *Collins* considers that it has a handle, whereas for the *SOED* this is optional, and *Collins* considers that what it is made of is important ('usually earthenware') whereas the *SOED* does not.

The lack of precise boundaries for the meaning for words is normal, and accounts for their flexibility. It is often possible to specify a central component of meaning for a word, such as 'drinking vessel' for *mug*, and to then specify a number of additional meanings that have different probabilities of applying, depending on the context in which the word is used. The existence of a handle, or being made of earthenware, are perhaps rather less central aspects of the meaning of *mug* in most contexts.

We shall return to this point below. For the time being, we shall simply repeat what we hope this section has shown: that although words can be seen as symbols, the relationship between a word and the aspects of the world that it symbolises is extremely complex.

Sense relations

So far, we have been discussing the meaning of words in terms of their relationship to the entities or concepts that they symbolise. This type of relationship can be termed 'reference', as we saw above. Like all symbols, however, the meaning of a word is determined (in part, at least) by the syntagmatic and paradigmatic relationships that the word enters into with other words in the language. (*Syntagmatic* and *paradigmatic* relationships were discussed in section 3.3; if you have not yet read this section, look now at this discussion.) The meaning relationships that different words in the vocabulary of a language have with each other are termed *sense relations*. The rest of this section will describe this aspect of word meaning.

SEMANTIC FIELDS

Just as the meaning of a yellow traffic light is determined by its place in the three-term system of red, yellow and green traffic lights, so the meanings of many words are determined by their place in different *word systems*. We can see this very clearly if we consider the meaning of *good* in different areas of our culture. In an examination system there might be four grades — *poor*, *fair*, *good* and *excellent*; in a grading system for hotels in a tourist brochure, on the other hand, the grades are more likely to be *good*, *very good*, *excellent* and *outstanding*. The relative meaning of *good* is different in these two instances, because of the relationships that it enters into with the other words in the *semantic fields* of examination grades and hotel classifications.

Sometimes a semantic field is divided up differently by different varieties of the same language, to reflect distinctions that are important in a particular community. In some sheep-farming communities in mid-Wales, for instance, (and probably in other parts of Britain, too) the semantic field of 'sheep' includes the words *tup*, *ewe*, *wether* and *hoggart* — distinctions that are not usually made in non-farming communities, where they have no cultural relevance.

The way that the vocabulary of a language divides up semantic 'space' can often be clearly seen when we try to translate words from one language to another. The English word *cousin*, for example, has to be translated into French by either *cousin* or *cousine*, depending on whether the cousin is male or female. The French kinship terms make a distinction that the English term does not; and the precise meaning of the French word *cousin* is therefore different from its English counterpart, because it stands in a different relationship to other words in the semantic field of kinship terms.

The distinctions that are made by the vocabulary of a language very often reflect a society's beliefs and values. In ancient Greece the words for *carpenter*, *physician*, *shoemaker* and *teacher*, for example, all fell within a semantic field of 'occupations that require specialised knowledge'. These were all included in the term *demiourgos*. We usually translate this as *artisan* or *craftsman*, but in modern English there is no term that is exactly equivalent in scope to the Greek *demiourgos* — we tend instead to think in terms of *the professions* and *trades*, and our vocabulary reflects this distinction (Lyons, 1977).

The way in which a word fits into different semantic fields can be illustrated by substituting it for other words in a fixed linguistic context. Gannon and Czerniewska (1980) give the following example for the word *struck*, which can be considered as contributing a different meaning to each of the sentences below:

the clock $\left\{ \begin{array}{l} \text{struck} \\ \text{chimed} \\ \text{tolled} \end{array} \right\}$ twelve

the miner $\left\{ \begin{array}{l} \text{hit} \\ \text{struck} \\ \text{found} \\ \text{discovered} \end{array} \right\}$ gold

$$\text{the umpire} \left\{ \begin{array}{l} \text{struck} \\ \text{hit} \\ \text{punched} \\ \text{slapped} \end{array} \right\} \text{the spectator}$$

Where a semantic field seems to be a naturally occurring one, such as, perhaps, the colour continuum, then its scope can be precisely stated. The exact nature of the 'semantic space' that our vocabulary divides up for us, however, is not always so easily formulated (consider, for example, the nature of the semantic space that is divided up by the words that *struck* relates to, in the three examples above — 'announcing time'? 'discovery'? 'physical violence'?). In view of the fuzziness in our beliefs about word meaning, some vagueness in the formulation of the scope of a semantic field is inevitable.

Despite the difficulty of delimiting a semantic field, this approach to the analysis of word meaning has been very useful for some areas of the vocabulary. At the very least, it shows clearly how the meaning of a word depends in part on the syntagmatic and paradigmatic relationships that it enters into with other words in the language.

COLLOCATION

Syntagmatic relationships are particularly important in determining word meaning, since the linguistic context in which a word occurs often identifies which of several related meanings is intended. Dictionaries often give a context in order to help to define a meaning, as you may have noticed during Activity 4.2. A clear example is the meaning of the word *white*, which refers to a different colour in the phrases *white coffee*, *white wine*, *white paint* and *white skin*, and to a different semantic field altogether in the phrases *white light* or *white noise*.

Languages differ in the *collocational* ranges of their words. For example, in English we distinguish between wiping our nose, brushing our teeth and polishing our shoes, whereas in German the term *putzen* can be used for all these activities (Stork and Widdowson, 1974).

Clichés are born when a word occurs very frequently in a particular collocation. The word may then lose some of its semantic 'force', because we become used to thinking of the phrase as a single unit. Some examples from everyday English are 'last but not least' and 'the more the merrier'. Different professions tend to coin their own clichés: estate agents, for example, talk of 'a wealth of exposed beams' and 'tastefully decorated throughout'; in education, a current cliché is the phrase 'caring schools'.

Habitual collocations often reflect social conventions and social attitudes: the collocations of the words *pretty* and *handsome*, for example, indicate that we categorise good looks for men and women separately. This is one way that language can perpetuate social divisions.

OPPOSITES

Another structural relationship that helps to determine word meaning is the relationship of 'opposites'. This is a paradigmatic relationship, as is the relationship between words in a semantic field, but it is between only two items. There are, however, various kinds of opposite relationships.

Complementarity Take the pairs *alive* and *dead*, and *asleep* and *awake*. If someone is alive, then, by definition, they are not dead; similarly, if someone is awake, then they cannot also be asleep. The term used to describe this type of relationship is *complementarity*.

Antonymy As with all our attempts to impose order on language, there are various difficulties even with this apparently straightforward relationship. Although strictly speaking the real world relationship between *awake* and *asleep* is one of incompatibility, we do sometimes use the words as though they were not incompatible. We talk of someone as being 'half-awake' or 'half-asleep', or even 'three-quarters asleep', or as being 'more dead than alive'. When we do this we are using the words as if their relationship were one of *antonymy*. Like complementarity, antonymy is a paradigmatic relationship of opposites in a two-term system, but this time we can imagine the words in the pairs as being at opposite ends of a continuum. For this reason, they are said to be *gradable*. For example, the pairs *old/young*, *high/low*, *clever/stupid*, or *dark/light* are incompatible (if we are young, then we are not old) but there are intervening degrees between the polar opposites (we can be very young, fairly young, not so young, and so on).

Antonyms can be explicitly graded by using words such as *very*, *fairly* or *not so*, but in fact they can be thought of as always being implicitly graded. We only interpret words such as *old*, *wide* or *big* in terms of being older, wider or bigger than something else. The 'norm' against which we interpret them, however, varies depending on what is being described. The 'young businessman of the year', for example, may be in his 40s. This implicit grading can be made use of in advertising: products are often described as *new*, *good*, *clean* or *bright*, which are all adjectives that imply a favourable comparison with other products.

Markedness Another characteristic of antonyms is that one member of the pair functions as the *semantically unmarked* or 'neutral' member. For example, if we want to ask about someone's age, we ask them how *old* they are; if we want to know if there is headroom for our bus to pass under a bridge we ask how *high* the bridge is. No assumptions are implied about the height of the bridge or the age of the person. In the same way, we can use the word *dog* to refer to an animal that is female as well as to one that is male.

If the other member of the pair is used, however, then assumptions *are* made. If we ask how young someone is, then the implication is either that they are not young, or that they are too young; if we ask how low a bridge is, then we imply that it is low rather than high. Similarly, a bitch is unquestionably a female animal; people sometimes speak of a female dog, but they would be most unlikely to speak of a male bitch. Often there is a noun derived from the unmarked term, but not from the marked term. In English, for example, we have a noun *height*, but no corresponding term derived from *low*. The term that is used as the unmarked member of the pair seems to vary in different languages; for example, where English speaks of a *thickness gauge*, Japanese has a *thinness gauge* (see Palmer, 1981). It can be very revealing of society's values to consider which of a pair of antonyms is used as the unmarked one.

Some pairs of words that are 'opposite' in meaning are *formally marked*. For example, *truthful* and *untruthful* can be analysed as complementary in meaning (though they are often used as antonyms, like other examples mentioned above); and in this case the opposition is formally marked by the prefix *-un*. This prefix is often used as a formal marker of 'oppositeness' (some other examples that come to mind are *helpful/unhelpful* and *happy/unhappy*). In English *in-* and *dis-* are used in a similar way, as formal markers of oppositeness: so that we have pairs such as *appropriate/inappropriate*, *eligible/ineligible*, *like/dislike* and *approve/disapprove*. These prefixes do not always mark a relationship of oppositeness, of course: for example, the words *disappoint* and *dismay* do not have corresponding opposite forms **appoint* or **may*. Sometimes a marked member of a pair is formally marked by a suffix, such as the *-ess* suffix in the pairs *host/hostess*, or *lion/lioness*, or the *-ette* suffix in *usher/usherette*. Prefixes and suffixes of this type are described in more detail in Section 3.5, on word structure.

Converses A further relationship of opposites involves pairs of words where one implies the reversal of the other. In English this includes terms such as *husband/wife*: and *borrow/lend*. For instance, if Paul is June's husband, then this implies that June is Paul's wife; if we say that Ann has borrowed £5 from her mother, then this implies that her mother has lent Ann £5. Of course, it is possible to use the word *borrow* in a way that does not imply a converse relationship; we could be speaking loosely, and be trying to make light of the fact that Ann has stolen £5 from her mother (in which case her mother would not, of course, have lent Ann the money!). The possibility of using words in many different ways is always there, as part of the flexibility of word meaning.

In some languages the same word may express both aspects of the relationship; in fact, this may even be the case in different varieties of the same language. In many parts of the British Isles, for example, people use the word *lend* in phrases such as *Can I lend £5?* (meaning 'Please give me a loan of £5') as well as in phrases such as *I'll lend you £5* (meaning 'I'll give you a loan of £5').

On the other hand, there are some languages that make distinctions where English does not. For example, English uses the same word *marry* whether the person who is the subject of the verb is the husband or the wife. In many languages, though, there are two words — one that is used when the subject is the wife (as in *Mary married John*) and another that is used when the subject is the husband (as in *John married Mary*). Italian, for example, would use the verb *maritarsi* in the first case and *ammogliarsi* in the second. Again, the relationships that the language specifies in its vocabulary (or that it *lexicalises*) can often be very revealing of cultural attitudes.

HYPONYMY

A paradigmatic relationship of a different kind is *hyponymy*. This is a relationship of 'inclusion'. The meaning of the word *flower*, for example, is included in the meaning of the word *daisy*, since daisies are flowers; similarly, the meaning of the word *emotion* could be said to be included in the meaning of *joy*, or of *sadness*. Hyponymous relationships are hierarchical, and can be displayed in the form of a tree, as in the diagram below:

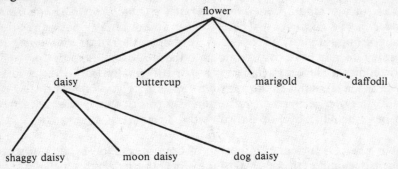

The upper term is called the *superordinate* (in the diagram this is *flower*) and the lower term is called the *hyponym*. In the diagram, *daisy*, *buttercup*, *marigold* and *daffodil* are all hyponyms of *flower*, and we have given *shaggy daisy*, *moon daisy* and *dog daisy* as hyponyms of *daisy*. Someone with a better knowledge of different species of flowers could also give hyponyms of *buttercup*, *marigold* and *daffodil*. Tree diagrams for hyponymy reflect the way in which language users attempt to organise their world, categorising things in order to make sense of them. It is often very revealing, therefore, to analyse the different hyponymous relationships in different languages. We mentioned earlier an example from ancient Greek, where there was a superordinate term to include a variety of professions and crafts, such as carpenter, doctor and flute player. English has no such superordinate term. These differences in semantic structure seem to be related to differences in the way that the two cultures have evaluated various occupations.

It can be equally revealing to analyse the different hyponymous relationships for 'pairs' of words in the same language. Todasco *et al* (1973) found 89 nouns and 120 adjectives to refer to a promiscuous woman, but only a few to refer to a promiscuous man!

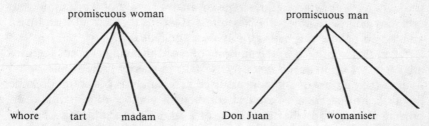

The categories that are reflected in the language can be refined as required by the occasion. In everyday English, for example, we use *beetle* as a hyponym of the superordinate *insect*, but in entomology the term *beetle* is itself a superordinate for over 200,000 different species of what a layperson might call a beetle (Eco, 1984).

Some of the words that we mentioned earlier as examples of semantic markedness can also be usefully analysed as examples of hyponymy. *Dog*, for example, is the unmarked member of the pair of words *dog* and *bitch*, in that it can be used to refer to the animal when its sex is not known, or when there is no need to mention its sex. The word *dog*, therefore, is both a superordinate and a hyponym:

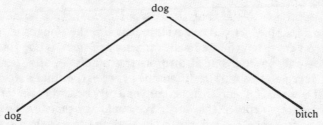

Similarly, the word *man* may function as both a hyponym and a superordinate, and it is not surprising that this can give rise to difficulties of interpretation.

COMPONENTIAL ANALYSIS

Another useful way of analysing word meaning is in terms of *semantic features*, by trying to specify the different components of meaning that make up a word. This approach can be used to analyse several of the meaning relationships that have been discussed so far. Components are usually treated as binary, so that meanings can be economically represented as (+) a feature or (−) the feature. For example, hyponyms can be said to contain the more general, superordinate concept, so that *daisy*, *buttercup* and *marigold* all have as one of their components

[+ flower]; similarly, antonyms and complementaries can be analysed
as differing from each other by the presence or absence of a component
feature, so that *alive* could be analysed as containing the component
feature [+ alive], and *dead* as containing the feature [− alive]
(though, as we saw above, this type of analysis will not work in normal
everyday language, where the flexibility of words is often fully exploited
and where people can be 'half alive' or 'half dead').

When this approach to the analysis of word meaning is used, features
are often set up in an *ad hoc* way, so that in theory there would be no
limit to the number of components used in an analysis of meaning. Some
linguists, however, have searched for a small number of semantic components that can provide definitions for a large number of words, hoping
to establish semantic primitives, or universals of meaning. These semantic primitives (sometimes called 'primes') would be components that are
essential to the word's meaning. For example, we might decide that
animal has the component [+ animate] as an essential component of
its meaning, but not, perhaps, the component [+ furry]. Many animals
are furry, but some (pigs, for instance) are not; there are no animals,
however, that are not animate — though as always, it is possible to think
of occasions when the word could be used without this apparently essential aspect of its meaning. This approach has something in common with
the concept of 'core' meaning, mentioned earlier. The idea of core meanings, however, does not necessarily assume that the core meaning is a
semantic universal.

This approach to the analysis of word meaning has sometimes been
used to describe semantic development in the language of young
children. Very often children will learn a word such as *dog*, but use it to
refer not only to dogs but also to other animals — cats, perhaps, and
horses, sheep and cows. The difference between the child's word *dog* and
an adult's word *dog* can then be conveniently described in terms of the
semantic components of the word. We could say that for the child, *dog*
has the component [+ animal]; whereas for the adult it has the two
components [+ animal] [+ canine], and the second component
differentiates it from other words in the adult's vocabulary that share the
feature [+ animal]. Similarly, some children use the words *mummy*
and *daddy* interchangeably; for them, both words seem to have a component such as [+ parent], and in time they will presumably acquire the
additional components [+ female] and [+ male] which the adult
words *mummy* and *daddy* can be said to have.

Componential analysis can analyse *underextended* meanings as well as
the *overextensions* we have just described. For example, a young child
may use the word *bottle* to refer to its own drinking bottle but not to any
other kinds of bottle; in this case the word could be said to have the components [+ container] [+ drink], whereas for the adult the word could
be said to lack the [+ drink] component. Of course, we cannot claim
to have given an adequate account of the meaning of *bottle* by simply

saying that it contains the components [+ container] [+ drink]. It can often be difficult to know which components to specify as the essential features of a word's meaning. Nevertheless, this approach to the analysis of word meaning can be a neat way of representing the meaning relationships that exist between some words in the vocabulary, and it has had a useful application in describing some of the differences between children's and adults' uses of certain words.

Activity 4.3

If you know a child of about two years old, look through a picture book with the child and ask them to name some everyday things that are in the pictures. Note the words that seem to be underextensions or overextensions of adult usage, and try to specify the semantic features that the child has but that adults do not have, or that adults have but that the child does not.

Although componential analysis has its uses as an *ad hoc* descriptive device, it has several problems. We said above that it is economical to treat components as binary, so that certain words can be said to differ from each other by the simple presence or absence of a semantic feature. Binary relationships of meaning are important in the vocabulary of a language (as we have already seen in the analysis of opposites) but there are other types of relationship that are equally important and that cannot be analysed in this way. For example, words such as colour terms and days of the week cannot be analysed as differing from each other by the simple presence or absence of a particular semantic feature. Furthermore, it is not necessarily particularly revealing simply to list the semantic components of a word, as we saw earlier with *bottle*; and even if it does seem that this can be done, we may need to say how the components are combined. An example that is often given is the word *kill*, which can be analysed into the components [cause], [become], [-alive] but for which we need, in addition, to specify that the components are ordered in a hierarchical relationship:

[cause]
$\downarrow$
[become]
$\downarrow$
[− alive]

and to specify the participants (for example X [cause] Y → Y [become] → [− alive]).

A further difficulty is that, although it is economical to represent semantic features as being present or absent, it is not necessarily helpful to give the meaning of a word in terms of what it is not, rather than in terms of what it is. The meaning of the word *girl*, for instance, has been analysed in terms of the features [− adult] [− male], which do indeed distinguish it from *boy* ([− adult] [+ male]) and from *woman* ([+ adult], [− male]) but which do not tell us a great deal about the meaning of *girl*! In fact, there is no obvious reason why *girl* should not be analysed as containing the features [+ child] [+ female] and *boy* as [+ child] [− female]. Sometimes it is the semantically un-marked term or the formally unmarked term that is chosen as the positive pole — and this may account for the choice of [+ male] rather than [+ female]. However, the choices that analysts make are unlikely to be arbitrary or objective. Like anyone else, analysts will be influenced by the norms and values of their society.

Activity 4.4

You may find it helpful to test your understanding of the different types of relationships between word meanings mentioned so far. You can do this by deciding which of the different types of structural relationship we have discussed is most helpful in trying to analyse the meanings of the following words:

   calf
   addled
   chaffinch
   innocent
   buy

There is no right or wrong way to analyse word meaning, but since mean-ing relationships are of several different kinds, some words may lend themselves to a particular type of analysis better than others. The most helpful forms of analysis for the words above seem to be:

calf Since this is the word used to refer to a young male bull, this can be economically analysed as containing the components [+ cattle], [+ male], [− adult] — if we use the conventional 'positive' features. It then contrasts with

bull [+ cattle], [+ male], [+ adult]
cow [+ cattle], [− male], [+ adult]
heifer [+ cattle], [− male], [− adult]

In fact, componential analysis was first used by anthropologists to analyse kinship terminology, and it is often a useful way of representing 'family' relationships such as this one.

addled This word occurs almost exclusively in connection with the words *eggs* and *brains*. Its meaning can, therefore, be usefully analysed in terms of its collocations.

chaffinch Since this is one of the species of birds that we identify as a separate type, its meaning can be represented as a hyponymous relationship, with *chaffinch* a hyponym of the superordinate *bird*.

innocent This can be considered to be in a complementary relationship with *guilty*, since in principle it is not possible to be both innocent of something and guilty of it.

buy This can be considered to be in a converse relationship with *sell*, since the two are reverse activities. In the normal course of events someone can only buy an object if it is sold to them.

4.3 WORDS IN CONTEXT: SENTENCE AND UTTERANCE MEANING

Analysing word meaning is useful, but there is more involved in communication than simply adding together the meaning of individual words. Linguistic context can be all important in determining which of a number of meanings of a word is intended: compare, for example, the two phrases *here's a mug of coffee* and *he's an ugly mug*! The linguistic context alone is still not adequate, however. The phrase *here's a mug of coffee* can have many different meanings depending on such factors as the way in which it is uttered, what has been said before, and the general situational context. It could be a straightforward piece of information mentioned by a speaker as they pass across a steaming mug; but at the end of a party it could be a polite hint that it is time the guests were leaving; or it could be a not very polite way of telling someone they have had more than enough to drink and that they ought to sober up. Many other interpretations are possible in different contexts.

It can be helpful to make a distinction between *sentence meaning*, which can be described in terms of the words and the syntax of what is said, and *utterance meaning*, which takes account of other features of the linguistic context (such as intonation) and of the situational context. However, it is not always easy to draw a clear-cut distinction in this way, and when we interpret language these two aspects of meaning are usually interrelated. Listeners and readers need actively to interpret what is said — to make inferences about the meaning of utterances using both their linguistic and their cultural knowledge. In this section we will not attempt to make a clear distinction between sentence meaning and utterance meaning, but we will discuss approaches to the analysis of meaning which take account of the need to interpret words in context.

Speech acts

Speech act theory focuses on the communicative function that a particular sentence has when it is uttered, or the 'act' that it performs. It is possible to identify sentence types on the basis of their syntactic structure. In section 3.4 for instance, four sentence types were identified: statements, interrogative sentences, imperatives, and exclamations. These often correlate with the acts of giving information, asking questions, giving orders and exclaiming.

Statement	You will have to go.
Interrogative	Do you want to go?
Imperative	Go away!
Exclamation	What a good idea!

The relationship between the form of a sentence and the speech act that it performs is more complex than this, however. Although the four sentence types above do often have these semantic functions (some analysts have argued that they always do, though they may have other functions too) there is not necessarily always a one-to-one correlation. Consider, for example, the sentence, *It's hot in here*. This may have the semantic function of giving information (that the speaker thinks that it is hot), but it could also function as an order or as a question, depending on the circumstances in which it was said. If said by someone in authority it could mean 'will you open the window?' or even 'open the window immediately!'. In this case we can say that the sentence is an indirect speech act.

There are, of course, more functions than the four mentioned above (giving information, asking questions, giving orders and exclaiming). The same sentence, *It's hot in here*, could be an apology (if said to visitors in your home), a complaint (if said by a visitor in a hotel) or even a warning (for example, if the speakers are in a room where nitroglycerine is stored!). It can perform several speech acts at the same time: this same sentence, for instance, could be both an apology to visitors and a complaint that someone had not opened the window, as well as a request that someone should now do so. The philosopher Austin suggested that there could be as many as 10,000 different functions of sentences and others have suggested the number is infinite! These functions are performed by a relatively small number of syntactic structures.

The sheer number of different speech acts that sentences can perform makes it very difficult to analyse this aspect of language. A further problem is to decide whether to categorise speech acts in terms of the speaker's *intentions*, or in terms of the hearer's *perceptions* of the speech act. These do not always coincide, as the example below, adapted from Gumperz (1982), illustrates. A mother is talking to her eleven-year-old son, who is about to go out in the rain:

Mother: Where are your boots?
Son: In the closet
Mother: I want you to put them on right now!

The mother intended her first sentence to be an order for her son to put his boots on (an indirect speech act). Her son interpreted her sentence not as an order but as a question, to which he responded — or perhaps he only pretended to interpret it in this way, in order to joke with his mother. His statement was then interpreted by his mother as a refusal to obey her order. Alternatively, she may have wanted to communicate that joking was not appropriate at that moment. It is even possible that all of these functions were present. We cannot say exactly what went on in this transaction, since we cannot know the intentions or the emotions of the people involved.

Because of these problems, speech acts are often categorised in terms of the act that is performed by speakers when they say a particular utterance, rather than in terms of the speaker's intentions. This is easiest to see when a sentence contains a *performative verb*. In this case it is the utterance of the sentence that performs the act, and it is less necessary to take into account the speaker's intentions and the hearer's perceptions. Some clear examples are:

Act of marriage	I hereby pronounce you man and wife.
Act of naming a ship	I name this ship the *Saucy Sue*.
Act of closing a meeting	I declare this meeting closed.
Act of a wager	I bet you a fiver.
Act of apology	I apologise.

In all these sentences there is a first person present tense verb, the sentence has the syntactic structure of a statement, and it would be possible to include the word *hereby*. Of course, for the utterances to fulfil their function the circumstances have to be right: not just anyone can pronounce two people man and wife; one has to have the authority to do this. Even in apparently clear-cut examples such as these, the social circumstances of the participants and the situation have to be taken into account.

When a performative verb is not present, the number of potential functions of an utterance greatly increases. However, the situation in which an utterance occurs helps the communication to go smoothly, for our shared social and cultural knowledge provides us with clues about what to expect. For example, we know that a teacher who says to a class of pupils *I can hear someone talking*, is more likely to be giving an order for that person to stop talking than to be simply giving information (though these functions probably overlap to some extent). We know, too, that the sentence *Can you swim a length, Mary?* is likely to be a question if it is said by a teacher to a pupil in a classroom, but that if it is said by a teacher to a pupil at a swimming pool it is more likely to be a command, and to be followed by a splash! (see Coulthard, 1977). If the people involved do not have the same social and cultural knowledge, however, problems of interpretation can arise. Some illustrations of miscommunications between people from different cultural backgrounds can be found in Gumperz, 1982.

Activity 4.5

Identify both the syntactic form (e.g. the four sentence types identified earlier) and the semantic function (e.g. 'asking a question' or 'giving an order') of each of the following utterances. Where more than one semantic function is possible, think of a context in which each possibility might occur.

(1) Be there at four o'clock
(2) I name this child Elizabeth.
(3) Are you going to do that washing-up?
(4) Come upstairs.
(5) I bet you a fiver it snows before Christmas.
(6) I sentence you to six years' heavy labour.
(7) I run round the block every morning.

Sentences (1) and (4) have the form of an imperative sentence, sentence (3) of an interrogative sentence and the other sentences all have the form of statements.

The semantic functions of sentences (2), (5) and (6) are unambiguous. They all contain a performative verb (*I name*, *I bet* and *I sentence*) and they perform, respectively, the acts of baptising, betting and sentencing (if the social circumstances are right). The semantic functions of the other sentences are potentially very numerous: for example, sentence (1) could be an invitation, if said by one friend to another, a command, if said by an army general to his subordinate, a plea, a warning and many other things.

Note that sentence (7) does not contain a performative verb despite the fact that is has a first person present tense form. To say *I bet* constitutes the act of betting, but in order to perform the act of running we have to do more than say *I run*! A test for performative sentences is to see whether the word *hereby* can be added: it could, to *I bet*, but not to *I run*.

Inferential meaning

We now examine three types of inference that may be drawn from utterances: *entailment*, *presupposition* and *conversational implicature*. As you will see, the inferences become progressively more dependent upon the non-linguistic context.

ENTAILMENT

This is perhaps the most straightforward inference. Entailment refers to a logical relationship that holds between a sentence and a proposition that the sentence expresses (this relationship should hold irrespective of the context in which the sentence is actually realised and it can be considered, therefore, as an aspect of sentence meaning as opposed to utterance meaning). Entailment is often described using logical formulae but, in more everyday language, a sentence *entails* a proposition if, under every condition in which the sentence is true, the proposition is also true. Thus the sentence

S Mary has a cat and a dog

entails the proposition:

S_1 Mary has a cat

since if S is true, so is S_1.

Note that although entailment here refers to certain propositions that may be deduced from sentences it is also a way of handling many of the *sense relations* discussed in Section 4.2 above. In the relation of *hyponymy*, for instance, *x is a rose* entails *x is a flower*, but *y is a flower* does not entail *y is a rose*.

PRESUPPOSITION

Entailment is of limited usefulness in handling inferences listeners may draw from utterances of a particular sentence. It only really applies to sentences that have a *truth value* (i.e. that are either true or false), which rules out non-declarative sentences such as: *Who ate those cherries?*

Someone who heard this uttered might conventionally infer that the speaker believed *someone* had eaten the cherries but the sentence cannot *entail* this proposition as it does not have a truth value (it is not possible to say that a question is either true or false). Such inferences, which depend upon the meanings that a listener would conventionally attach to the utterance of a particular sentence, have been termed *presuppositions*.

There has been some argument over the need to distinguish presupposition and entailment. A classic case concerns the sentence

S The king of France is bald.

Some analyses suggest that this sentence entails the proposition:

S_1 There exists a king of France.

If, as nowadays, the proposition S_1 is false, then so is the sentence S. An analysis based upon presupposition, however, would claim S *presupposes* S_1. If S_1 is false S is neither true nor false — it's simply based upon an erroneous presupposition. Unlike entailment, it's argued, presupposition holds good under negation and in question forms:

S the king of France is not bald
S is the king of France bald?

still presuppose S_1.

Presupposition has been used to describe other inferences that derive from the (linguistic) meaning of a sentence — for instance, those that derive from verbs such as *know, realise* and *regret*: *Eve knew Adam's fig leaf was loose* presupposes: *Adam's fig leaf was loose.* (Contrast: *Eve believed Adam's fig leaf was loose*).

Presupposition does have characteristics in common with entailment — for instance if a presupposition is overtly contradicted, an utterance will not (normally) make sense: *Adam's fig leaf wasn't loose but Eve knew Adam's fig leaf was loose.*

Semantic theorists have often been dissatisfied with the notion of presupposition — it has proved very difficult to define in a watertight way which includes everything one intuitively feels is a presupposition while excluding everything else. For instance, it's been argued that presuppositions need not hold constant under negation. One might legitimately say: *Of course the king of France isn't bald: there isn't a king of France.*

Kempson (1977) discusses some of the problems associated with presupposition from a theoretical point of view and argues that it is more straightforward to handle all such relations in terms of entailment. This, however, seems not to account adequately for a common-sense understanding speakers and listeners may have that a sentence can presuppose something it does not directly assert. An alternative suggestion (e.g. Lyons, 1977) is that we should allow presupposition some measure of *context dependency*. For instance, imagine a conversation between X and Y in which X says that, to her certain knowledge, no reigning European monarch is bald. If Y responds seriously that *The king of France is bald*, X could well retort *That's not true: there isn't a king of France.* What is being denied here is Y's assertion that the class of European monarchs contains the king of France. In other contexts, however, *That's not true* would be taken to deny the assertion that the king was bald. (For a fuller discussion of this and other examples, see Lyons, 1977, pp. 601–5).

CONVERSATIONAL IMPLICATURE

The notion of conversational implicature is based chiefly on the work of Grice (see Grice, 1975). Grice identified two kinds of implicature: *conventional* and *conversational implicature*. The distinction between these is not always straightforward but, roughly, conventional implicature refers to implications in an utterance that depend upon the conventional meanings of words and expressions. (These shared conventions were mentioned in section 4.2 and we saw there that they can sometimes be decidedly fuzzy.) Conversational implicature, with which we shall be concerned here, takes into account not only the literal meaning of a sentence, but also the context in which it is uttered, the background knowledge of speaker and hearer and general principles governing the conduct of conversation. Grice suggested that each participant's contribution is governed by these four principles (sometimes termed *Grice's maxims*):

Quantity: don't provide more or less information than is required
              for the current purposes of the exchange;
Quality: speak the truth;
Relevance: be relevant;
Manner: be clear.

For instance, the utterance of the sentence *I think the car's still there* might imply that the speaker is not *certain* the car is still there since according to Grice's maxim of *quantity* a speaker would normally be expected to be as informative as was necessary. In most contexts it would be preferable to provide more definite information: *The car's still there*, if one had this information. Similarly, if a motorist tells a passer-by that she's nearly out of petrol and asks for directions to the nearest garage the reply *There's one just round the corner on the right* would be taken to imply that, as far as the passer-by was aware, the garage was open and had supplies of petrol — since, according to Grice's maxim of relevance one would normally be expected to say something that is relevant to the conversation in hand.

Unlike entailment and presupposition, some implicatures can be cancelled by the speaker. The utterance *I think the car's still there* might imply *I don't know it's still there*, but in response to a question *Do you think the car's still there*? a speaker could quite reasonably reply, *Yes — in fact, I know it is.*

The notion of implicature is, as Grice recognises, often imprecise — and the formulation of the conversational maxims themselves is somewhat vague. The distinction between presupposition and implicature is also not straightforward — and in fact, it's been suggested that presupposition can be handled in terms of conversational implicature. For instance the utterance *the king of France is bald* would normally flout Grice's maximum of relevance if there were, in fact, no king of France. However, it does not seem sensible to lump the two categories together, since conversational implicature is distinct from presupposition in assuming a speaker is providing information that is not part of the literal meaning of a sentence.

It may sometimes seem that participants are not conforming to these conversational principles (the first one, particularly, may often seem to be flouted!), but in fact these principles often help in the analysis of conversations that appear at first to be problematic. Consider, for example, this exchange:

A: Are you going to the cinema tonight?
B: Jim's away.

If we assume that both A and B are obeying Grice's four maxims, then B's response must be relevant to A's question, and must provide enough information to answer the question. For example, B could be married to

Jim and have two small children and no access to babysitters. A would have to know this background information about B, and B would have to know that A knew it.

INDIRECT SPEECH AND PERSUASIVE LANGUAGE

Persuasive language such as that used in advertising often depends in part for its effectiveness on propositions that are implied in an utterance rather than directly asserted. In a study of 800 video-taped advertisements broadcast on American television between 1978 and 1981 Geis (1982) found several occasions when part of the advertisers' message, which might have been difficult to support by evidence, was put across indirectly — obviously by visual means, since his sample of adverts came from television, but also through indirect uses of language, analysed by Geis in terms of presupposition and conversational implicature. Examples of presuppositions include:

a) *We're in the appliance department to find out why Sears is where America shops* — presupposes 'Sears is where America shops'.
b) *This Atra face-hugging action keeps twin blades at the perfect angle* — presupposes 'Atra twin blades are at the perfect angle'.

(Note: Geis terms these 'conventional implicatures' after Grice (1975), but since in this case they are identical to presuppositions, we shall continue to use this term.)

Geis argues:

> Since conventionally implicated propositions [i.e. presuppositions] are rarely defended in ordinary conversation, I submit that viewers will normally not expect to find them defended in advertising. Therefore, any advertiser who wishes to convey some proposition P but does not want to defend P or cannot defend P can simply use a construction that [presupposes] P with little fear that viewers will question P.

He compares utterance b) above with the following possibility, in which both propositions are formulated as assertions (Geis, 1982, p. 46):

c) *Atra twin hugging blades are set at the perfect angle and this Atra face-hugging action keeps them that way* and suggests that viewers would be much more likely to challenge the truth of the proposition that the Atra twin blades are set at the perfect angle had the advertiser said (c) instead of (b).

Examples of conversational implicatures include:

d) *They invented fluoride toothpaste to help fight cavities. Why hasn't somebody invented a better toothbrush*? implies 'somebody should have invented a better toothbrush — we later find out, of course, that somebody has.
e) *Wet feet*? *LOOK OUT FOR A COLD — gargle with LISTERINE QUICK* — an old advert from a study carried out in 1943. Geis

argues that the use of language in this advert conversationally implicates that Listerine can prevent colds — why otherwise would there by any need for quick action? Here Geis is using Grice's maxim of relevance, discussed above.

f) *We are building a reputation*, *not resting on one* — an advertisement for Ramada Inn. Geis tried out this claim on a number of respondents, virtually every one of whom took it to be suggesting:

g) Some leading competitor of Ramada Inn is resting on its reputation.

In fact, most of Geis' respondents assumed the leading competitor must be Holiday Inn. Geis (1982, p. 50) again argues this implication can be justified by the maxim of relevance: 'Why say you are not resting on your reputation unless someone has said that you are or you believe someone else is resting on his reputation?'

Geis draws conclusions from his study that have implications for practice — he wants advertisers to be responsible for what their adverts would normally be taken to imply, as well as for explicit assertions. In support of this he argues that, in speaking, people normally make inferences about meanings, and that they do not distinguish between semantic inferences (such as entailment) and pragmatic inferences (such as conversational implicature). This, of course, makes sense in ordinary conversation but can be played upon by users of persuasive language.

Activity 4.6

You may like to compare British advertisements with Geis's American sample. Record a sample of television adverts (say, five or six) broadcast during one evening. Listen to each carefully (you may need to replay your recording two or three times) and try to identify how many use 'indirect' language to convey their message. Can you analyse this usage in terms of presupposition and conversational implicature?

Note that this exercise is only a 'taster': to be able to say anything about British advertising in general you would need to analyse a representative sample, as Geis did in the USA.

4.4   THE ROLE OF WORLD KNOWLEDGE

In the previous section we described the types of inference that we draw from the utterances that we hear. In this section we will consider the way in which these inferences are dependent on our knowledge of the world.

Consider, as an example, the following sentences (from Bolinger, 1965):

Our store sells alligator shoes
Our store sells horse shoes

It is likely that you will interpret the first sentence as meaning that the store sells shoes that are made of alligator skin, and the second sentence as meaning that the store sells shoes that are for horses to wear. In part it is our knowledge of language that leads us to these interpretations. We can interpret the first sentence by comparing it with sentences such as:

> Our store sells leather shoes
> plastic shoes
> canvas shoes

and the second sentence by comparing it with:

> Our store sells tennis shoes
> curtain rings
> dog leads
> cat litter
> writing paper

In each case we make use of our knowledge of the syntagmatic relationships and the paradigmatic relationships in language: syntagmatic, by considering the relationships between the noun *shoes* and the adjectival nouns that describe the nature of the shoes; or between the noun *shoes* and the nouns that describe what the second set of nouns are for; paradigmatic, by comparing *alligator* in the first case, and *horse* in the second case, with other nouns and adjectives that could occur in this phrase. We need to draw on more than our knowledge of language alone, though, for this simply tells us that either interpretation is acceptable in terms of the structure of the language. It is part of our knowledge of the world that horses wear shoes and that alligators do not; and that alligator skins are used to make shoes whereas horse skins are not. We draw inferences from the words in the two sentences, and the inferences result from a combination of our knowledge of language and our knowledge of the world.

If we want to analyse the meaning of words in context, then we need to find a framework that will not only analyse the conventions governing the meaning of words and sentences, and the inferences that are drawn from them, but that will also analyse our knowledge of the world. This is a daunting prospect. Furthermore, it is not possible to draw a clear line between these two different types of knowledge, for they are interrelated. We could conceivably analyse *horse* as having as one component of its meaning the fact that in certain states of domesticity it is likely to wear metal 'shoes' (see Biggs, 1982) but if we take this line of analysis then the amount of information that we would have to include about all the entities in the world that we might like to talk about at some time would be immense. It would also vary from one person to another, since we all have different experiences of the world and we all have different amounts and types of world knowledge to draw on when we attempt to interpret language, as well as different amounts and types of linguistic knowledge.

Eco (1984) gives us a way of analysing how our interpretation of words in context depends on both our knowledge of language and our knowledge of the world. He uses the concept of 'frame', which comes from recent research into Artificial Intelligence, but which can be usefully applied to real intelligence, too (see also the discussion of 'frame' in section 7.4). The assumption is that we have an 'encyclopaedic' set of beliefs about the world, which we store in sets of frames. Eco gives as illustration the sentences below:

> John was sleeping when he was suddenly awakened. Somebody was tearing up the pillow.

When you read these sentences you undoubtedly made the inference that the pillow referred to in the second sentence is the pillow that John was sleeping on. It may seem that this is simply common sense. However, the goal of linguistic analysis is to make explicit the unconscious knowledge that we draw on when we communicate with each other, and so our common-sense interpretation is something that needs to be explained. After all, there is no mention of a pillow in the first of the two sentences. In part, of course, our interpretation depends on our linguistic knowledge: we know (unconsciously, perhaps, rather than consciously) that to say *the pillow* rather than *a pillow* implies that the speaker has a particular pillow in mind. This could be a pillow that had been mentioned in a previous sentence, in which case it is the linguistic context that provides us with the correct interpretation; or it could be simply a pillow that we might expect to be there, since we know that people conventionally go to sleep with their head resting on a pillow. In this case it is our world knowledge that provides us with the correct interpretation — coupled with our linguistic knowledge of the opposition between *the* and *a*.

If we go along with Eco's approach, seeing our knowledge of the world as stored in sets of frames, then we can share his view of the process that you may have used to make the inference that the pillow in his example sentence was the pillow that John was sleeping on (assume, in the quotation that follows, that you are his addressee):

> By resorting to this storage of competence, the addressee knows that human beings usually sleep in bedrooms and that bedrooms are furnished with beds, beds with pillows, and so on. By amalgamation of two or more frames, the addressee realizes that the pillow just mentioned can only be the one John was resting his head on (Eco, 1984, p. 71).

Eco gives a further example of the way in which we might use 'frames' in communication. He asks us to imagine that during the night, looking out of the window of her home in the countryside, a (presumably American) wife tells her husband: 'Honey, there is a man on the lawn near the fence!' The word *man* enters into a number of different meaning relationships with other words in the vocabulary. Some of these can be analysed using componential analysis: for example, *man* is related to *boy* (man is [+ adult], boy is [− adult]), to *tree* (*man* is [+ animate], *tree* is [− animate]), and to *dog* (*man* is [+ human], *dog* is [− human]). It also enters into relationships with other words, which cannot be analysed so neatly: if we imagine a 'semantic field' of 'strange things in the garden at night', for example, we might include in the semantic field such words and phrases as *alien invader*, *giant teddy bear* (left there by their children), *shadow of a tree*, and so on. The husband has to make a conjecture about the semantic properties of the word *man* that are important to his wife on this particular occasion. In this case it seems most likely that the woman was interested in the man as a possible threat to their safety. As Eco (1984, p. 79) says:

> Probably the wife was not interested in the fact that men are mortal or hot-blooded animals; she was interested in their being rational only insofar as to be rational means to conceive evil intentions. In other words, a man was to her something potentially aggressive, able to move inside. If the thing were a child, it would be felt as nonpotentially aggressive; if it were a dog, it would be felt as unable to intrude; if it were a tree or a giant teddy bear, it would be felt as unable to move. On the contrary, a spatial alien would be viewed as a moving and potentially agressive being. We can also suppose that each alternative elicits the retrieval of a given frame such as 'burglars in the night', 'lost child', 'space invaders', . . . and so on.

Eco's point is that each time we use a word we 'blow up' certain properties of the word, and 'narcoticise' other properties. In this case, as Eco says, the woman had presumably 'narcoticised' the component of the meaning of *man* that is [+ mortal] (i.e. *man* as the complementary of *god*), as well as various other possible components of the word's meaning. Instead, she had 'blown up' the component of [+ dangerous]. We would probably not consider this aspect of the meaning of *man* to be a central aspect of its meaning (unless, perhaps, we had had some particularly unfortunate experiences, which had given the word this connotation for us). It is certainly unlikely to be listed in a dictionary as part of the meaning of the word. However, if we think of words as having various components of meaning, both central and more peripheral, with each component having a probability of applying (as discussed in section 4.2) then we can see that in the situation that Eco describes — late at night, looking out into a dark garden — there is a higher than usual probability of this aspect of the meaning of *man* applying.

If the husband in this scenario wants to reassure his wife, it is not enough for him to answer 'No, honey, it's not a man', since this would leave open the other potentially threatening meanings of the word. Eco's suggestion is that the husband who interprets his wife's utterance correctly will make a spur of the moment 'hyponymy' tree for himself, to see how the word *man* fits into his wife's own current classification of things. He does this using his knowledge of the world (and this will include his knowledge of what he thinks his wife's knowledge of the world is). The result may be something like the hyponymy tree below:

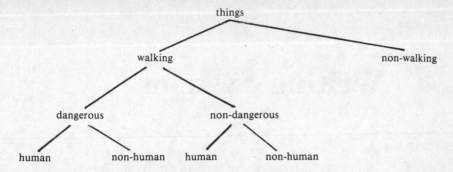

He can then look out of the window to see which of the objects in this *ad hoc* classification the object most resembles. This may then lead him to say something like 'No honey, it's not a man, it's a child' or 'a dog' or 'a teddy bear', so that he can exclude the [+ dangerous] component of meaning. Alternatively, if he wishes to scare his wife, he could say simply, 'No, honey, it's not a man', leaving open the possibility that the thing is, perhaps, a creature from Mars!

Eco's analysis gives us a way of analysing the flexibility of word meaning, and of describing the way in which our interpretation of meaning depends on both our knowledge of language and our knowledge of the world. In his own words: 'language is a flexible system of signification'. We still have not managed to give a framework that will allow us to systematise our knowledge of the world, though. Most linguists and philosophers would agree that this is an impossible task.

We can, however, take a view of human culture that has much in common with Eco's view of word meaning. The philosopher Quine gives an analysis of beliefs and their relation to language which fits in very well with this approach. Quine (1953; 1960) proposes that we share a tightly organised central set of beliefs and a more fuzzy periphery of beliefs. We have recourse to these beliefs when we draw inferences from what people say. Many of the conventions that we share about the meanings of words (their core meanings, for example, or the connotations that they have for us) are part of the central area of our 'world view'. Eco suggests that many of the superordinate terms that we use in our classifications of hyponyms (see section 4.2) are central beliefs: they have been part of the world view of our culture for millenia, and as a result they are taken for granted as true, and are very resistant to change.

For Quine, our beliefs about the world are similarly part of an interwoven network of inferences or beliefs. It is possible for the central beliefs to change, but for this to happen radical social changes are necessary.

5 Writing Systems

5.1 THE DEVELOPMENT OF WRITING SYSTEMS

The ways in which humans first learned to communicate with each other — by sounds and gestures — were ephemeral. There was no way of recording communications for archive purposes, or for transmitting to a person who was out of sight or earshot. It is easy to see why alternative ways were found to inscribe messages in a more permanent form.

The earliest known written messages were essentially *pictographic* in nature. That is, they sought to convey their meaning through the use of drawings in much the same way as a modern cartoon. Thus the picture might conjure up a whole sentence or linked ideas in the reader's mind. Figure 5.1 shows a letter sent in the last century by a North American Indian girl which is predominantly of this kind. You may well find it difficult to work out exactly what the letter meant, since you do not share the writer's cultural background or the recipient's expectations. This is how it was interpreted by a contemporary American ethnologist Garnick Mallery (cited in Gelb, 1963 p 31):

> . . . a letter written by an Ojibwa girl to a favoured lover, requesting him to call at her lodge. The girl is represented by the bear totem, the boy by that of the mud puppy. The trail leads toward the lakes, shown by the three irregular circles, whence it branches off in the direction of the two tents. Three Christian girls, indicated by the crosses, are encamped there. From one of the tents protrudes the arm of the girl inviting the Indian boy to call on her.

Apart from the cartoon, this kind of pictograph has contemporary counterparts in illustrated maps or in certain road signs — such as the one for 'quayside or river bank' which depicts a car falling from a solid surface into water. Although clearly representational, they embody certain conventions and assumptions about how a message is to be read.

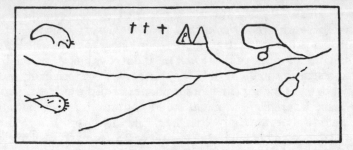

Figure 5.1.   Letter from an Ojibwa girl to her lover
Source: Reproduced in Gelb (1963)

Ancient writing systems seem to have developed from systems of pictographs by associating stylised drawings with particular words in the writer's language. Certainly, this is what seems to have happened during the development of the oldest known writing system, *Sumerian cuneiform*, which appeared in southern Mesopotamia towards the end of the fourth millenium BC. Pictographs became more stylised, streamlined, and hence more suited to inscribing on the clay tablets then used. The writing system is called *cuneiform* (from the Latin for 'wedge shape') because of the shape which the signs then acquired.

The meaning of the signs also changed as the writing system developed. The writing system was at first a *logographic* one — that is, a single sign denoted a single word — but this had the disadvantage that a new sign had to be learned and remembered for every word in the language. This was obviously not an insuperable problem, however. Indeed, there is at least one major world language — Chinese — whose writing system is basically logographic in character. (Japanese, which has a mixed script, also uses many logographs borrowed and adapted from the Chinese.) Some of the logographs are highly stylised pictographs. For example we find not only 木 for a tree but 林 for a wood and 森 for a forest. It is not difficult to imagine how the picture of a tree gradually turned into the symbol for a tree. But if we give the tree roots, it becomes 本 which originally meant literally 'a root' but has now come to mean 'origin' or, by extension, 'book' (the source of knowledge). As any reader of Chinese or Japanese will tell you, this is a very simple example. Some complex characters are very metaphorical indeed! But they have the advantage — in a vast country such as China, which has a variety of spoken languages — of being directly comprehensible, without needing to be 'sounded out' in any particular form of spoken language. If you can understand Chinese script, you can read the words aloud in English or Urdu or whatever spoken language you please. (Naturally, a full understanding of idioms would require greater familiarity with the culture.)

Two kinds of writing systems superseded the logographies in most parts of the world: the *syllabaries* and *alphabets*. It is believed that an intermediate stage in the transition from logography to syllabary may have been the adoption of the *rebus* (Latin for 'by things') principle. This allowed a sign to stand not only for the word it was originally intended to depict but also for any other homophone (a word which is *pronounced* in the same way). Thus ⊙ might stand not only for 'eye' but also for 'aye' and 'I'; ⋛ not only for 'bee' but also for 'be'. Moreover, monosyllabic symbols could be combined to form polysyllabic words such as ⋛ ⅃ = eye + deer = 'idea' or ⊙ ∨ = bee + leaf = belief. This represented a fundamental break with the previous principle of a *semantic* link, however tenuous, between the picture and the word. (It is totally different, for example, from the process at work in the development of Chinese logographs.)

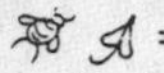

Gradually, fully stylised syllabaries evolved — as can be seen from the illustrations of Sumerian cuneiform script in figures 5.2 and 5.3, where the stylised picture of a bird, etc., has gradually evolved into the symbol for the sound 'bird' in whatever context. There are still a number of extant syllabaries, notably the Hiragana and Katakana scripts used for writing Japanese, which has a very regular syllable structure. They did not prove appropriate for all languages, however, especially those (like English) where syllable structure is more complicated.

The Sumerian cuneiform was not the only writing system used in the

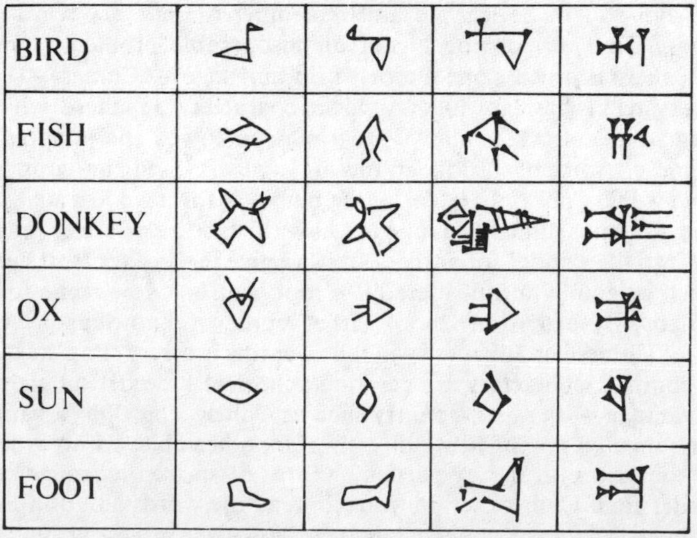

Figure 5.2.   Development from pictogram to wedge symbol in Sumerian cuneiform

Figure 5.3. Fully developed cuneiform found at the Palace of Assourhazirtal, Iraq

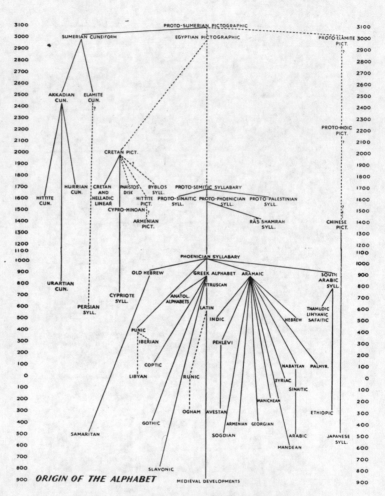

Figure 5.4.   The development of writing systems
Source: Gelb (1963)

ancient world. Although the first to appear, it was soon joined by a number of other more or less independent systems, such as the hieroglyphics used in ancient Egypt. Many of these rival scripts seem to have developed from a logographic to a syllabic system. But it was not until the ancient Greeks borrowed and modified a Semitic syllabic script that a true *alphabetic* system was devised. Alphabets require even fewer symbols than syllabaries by using — in an ideal system — only one symbol for each single phoneme (see section 2.3). Most of the world's writing systems are now alphabetic, although there are considerable differences in the shape of the symbols used in different alphabets. The evolution of the world's writing systems thus seems to have followed a similar pattern, as shown in Figure 5.4. This may misleadingly suggest, however, that alphabets are inherently superior to other systems, and that they will serve the needs of a literate society better. This is not altogether true. English, for example, makes use of an alphabet, but diverges in many ways from a strict alphabetic principle in the ways it spells words. As section 5.3 explains, most alphabetic systems are mixed ones, and incorporate some logographic features. What counts as an optimal writing system will very much depend on the structure and internal variety of a given language.

5.2 THE PATTERN OF ENGLISH SPELLING

If a writing system closely mirrors the spoken word, then differences in written forms will indicate differences in pronunciation and language usage, but anyone familiar with English *orthography* (its spelling system) will know that this is not always the case. Many teachers and learners of English have complained that English spelling seems hopelessly unsystematic. George Bernard Shaw — an ardent supporter of spelling reform — once claimed that it would be quite possible for the word *fish* to be spelled as 'ghoti'. His reasoning is given below:

gh as in 'rou*gh*'
o as in 'w*o*men'
ti as in 'na*ti*on'

Shaw was, of course, quite wrong — or at least mischievous. The absurdity of his suggestion comes precisely from the fact that we realise that English spelling does not allow such a representation, although we may not be quite able to put our finger on why.

English spelling today can be regarded as containing a number of conventions and systems for representing sounds. Many of these have arisen for historical reasons. In this section, we look briefly at the historical background and then outline several of the subsystems or principles which are inherent in modern English spelling. As we are examining the relationship between sound and spelling you may find the discussion easier if you have already read Chapter 2. See particularly Table 2.2 representing the sound system (phoneme inventory) of English.

Historical background

The oldest preserved inscriptions in English date from the early eighth century and, like Scandinavian inscriptions at that time, used the futhorc, or *runic alphabet*. Figure 5.5 shows a fragment of a poem ('The dream of the Holy Rood') which is inscribed on part of the Ruthwell Cross and written in the Northumbrian dialect of Old English — then the foremost literary variety.

The runic alphabet was, in spite of its appearance, based on an early Roman one, which was modified to make it more suitable for inscribing on stone or grained surfaces with an axe. The manuscript alphabet used in later Old English was not a direct development from the runic, though it retained one or two extra symbols:

a, æ, b, c, d, e, f, ᴣ, h, i, k, l, m, n, o, p, r,
s, t, þ, ð, u, ρ, x, y.

By the end of the eleventh century, Old English spelling had become very close to being phonemic, and there was considerable agreement between scribes in various parts of the country about the conventions to be employed.

This situation changed dramatically during the Middle Ages and the Middle English period (1066–1500). The scribes who copied the works of Chaucer, Lydgate or the Gawain poet seemed to spell words in various ways, often spelling the same word differently on the same page. English spelling became destabilised during this period for several reasons. Most scribes were trained in French and Latin, which used rather different conventions for representing sounds. They often used these conventions when copying or writing in English. (Hence þ (thorn) became *th*). There was very little original material being produced in English — most official documents were in French and Latin. Hence it was difficult to maintain a proper tradition of English spelling. The stability of the Old English spelling system contributed to its own undoing. The pronunciation of English was undergoing great changes, partly as a result of contact with French. This meant that fixed spellings were becoming less and less accurate as representations of speech. Under these various pressures, medieval scribes began to spell words roughly as they pronounced them in their varied dialects, and according to a variety of conventions.

SE FRAGMENT

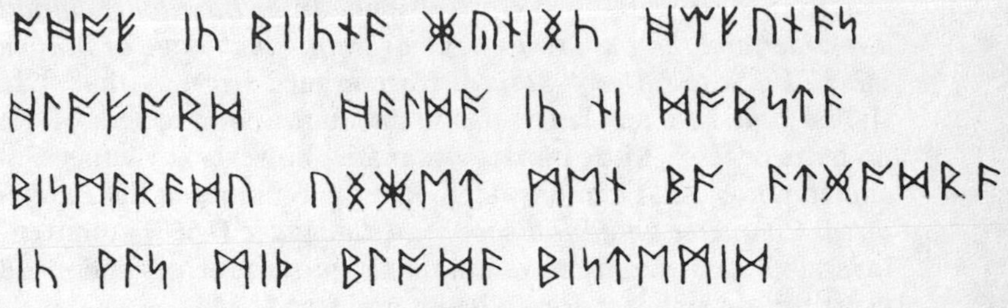

ᚠᚺᚠᚠ ᛁᚺ ᚱᛁᛁᚺᛏᚠ ᚲᛘᚺᛁᚷᚺ ᚺᛐᚠᚿᛏᚠᛋ
ᚺᛁᚠᚠᚠᚱᚺ   ᚺᚠᛁᚺᚠ ᛁᚺ ᛐᛁ ᚺᚠᚱᛋᛏᚠ
ᛒᛁᛋᚺᚠᚱᚠᚺᚿ ᚿᚷᚲᛘᛏ ᛘᛁᛐ ᛒᚠ ᚠᛐᚷᚠᚺᚱᚠ
ᛁᚺ ᛈᚠᛋ ᛘᛁᛈ ᛒᛁᚠᚺᚠ ᛒᛁᛋᛏᛘᛈᛁᚺ

TRANSLITERATION AND GLOSS

ahof   ic riicnæ k͡yniŋc héâfunæs hlafard hælda ic ni   dorstæ bismærædu uŋk͡et men
Lifted up I a great king,   heaven's Lord. Bow I did not dare.   Mocked   us two men

ba   ætg͡adræ ic wæs miþ blodæ bistemid
both together. I was with blood bedewed.

Figure 5.5 Runic fragment from Ruthwell Cross
Source: Algeo, J. (1972)

A number of other minor considerations also influenced scribal practice. One was the way certain spellings were modified to make words more legible in particular forms of handwriting. One common practice was to avoid the use of *u* when it was followed by *m* or *n* as this gave rise to a long series of identical vertical strokes, making it difficult to distinguish the individual letters. The problem was simply solved by closing the top of the *u* to make it like an *o*. To this habit we owe modern day spellings like *son* and *some*. But perhaps the most extraordinary practice was the habit of many lawyers' clerks to add superfluous letters in order to make words longer, because their work was paid for by the inch.

It was not until the advent of printing, however, that real attempts at recodifying English spelling were made, but what was fixed was often a mixture of the various spellings currently in existence. Furthermore, there was no single agreed dialect used.

The trend to fix English spelling by the printer Caxton and his successors had a somewhat similar result to the fixing in Old English times. That is, the pronunciation of English continued to change — indeed some dramatic changes to the vowel system have occurred since Caxton's period — but the spelling remained static. For this reason, many of our spellings reflect a medieval pronunciation better than a modern one. Our 'writing retains a regretful memory of its earlier days' (Bradley, 1913).

The lack of regularity in spelling was a continual source of grievance to scholars, many of whom tried to reform the system. One of the first was John Hart who, in 1569, published *An orthographic containing the due order and reason how to write or painte the image of Manne's voice most like to the life or nature*. Hart argued strongly that 'the writing should have so many letters as the pronunciation neadeth of voices and no more or less'. Little impact was made, however, by either Hart or his contemporaries. A century later, Bishop Wilkins, in his *Essay towards a real Character and a Philosophical Language* (1668) admitted that 'so invariable is custom, that we still retain the same errors and incongruities in writing, which our forefathers taught us'.

Indeed, some attempts at reform merely made matters worse. Further confusion arose from the over-enthusiastic attempts at respelling certain words by Renaissance scholars, who wished to make words look like their supposed classical origins. *Debt* and *subtle* acquired their *b* through this means, in spite of the fact that it is not pronounced to this day. Such respellings were more extensive than might appear — in many cases the word has since changed pronunciation in order to conform to its new spelling. Hence the *l* in words like *false* and *fault* is now pronounced.

Ironically, those who attempted to straighten out our spelling system were largely thwarted by the growing demand for fixing and codifying the language and ascertaining a 'correct' form which would last for all time. The eighteenth century was a period in which we narrowly avoided the setting up of an academy (like the Académie Française) — much to the disappointment of literary figures such as Jonathan Swift. In such a context, little sympathy was found for people who wanted to meddle further with the system.

Attempts at reform have continued, however, in both Britain and the United States. One of the most recent occurred in 1949 when Sir James Pitman and Mr Mont Follick introduced a Private Members' Bill in the House of Commons. This measure failed (by a narrow margin) but a revised and more modest proposal in 1953 *The Simplified Spelling Bill* — which promoted a new orthography suitable for use in schools — was successful. The new simplified spelling was called *Augmented Roman* — it later became known as the *Initial Teaching Alphabet* (i.t.a.).

The structure of present-day orthography

The history of English spelling may help explain some of the features we find today, but it does not provide a proper basis for describing present-day English orthography. People today are, by and large, unaware of the etymological origins of words and of medieval scribal practices. For modern users, therefore, the orthography has a particular structure which can be described entirely in its own terms.

Nearly all the complaints made through the ages about English spelling have been to the effect that it departs radically from a phonemic principle. A simple representation of speech is seen as being the optimal writing system. This, however, is probably short-sighted. It is a mistake to think that writing should necessarily reflect speech. This point has always been made, from the Middle Ages onwards, but has been very much a minority view. As Bradley (1913, p. 1) put it:

> Many of the advocates of spelling reform are in the habit of asserting, as if it were an axiom admitting of no dispute, that the sole function of writing is to represent sounds. It appears to me that this is one of those spurious truisms that are not intelligently believed by any one, but which continue to be repeated because nobody takes the trouble to consider what they really mean.

The historical discussion above has highlighted a basic dilemma with writing systems. Adherence to strict phonemic principles will mean that the spelling of words will necessarily change as the language changes, and spelling will vary according to the dialect of the speaker. On the other hand, a fixed spelling system, however regular at its inception, causes a gradual change in the way spelling relates to sound. Furthermore, speakers of different dialects will have to use different sets of correspondence rules to map pronunciation onto written forms. Where one has variety in language (whether socially, geographically or historically) one must also have either variety in spelling *or* variety in the correspondence rules which relate sound to spelling. Hence one drawback with a strictly phonemic writing system is that it can only represent *one* variety of a language, and puts at a disadvantage readers and writers who do not speak the chosen form.

A further problem with too literal a representation of pronunciation is that it may not be the most suitable system for rapid and efficient reading. Psychologists have shown that readers process words broadly in two ways. When their eye falls upon a word, they may form a mental representation of its pronunciation and use this to locate the meaning of the word in their mind. It has been shown that words which are spelled regularly are processed faster than irregularly spelled ones. Very fast and fluent readers, however (and nearly everyone when confronted by a very familiar word), use a different strategy. The whole word will be recognised as a single entity from its orthographic shape, and its meaning located without the intermediate process involving pronunciation. This strategy has been shown to be faster and more efficient. It could be argued, then, that the optimal writing system is one which maintains a distinct and easily recognisable visual shape to words, even at the expense of regularity in spelling.

For whatever reasons, it is very common for alphabetic writing systems to depart from strict phonemic principles and become systems which are patterned visually. This then, is a key to understanding the structure of English spelling today. It is partly based on representations of pronunciation, and partly based on graphic regularities.

REPRESENTATION OF SOUND

An ideal phonemic alphabet would contain one symbol for each phoneme in the language. There are however, around 44 phonemes in British English (the exact number varies from dialect to dialect) and only 26 letters in our currently used alphabet. Clearly, then, the spelling system must incorporate a more complex way of relating spellings to sounds than on the basis of one symbol, one sound. These relationships are described in terms of *phoneme to grapheme correspondence rules*. Whole books (for example, Veneszky 1970) have been devoted to the analysis of such rules, but the basic principles are easily described.

1. Certain new symbols can be constructed by putting together two of the existing ones. This forms a *digraph* such as *th* or *ch* which are used to represent single phonemes. This may lead to a minor problem, since readers need to distinguish between the digraph and the sequence of *t* and *h* (as in *lighthouse*), but these confusions rarely occur, and it is usually possible to recognise them on other grounds — such as the fact that the digraph does not occur over a morpheme boundary.
2. One symbol may be used to represent more than one phoneme. For example, *th* variously represents /ð/ (as in *this*) and /θ/ (as in *theatre*).
3. One symbol is made to represent more than one phoneme, but exactly *which* phoneme will depend on the context of other letters. One of the most familiar examples of this is the so called 'magic *e*' which influences the quality of a preceding vowel, but which is not sounded itself. Examples are *pane* versus *pan* or *pine* versus *pin*.

This last principle is the most widespread of all in English, and most of the attempts at describing the correspondence rules have been devoted to identifying the different contexts and sequences which affect the way letters represent sounds. It can be shown through such studies that, although the correspondence rules for English spelling are extremely complex (partly because of the variety of historical changes in pronunciation which created them), they do at least exist. There is also some evidence that although people are not consciously aware of them, they make use of such knowledge when reading (Smith and Baker, 1976).

For example, if we return to Shaw's problem with the word 'ghoti', we can rapidly establish that very few words indeed begin with this sequence of letters in English. Furthermore, initial *gh* sequences are never pronounced as /f/. The correspondence of *o* as /ɪ/ is also extremely rare. Since it results from the medieval scribal practice of closing a 'u' in certain contexts it could not occur before *t*, but only before *m* or *n*. Lastly, the correspondence between *ti* and the sound /ʃ/ is also contextually determined, and only occurs in certain places where *ti* begins a syllable. In fact, it might be better to think of the whole unit *-tion* = /ʃən/as a frequent but indivisible sequence.

Context-sensitive correspondence rules such as these may not always guarantee a single possible pronunciation. They will, however, usually limit the possibilities to two or three, of which one will be by far the commonest.

GRAPHIC REPRESENTATIONS

It could be claimed that an ideal writing system should not exclusively focus on phonemes, but should preserve intact higher-level linguistic units. This is, in fact, an important principle in English spelling and it often resolves apparent difficulties in phoneme to grapheme correspondences.

One important higher-level unit is the *morpheme*. The plural morpheme in English is variously pronounced as /s/, /z/ or /ɪz/ (as in 'cats and dogs and houses'), but our spelling ignores this alteration and always uses *s*. Words like *sign* and *signal* or *medicine* and *medical* retain the shape of their shared stem morpheme, which would be obscured by a strictly phonemic system.

In some respects, the English writing system incorporates a logographic principle. We have already mentioned the fact that some words are processed as single units by readers (i.e. as logographs), but there are a number of words in English, often very common ones, where there is no attempt to represent pronunciation. Examples are contractions such as *Mrs* or *St* which in the house style of most publishers (including the one which published this book) are not given a full stop. There are also some words which are apparently so irregular in spelling that they can be treated as logographs (e.g. *yacht*).

Conclusion

The English spelling system is not by any means transparent in the way it operates but it contains a great deal more structure and regularity than might be supposed. Some linguists (Chomsky and Halle, 1968) have deemed it near optimal in the way it represents underlying linguistic regularities rather than superficial ones. This seems perhaps an overstatement of the case. Nevertheless, English spelling represents a balance between the various competing demands which any writing system must satisfy, and the solutions which have been found are common in other languages. As Stubbs (1980, p. 49) observes:

> All alphabetic systems which have evolved naturally are mixed systems which involve compromises between phoneme–grapheme correspondence and the correspondence of graphemes to higher morphological and syntactic levels. There must be powerful reasons why the end point of the development of writing systems in the five or six thousand years or so since true writing was invented, and over the many languages to which it has been applied, is alphabetic systems with an admixture of morphological and/or syntactic information.

6 Face-to-face interaction

6.1 INTRODUCTION

This chapter is concerned with various aspects of spontaneous communication in face-to-face interaction. Such talk has a number of special characteristics. One is that people will be able to use and look out for many signals which are communicated through body movement of one kind or another. Another is that people need some way of working out when they are expected to speak, and when to listen. Ordinary conversation, by its very nature, is extremely *ad hoc*, but people send out and receive an immense amount of systematic non-verbal information. Some of this is quite independent of what is being said, but much is in support of it and helps the smooth flow of conversation.

Section 6.2 reviews the research literature on non-verbal behaviour. This literature is surprisingly vast, but rather fragmented. Here we restrict ourselves to an overview of the basic areas and functions of non-verbal communication.

Section 6.3 examines various aspects of the 'management' of spontaneous talk — which might be described as how to get a word in edgeways without interrupting. The detailed mechanism which allows people to synchronise their turns is examined, together with the ways in which turns are allocated to different speakers.

Section 6.4 provides a very practical introduction to methods of transcribing spontaneous talk — in preparation for the kinds of analysis described in Chapter 7.

6.2 NON-VERBAL COMMUNICATION

Non-verbal communication (often abbreviated to NVC) includes all means of human communication *other* than words (in fact, other than what we conventionally regard as language). We include the topic in this

book because NVC is often intimately bound up with spoken language
— our understanding of face-to-face conversation, for instance, may be
impoverished if we do not take account of the non-verbal component.
Despite its importance, the literature on NVC is rather fragmented and
results from research are sometimes inconclusive — even contradictory.
Our survey here covers some of the more important functions of NVC
in interpersonal interaction and looks at interpretations that may be
made of different non-verbal signs. It does not, however, attempt to
impose a consensus in those areas where none exists.

NVC can utilise any of the five senses — visual, auditory, tactile,
olfactory and even taste. This section looks at a more restricted range of
phenomena, mainly connected with body movement, that are particularly relevant to face-to-face communication.

NVC performs three rather different functions in face-to-face interaction. First, it can communicate quite specific meanings through the use
of conventional gestures and movement. Second, it serves as a complex
channel of communication which enables people to let others know their
emotional disposition. Information from either kind of non-verbal
behaviour may be duplicated by the spoken channel (as when someone
smiles and says *Hello* or says *Ooh no, I don't like that* whilst pulling a
face) but such messages may, in principle, stand on their own. Third,
NVC may play an important supporting role in speech — it helps
speakers to coordinate their turns, for example, or allows speakers to
add emphasis (as when the preacher thumps the pulpit at a shaky point).
This third function of NVC is dealt with more fully in section 6.3.

If we restrict the term non-verbal communication to those aspects of
body movement which have been shown to carry meaning, we can identify six areas of specific interest: gesture; proxemics; body contact;
posture and body orientation; facial expression; and gaze.

Gesture

Gesture is perhaps the most obvious and familiar way in which people
convey meanings without using words. Morris *et al.* (1979) made an
intensive study of twenty ritual gestures which are used in various parts
of Europe, often with different meanings. For example, the V-sign (made
with the palm facing inwards towards the signer) forms an obscene
gesture in Britain, but is taken elsewhere to be a sign of victory. Such
gestures are made intentionally and apparently with specific meanings.
Like words in verbal language, their meanings are essentially arbitrary
and symbolic:

> If a man taps his temple with the tip of his forefinger, it can mean one of
> two things, either 'crazy' or 'intelligent' — two opposing meanings, but
> both relevant to this particular gesture. There is no mimicry involved. A
> simple hand action stands for — symbolizes — an abstract quality —

craziness or intelligence. In a culture where this particular symbolic convention is totally absent, the gesture might well be meaningless (Morris et al, 1979, p. xvii).

This rather simple view of the relationship between gestures contrasts with that presented in less popular research literature. A hand salute, for example, might be regarded as a symbolic gesture with a well-defined meaning, but Birdwhistell (1970, p. 119) argued that it was far more complex a phenomenon than this view allows:

> Although they [gestures] have an apparent unitary and discrete quality, they prove consistently to carry the instruction to look elsewhere in the body behavioral stream for their modification or interpretation. A salute, for example, depending on the integrally associated total body or facial behavior, may convey a range of messages from ridicule and rebellion to subservience or respect.

Birdwhistell favoured a close analogy between the way gestures worked and the way spoken language worked. A small number of movement types combined to form larger structural units (Birdwhistell, 1970, p. 119)

> Gestures are forms which are incapable of standing alone — except of course, where the structural context is provided by the questioner. Just as there is no 'cept' in isolation in American English, an informant may be taught how to produce it together with pre- or con- and -tion.

Not all gestures have such clear intentional status, but they may have communicative significance nevertheless. People often gesture with their hands when talking — even when on the telephone. Such movements may be mannered rhetorical devices (see Figure 6.1) or they may be less obtrusive and spontaneous gestures. In each case, the function is the same — to add emphasis and help identify the structural units of utterances in much the same way as intonation or stress in the spoken channel.

Schegloff (1984) observed that 'Hand gesturing is largely, if not entirely, a speaker's phenomenon'. That is, people listening tend not to gesture with their hands. 'This close relationship between speakership and gesturing with the hands does not extend in quite the same way to other gesturing body parts, like the head' (Schegloff, 1984, p. 273). Schegloff demonstrated that the timing of gestures was intimately synchronised with the spoken delivery, a fact which has been repeatedly observed by researchers in non-verbal behaviour.

The various kinds of gesture which we have identified here have been classified in many different ways by different authors, but most distinguish between those which seem relatively autonomous from speech and those which support speech. Salutes and V-signs belong to the first category and depend on an observer construing the gesture as a deliberate communicative act. Speech-supportive gestures seem to depend less on intentionality for their communicative function.

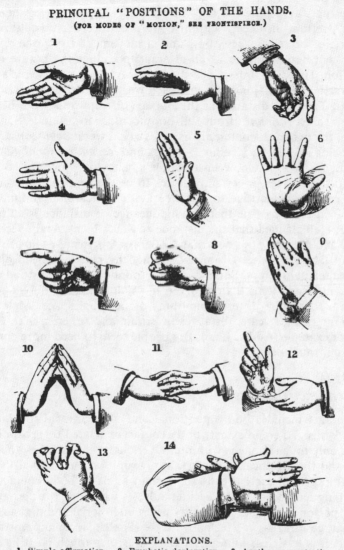

PRINCIPAL "POSITIONS" OF THE HANDS.
(FOR MODES OF "MOTION," SEE FRONTISPIECE.)

EXPLANATIONS.

1. Simple affirmation.   2. Emphatic declaration.   3. Apathy or prostration.
4. Energetic appeal.   5. Negation or denial.   6. Violent repulsion.   7. Indexing
or cautioning.   8. Determination or anger.   9. Supplication.   10. Gentle entreaty.
11. Carelessness.   12. Argumentativeness.   13. Earnest entreaty.   14. Resignation.

Figure 6.1   Victorian recommendations for rhetorical gestures
Source: Bell and Bell (1892).

Proxemics

The term *proxemics* was first used by the anthropologist E. T. Hall to describe the way people use and interpret physical distance when they interact. Certain distances, within a given culture or sub-culture, are appropriate for certain activities, and a movement from one zone to another will be interpreted as an attempt to change the nature of the interaction. Hall (1963) described the North American proxemic system as embracing four major positions (each with a 'close' and a 'far' sub-division). The most distant was the *public* (12ft upwards from hearers) and the nearest *intimate* (from full body contact to around 18 in.). In practice, the two most commonly used distances were *social-consultative* (close being 4–7 ft: far being 7–12 ft) and *casual-personal* (close is 18–30 in; far is 30–49 in. Whilst people's behaviour may not conform neatly to these zones, it certainly seems to be the case that interactants can be extremely sensitive to distance as an indicator of intimacy or threat. It also seems true that the significance of distance is culturally variable. Hall claimed that the distance at which many Arabs feel comfortable at conducting business may be felt by Americans as invasive and uncomfortably intimate. Distances adopted by people depend also on many contextual factors. Sommer (1962) found that people stood closer together in large rooms than they did in small rooms. Different people also seem to require different amounts of personal space. Male pairs seem to interact at greater distances in Britain and America than female pairs, for example (Addis, 1966). Big people seem to need more personal space than small people.

Body contact (haptics)

Body contact includes both intentional and unintentional touching of various kinds. To some extent, body contact is related to proximity — one can only touch if one is within close enough range of the other person — and the significance of certain proximities may derive, in part, from the potential each affords for certain kinds of body contact.

Touching may occur either accidentally, as when one brushes against another person in a queue, or it may be an intentional and perhaps conventional gesture, as when one shakes hands. In many instances, however, it is less clear quite what the status of a touch is. It has been found, however, that people do not have to be even conscious that touch has occurred in order to be affected by it. Fisher *et al.* (1976) showed that women, in particular, responded more warmly and positively to a library assistant who made hand contact when returning a library card even if they reported being unaware that a touch had occurred.

The amount of touching that can be seen going on in public varies greatly from culture to culture. Jourard (1966) reported observing around 110 touches per hour in Paris, as opposed to none at all in Lon-

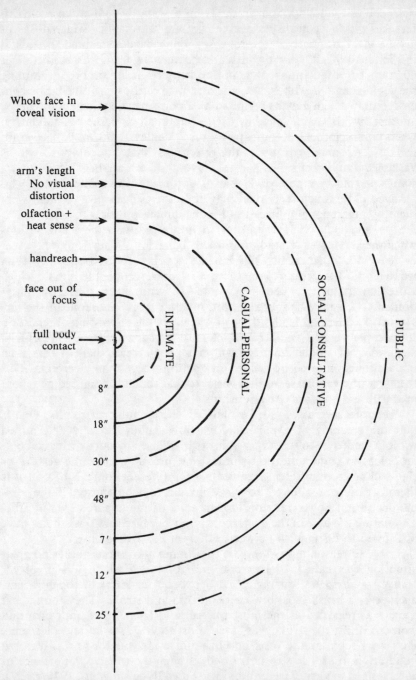

Figure 6.2. Hall's analysis of proxemic distances for white North
Americans

don, and around 2 per hour in the United States. There are also big differences within a culture between the amount of touching which different people give and receive. Several researchers have attempted to explain this in terms of differential status and power. Henley (1973) studied over 60 hours of observations made in public places in Baltimore, examining the socio-economic status, sex, age and race of those involved. She concluded that 'touch may be regarded as a non-verbal equivalent of calling another by first name, that is, used reciprocally it indicates solidarity: when non-reciprocal, it indicates status' (Henley, 1973, p. 93). Overall, the results seemed to support the hypothesis that 'touching is a status variable, with higher status persons having touch "privilege" over lower-status persons'. A part of Henley's argument was that women, who received more touch from men than they themselves gave to men, were thereby interactionally placed in a subordinate position to men.

Stier and Hall (1984) were not so impressed with these conclusions when they reviewed 43 studies of touch behaviour. They found no great evidence that men really did initiate touches more frequently than women and, furthermore, the thesis that powerful people initiate touch more than unpowerful people may itself be in doubt: 'at times, the initiation of touch may be more important, and more common, in the less powerful'. Stier and Hall did, however, make the interesting observation that people's beliefs and perceptions may run contrary to observed facts. A number of studies have shown that people really believe that men initiate touch in opposite-gender interactions more than vice versa. This seems, at the very least, to demonstrate that touch is regarded as salient in status and solidarity relationships.

There are several ways of explaining these equivocal results. One is that the meaning of a particular gesture cannot be fully determined without reference to the larger context in which it occurred. It is a commonplace in communication studies that precisely the same gesture or sign will be given different significances in different contexts of use. It is therefore quite possible for touch behaviour to be implicated in the communication of power relationships in spite of the apparently contradictory nature of some of the evidence, simply because very few studies have attempted to distinguish between different contexts of use.

A second reason may simply be that in many of these studies no great attention was paid to the precise *kind* of touch which was involved. Nguyen *et al.* (1975) distinguished between four kinds of touch: a pat; a squeeze; a brush (possibly accidental); and a stroke. They found that a pat was regarded as the most playful and friendly by both men and women, whilst the stroke was rated most 'loving, sexual and pleasant'. However, subjects also took into account *where* the touch was directed in addition to *how* it was performed, though the relative importance of each seemed to vary. The authors concluded (Nguyen *et al.*, 1975, p. 97): 'subjects relied more on the mode than on the location of a touch to determine how pleasant, playful, and warm/loving a touch was, but they relied more on location to determine whether or not it conveyed sexual desire and friendship/fellowship'. In addition there seemed to be some evidence that men were, on the whole, rather more attuned to the *kind* of touch involved, whereas women were slightly more concerned with *where* the touch occurred.

Posture and body orientation

The way people hold themselves, how they sit or stand, has long been understood as evidence of their innermost feelings and the state of their relationships with others. Some researchers have attempted to isolate particular postural behaviours, such as direction of lean when seated or openness of arm and leg positions, and assign to them particular interpretations. Scheflen (1964) commented: 'such [postural] behaviors occur in characteristic, standard configurations, whose common recognisability is the basis of their value in communication'. Such postures were, he claimed, governed by rules which determined where and when they could occur: 'a posture such as sitting back in a chair rarely occurs in subordinate males who are engaged in selling an idea to a male of higher status'. Scheflen was keen to establish a parallel between the workings of a supposed 'vocabulary' of postures and verbal language. The repertoire of postures varied from one part of the community to another, and thus identified a person's group membership rather like a dialect. All members of the culture, however, would recognise the various categories of posture being displayed, even if the exact manner of the display varied.

The idea that particular postures can be isolated in this way is an attractive one, but the results of approaches based on this premise have not been very conclusive. Such models are still appealed to in social skills training, however, where patients or clients may be taught to adopt certain postures at certain moments in an interaction in order to gain control or to signal certain meanings.

Probably more important are rather general features of tenseness and relaxation in posture. Mehrabian (1969) concluded that people were most relaxed in the presence of someone of inferior status, and most tense when facing a superior. It remains an interesting question whether such postures reflect a person's anxiety or stress or whether they form part of conventional ways of signalling attention and status.

POSTURAL ORIENTATION

Postural orientation seems to be one exception to this general rule in that specific behavioural changes can be shown to have particular communicative values. At one extreme, people will 'turn their backs' on a person with whom they wish to avoid interaction. People working cooperatively — whether on a joint task or supporting each other in a group discussion — will often be found side by side. An angle of 90 degrees is found by most people to be the most comfortable for casual but friendly interaction. Face-to-face orientations often indicate some more earnest discourse, perhaps between a doctor and patient or between lovers, according to Scheflen (1964).

POSTURAL CONGRUENCE

It has often been observed that when people interact they will fall into postures which are the same or mirror images of each other. If one person in a group leans back, then it is likely that some other member will, without realising it, move to adopt the same posture. Scheflen (1964, p. 241) termed this *postural congruence*:

> Since an individual in a given culture can only sit in a limited number of postures, one immediately wonders whether postural congruence is purely coincidental. But even a very few continued observations of a group quickly end any theory of coincidence. Two, four, even six people often sit in postural congruence. When one member of a congruent set shifts posture the others quickly follow suit, so that the congruence is maintained through repeated changes of body positioning.

Congruence, Scheflen argued, often showed who was allied to whom in discussions, even when this was not apparent in what they were saying. Or old friends may shift into congruence when temporarily arguing as if to confirm the ultimate continuity of their relationship. Congruence is also often a sign of peer status (Scheflen, 1964, p. 241):

> When some member of an alliance differs markedly in social status from the others, he may maintain a posture which is quite unlike that of the others.... In doctor–patient, parent–child or teacher–student reciprocals, where it is important to indicate different status, congruence is unlikely to occur.

A strenuous validation of these findings was undertaken by Beattie and Beattie (1981) who spent five hours a day for a fortnight on a beach on the French Riviera. Observations were made every five seconds of the postural positions of couples lying on the beach. The researchers found that male–female couples spent more than half the time in congruent positions. They concluded (Beattie and Beattie, 1981, p. 51): 'This study has shown conclusively that postural congruence in a naturalistic setting is a very real, common phenomenon, and is not simply the result of the chance coincidence of the relatively small number of postures normally displayed by individuals.'

POSTURAL SHIFTS

It might be thought that a person would shift posture on a fairly random basis, perhaps when feeling uncomfortable or just bored. Scheflen (1964) suggested that posture shifting was far more regular than this and was used to mark important boundary points in an interaction. For example, syntactic boundaries (ends of sentences) were marked by small head movements and gestures, as can be seen in Figure 6.3. A rather larger shift in head posture marked the completion of each point being made in discussion (Scheflen, 1964, p. 231):

> When an American speaker uses a series of syntactic sentences in a conversation, he changes the position of his head and eyes every few sentences. He may turn his head right or left, tilt it, cock it to one side or the other, or flex or extend his neck so as to look toward the floor or ceiling. Regardless of the kind of shift in head posture, the attitude is held for a few sentences, then shifted to another position. Each of these shifts I believe marks the end of a structural unit at the next level higher than the syntactic sentence.

A number of such points might be made in support of what Scheflen termed a 'position'. A shift of gross body position marked the boundaries of such episodes in the interaction.

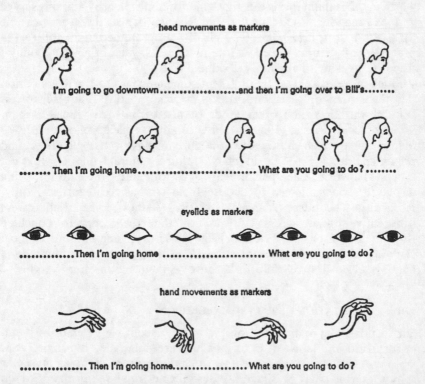

Figure 6.3. Body movement markers of American syntactic sentences
Source: Scheflen (1964)

Facial expression

'As a part of our primate heritage', one researcher observed, '*Homo Sapiens* has a mobile, labial visage with which to signal conspecifics' (Mackey, 1976, p. 128). This statement alludes to the two most interesting issues in the poorly researched area of facial expression. The first is the extent to which our facial responses to emotional stimuli are innate and similar to animal behaviour (particularly that of primates). The second is the question of how expressions convey meaning to people. Behind the rather pompous statement lurks the possibility that more than a century of research in the area has yielded very few insights beyond the obvious fact that our faces are capable of betraying our feelings, but that nobody quite knows how it is done.

THE BIOLOGICAL BASIS OF FACIAL EXPRESSION

Darwin's important book *The Expression of the Emotions in Man and Animals* (1872) was preceded by a couple of centuries of speculation by anatomists and physiognomists which Darwin summarily dismissed as worthless. His main thesis was that emotional displays by animals served various functions which aided species survival. It was therefore possible that certain displays were biologically programmed and subject to processes of natural selection in the same way as other behavioural dispositions which had survival value. ·

Much more recent research has lent some credence to Darwin's notion that the expression of emotion through facial posture is subject to less cultural variation than other kinds of non-verbal behaviour. Ekman, Sorenson and Friesen (1969) sifted through over 3000 photographs to obtain 'those which showed only the pure display of a single affect' and presented these to people in many cultures, literate and pre-literate, around the world. Each person was asked to identify the emotion being displayed, being allowed to choose from six basic categories: happy, fear, disgust—contempt, anger, surprise, sadness. The results were sufficiently similar across cultures for the researchers to conclude (Ekman, Sorenson and Friesen, 1969 p. 87) that 'our findings support Darwin's suggestion that facial expressions of emotion are similar among humans, regardless of culture, because of their evolutionary origins'.

THE CLASSIFICATION OF FACIAL EXPRESSION

Such studies beg many questions as to how such 'single emotions' can be identified and labelled. Emotions are rarely signalled by single facial gestures (such as raising an eyebrow or smiling) but by complex muscular responses which may be difficult to describe and analyse. Ekman, Friesen and Ellsworth (1972, p. 1) suggest that 'man's facial muscles are sufficiently complex to allow more than a thousand different facial appearances'. Other authors have hazarded a guess that the figure is nearer 20,000 (Thompson, 1973).

There have been two rather different traditions in attempts to describe and classify these possible expressions. The first has tried to isolate a few basic dimensions, such as 'pleasantness' or 'intensity'. Such dimensions are continuous variables which allow any one expression to be coded according to its score on each dimension. By and large, such attempts have met with failure, with different studies of people's reactions to photographs and video tapes arriving at different factors and different numbers of dimensions.

An alternative, and perhaps more obvious, approach has been the establishment of categories such as the ones used in the experiments by Ekman and his associates above. These six categories, which were later increased to seven by the addition of 'interest', were regarded as descriptive of the primary emotions which gave rise to particular expressions, rather than descriptive of the expressions themselves. In some ways, the fact that such categories work at all must be some vindication of the pan-cultural hypothesis. It may not be surprising that the repertoire of facial expressions is similar across cultures since everyone's facial musculature is roughly the same and allows similar expressive possibilities, but a category system based on the motivating emotions can only work if all cultures represent and recognise similar basic emotions in similar ways. The identification of the primary emotions was, in this case, based on earlier independent research on *affect*.

In addition to the primary emotional categories, however, certain expressions were to be regarded as *affect-blends*. 'Smugness', for instance, seemed to be a blend of 'happy' and 'angry' expressions according to Ekman, Friesen and Ellsworth (1972). This suggests that the facial expression is a mixture of those expressions associated with 'happiness' and 'anger' but, in principle, does not suggest that the emotion of 'smugness' is a mixture of happy and angry feelings. In practice, however, the emotional states and facial expressions are too closely connected within such a model to escape this consequence.

THE CULTURAL BASIS OF FACIAL EXPRESSION

Not all researchers have accepted the Darwinian hypothesis about the biological basis of facial expressions. Birdwhistell (1970), for example, argued that they are culturally learned:

> Although we have been searching for 15 years, we have found no gesture or body motion which has the same social meaning in all societies. . . .
> That is, we have been unable to discover any single facial expression . . .
> which conveys an identical meaning in all societies.

Birdwhistell even suggested that the general facial expressions of those in close relationships will be found to be similar. Such an observation may be no more than folk wisdom (as embodied, for instance, in jokes about old people's faces looking like those of their dogs) but even if true could be explained in various ways. If it is argued that a couple in a close relationship will tend to fall into similar emotional states then the Darwinian hypothesis is left unscathed. A clearly socially motivated explanation, however, might explain the effect as an extreme form of postural congruence.

The issue is not, in fact, a clear-cut one since the proponents of the Darwinian hypothesis accept that there may be a cultural component. Such a hybrid explanation was put forward by Ekman (1973) in his *neuro-cultural* theory. Displays of emotion had an innate basis, but were filtered by cultural learning. Such cultural learning allowed people to 'manage' their public faces according to socially appropriate display rules (Ekman, Sorenson and Friesen, 1969, p. 87):

> Past impressions of cultural differences in facial displays may represent a failure to distinguish what is pan-cultural (the association of facial muscular movements with each primary affect) from what is culturally variable (learned affect evokers, behavioral consequences of an affect display, and the operation of display rules). Display rules were defined as procedures learned early in life for the management of affect displays and include deintensifying, intensifying, neutralization, or masking affect display. These rules prescribe what to do about the display of each affect in different social settings; they vary with the social role and demographic characteristics, and should vary across cultures.

In other words, one reason why the 'meaning' of a particular facial expression may vary across cultures is that in each culture the social contexts in which such an expression could be freely and appropriately displayed will be very different. The primary affect and facial expression of a bereaved person, say, may be, in principle, similar around the world but some cultures may construe death as an occasion for celebration not distress, or may require the bereaved person to censor or exaggerate their display of emotion.

HOW EXPRESSIONS WORK

The question of how expressions work is perhaps the most interesting of all, and yet it is the least well understood. Two aspects have, however, been identified.

Boucher and Ekman (1975) took photographs of people displaying various emotional states, and cut them into sections. Subjects were then shown one portion of the facial expression and asked to identify the emotion being displayed. The researchers concluded that different parts of the face were important for the display of different emotions. The area around the eyes was important in detecting fear and sadness; happiness was seen more in the cheek and mouth area; surprise from any of the three areas; and anger required more than one area to be visible before it could be reliably recognised.

Ekman and Friesen (1967) suggested that facial expressions were quite good at communicating *how* people felt, but not so good at indicating the *intensity* of the emotion. This was signalled by other aspects of body movement and posture. To get the whole picture, people must take into account the way facial expression was associated with other aspects of non-verbal behaviour.

Gaze

People are remarkably sensitive to what others are doing with their eyes — no other aspect of non-verbal behaviour, except direct physical encounters, is capable of arousing quite the same intensity and subtlety of reaction.

When one person directs gaze at another it is generally termed *looking* in the research literature. When the person looked at simultaneously looks back then a situation of *mutual gaze* or *eye-contact* is reached.

Eye-contact can have an important but simple interactional function in obtaining the attention of someone in order to begin an encounter. It has often been remarked that waiters and officials are very good at avoiding eye-contact, thus avoiding beginning a service encounter until they themselves feel ready to do so. Teachers may silently stare in the direction of a child until eye-contact has been made, or may use eye-contact more subtly during lessons to select a child to answer a question or give permission to speak. In informal interactions, Goodwin (1981) has shown that people will often restart or delay continuing a speaking turn until mutual gaze and hence the attention of the other person is obtained.

Once an interaction has successfully begun, then looking and eye-contact continue to serve important functions, but in a rather complex manner. Kendon (1967) found that people look nearly twice as much when they are listening as when they are speaking, possibly because eye-contact seems to increase the cognitive processing load to an extent that makes it incompatible with simultaneous planning of speech. Whatever the reason, it seems that an increase in looking towards the end of a speaking turn can signal that the speaker is ready to hand over the turn to another. (This is discussed more fully in section 6.3).

People are sensitive to changes in this expected pattern of looking and looking away. An increase in looking may be interpreted variously as liking, as sexual interest, or as hostility. Exactly which interpretation is given will depend on other contextual factors and non-verbal behaviour. A reduction in looking may indicate that a person is rejecting the construction of the relationship being proposed.

For example, Jellison and Ickes (1974, p. 449) argued that an increase in looking indicated a desire to obtain more personal information about the other person:

> If two people like one another, mutual eye contact may support or validate the mutual liking. On the other hand, if the two people dislike one another, the other's gaze may be interpreted as a desire for information and knowledge to be used against the person.

A more specific extension of the idea that mutual gaze can be threatening is the idea that the person who is first to break gaze is yielding dominance to the other and admitting inferiority.

Another factor which may disturb the pattern of looking and looking away has to do with what is being signalled through other non-verbal channels. As we have seen, information about liking and interpersonal status can be signalled through such things as proximity. Argyle and Dean (1965) have shown that the amount of looking decreases if a speaker stands closer to the listener than would normally be comfortable.

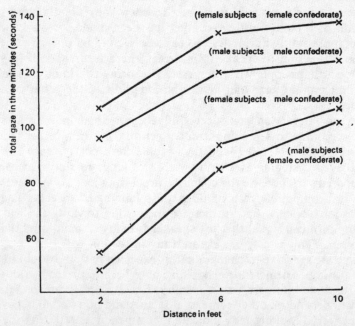

Figure 6.4 Relation between eye contact and distances for different combinations of confederates and subjects
Source: Argyle and Dean (1965)

This reduction (see Figure 6.4) was in proportion to the increase in proximity. The two channels thus worked together to signal information about current states of the relationship.

The study of gaze demonstrates several important points which are generally applicable to non-verbal behaviour. One is that the same behaviour may simultaneously be serving several functions. Another is that similar behaviours may serve rather contrary functions, and exactly which will depend on the precise context in which the behaviour occurs. For example, breaking eye-contact may be interpreted as yielding dominance in some contexts, but if it occurs in a listener as a speaker approaches the end of a turn, it may be interpreted as a preparatory gesture to taking over the turn. Finally, gaze behaviour demonstrates the way that non-verbal behaviour must be understood as a series of channels of information which work together to signal meaning.

Integrated descriptions of non-verbal behaviour

Non-verbal behaviour is such a complex phenomenon that it presents many problems of description and analysis to researchers. Much research has attempted to make the task more manageable by examining only one aspect of non-verbal behaviour in isolation, usually in laboratory experiments. It is clear however, from the descriptions above that in a number of cases the communicative significance of body movement is only apparent when all channels have been taken into account. This then raises the question of how easily we can generalise from the limited kinds of experiments which have been done to a proper and integrated understanding of how people behave in everyday life.

Many scholars would approach this question cautiously, observing that although much is now understood, it is still insufficient to make such an integrated description anything other than speculative. This has not prevented many more popular works on body language from attempting what are essentially caricatures based on behavioural stereotypes and gleanings from unconnected research studies. On the body language of politicians, for example, Wainwright (1985, pp. 121–3) says:

> In sitting position, the politician tends to adopt a forward lean. This indicates a desire to cooperate with the listener in discussion. He often uses more eye contact when he is speaking than is normal. ... Politicians will have a firm, warm handshake. They will nod frequently when listening ... They will place a protective arm around your shoulder ... The typical Conservative male wears a dark suit, shirt and tie, has a smart hairstyle and polished shoes. His skin is smooth and he has the air of being well-fed. ... His gestures are restrained and his posture either upright or casually asymmetrical. ... The Labour male is a rougher hewn individual with less of an interest in appearance. ... Posture is more hunched and gestures made with less thought for their effect. They tend to stand closer than their Conservative counterparts and they use the head cock of interest more.

> The Labour female is more likely than a Conservative to wear casual clothes and not to wear a bra. ... Gestures will be more like the man as whose equal she rightly regards herself and she makes a great deal of use of the head nod and the head cock.

Such material demonstrates the dangers and limitations of work in non-verbal communication which arise from its fragmentary and partial nature.

6.3   CONVERSATION MANAGEMENT

An important feature of ordinary conversation is its improvised nature. If participants make it up as they go along, however, they will need certain basic management skills which will allow them to integrate their performance with those of other speakers and listeners. The ability to get through a conversation without interrupting or overlapping with another speaker but still getting to talk where desired has been likened to the problem of how people walk down a busy street without bumping into one another (Duncan, 1972). In other words, the skills involved appear at first sight to be so commonplace that they seem also to be trivial, but a closer inspection shows that listeners and speakers exchange complex signals which guide their behaviour in conversation.

Sacks *et al*. (1974) listed a number of facts which they felt any model of conversational turn-taking would have to accommodate. They included the following:

> Speaker change occurs and (usually) recurs.

> Only one person usually speaks at a time.

> People will take turns which vary in length so a means of identifying when a speaker has completed a turn is needed.

> Places where more than one person talks simultaneously are common but do not last long.

> Transitions (from one speaker to another) are commonly made without gap or overlap.

> The order in which people talk is not fixed in advance but varies. Therefore some means of allocating and distributing turns must be used.

In this section we will examine some of the basic mechanisms which conversationalists seem to employ to achieve smooth turn-taking and turn allocation.

Turn exchanges

Psychologists and linguists have long been fascinated by the way speakers are able to take over from each other smoothly and rapidly. For example, Beattie (1983) has shown that in over a third of the speaker transitions in his data, the silent gap was equal to or less than a fifth of a second. Such gaps are less than many of the gaps and slight hesitations in normal speech which do not normally give rise to a new speaker taking over the turn. They are also below the reaction time of most people. Hence it is obvious that listeners can recognise whether a speaker is approaching the end of a turn and can anticipate precisely the point at which the turn will finish.

TURN-ANTICIPATION CUES

Sacks *et al.* (1974) invoked a notion of *projectability* to explain prompt turn exchanges. Although turns may consist of a variety of lengths and kinds of structure — from one word to a long monologue — listeners may be able to recognise the type of turn early on. This would then give them a basis for estimating when it will be completed and for recognising that completion promptly when it does occur. Sacks *et al.* largely left open the question of how such projection was accomplished. Listeners, however, can draw upon various kinds of knowledge allowing them to anticipate with different degrees of precision what kind of utterance will be made next.

General script or frame. Participants may recognise the nature of the speech event as one for which they already have a particular script (discussed more fully in section 7.4) which broadly guides who says what. Consider, for instance, the conventional routines associated with buying something from a shop assistant, consulting a doctor about an ailment or being interviewed for a job.

Discourse structures. Listeners can draw on their knowledge of discourse structures such as an *adjacency pair* or the *Initiation–Response–Follow-up* pattern found in classroom talk (see section 7.3). For example, once one part of an adjacency pair (such as a greeting or question-and-answer sequence) is produced then there will be a strong expectation that the second part of the pair will occur next.

Grammatical structure. Knowledge of grammatical structure will help the anticipation of the end of a particular turn since it is possible to tell when a sentence is grammatically complete, or potentially complete.

Sometimes, it is the existence of mistakes (interruptions and overlaps) which reveal that such knowledge is being used (Sacks *et al.* 1974, p. 702):

```
Desk: What is your last name, ⌈Loraine
Caller:                       ⌊Dinnis
Desk: What?
Caller: Dinnis
```

(Note: Square brackets indicate simultaneous speech.)

We can note that enquiry desks follow routine patterns of questioning and information-giving which can be anticipated by any caller. Hence the caller anticipated the end of the desk's turn by offering 'Dinnis'. The final address term 'Loraine' was unnecessary either to the grammatical completeness or to the illocutionary force of the desk's turn and it is revealing that the caller came in without waiting to see if the desk actually had anything further to say. Since the caller's name was lost in the overlap, the desk asks for a repetition. The question *What?* now demands a response whose nature and length can safely be predicted. If the caller had continued (by spelling out her name, for instance) then one might hypothesise that the desk would interrupt at this point anyway.

The data thus show how expectations which derive from knowledge of scripts, discourse structure, and grammar can be used by listeners to identify a possible completion of a turn by a speaker. The data also show, by demonstrating an overlap, that there may be more *possible* completion places than actually get used for turn exchange. Such a possible completion point was referred to by Sacks *et al.* (1974) as a *transition-relevance place*.

The notion that turns contain such transition-relevance places is an attractive one, since it allows us to specify more exactly the nature of the coordination problem. Listeners must first recognise that a transition-relevance place is coming up (the projection problem) and must then synchronise their entry precisely when the transition-relevance place arrives.

Although the model put forward by Sacks *et al.* (1974) does not go into detail about the precise cues used by listeners when they project a transition-relevance place, it does seem to be assumed that they are broadly of the kind discussed above. In other words, they derive from a listener's monitoring of the discourse and syntax and will be fully visible in written transcripts such as the one above. The model is unsatisfactory, however, in that it fails to explain adequately how it is that listeners can take over a turn almost instantly. Discourse cues of the above kind will allow only an approximate estimation of a turn ending, whereas turn exchanges may be completed within 50 milliseconds of a speaker finishing.

TURN-YIELDING CUES

Some psychologists have suggested that speakers give out complex non-verbal cues to indicate that they are about to finish and wish to yield their turn. Such turn-yielding cues help the prompt recognition of an end of turn, and help participants synchronise their turn exchanges with precision.

GAZE DIRECTION

Kendon (1967) suggested that speakers and listeners use *gaze direction* to coordinate turn-changeovers. He noted, in an analysis of seven two-person conversations which were filmed and recorded, that a listener tended to look at the speaker for longer periods of time than the speaker looked at the listener (see Figure 6.5). He suggested that when people are engaged in planning their next utterance (such cognitive planning may not be conscious) they cannot simultaneously deal with the processing load caused by making eye-contact. As speakers came to the end of long utterances, Kendon reported, their looking increased and the utterances were completed with steady gaze directed at the listener. Listeners, on the other hand, who have been gazing much more at the speaker (possibly to monitor for turn-yielding cues as well as to show attention) looked

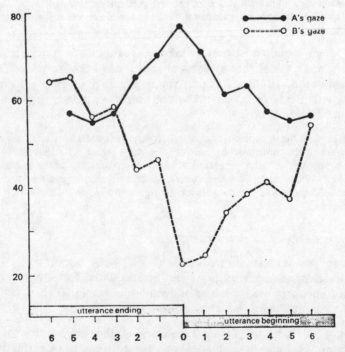

Figure 6.5.   Direction of gaze and the beginning and ending of long utterances. Frequency of *q*-directed gazes at successive half-second intervals before and after the beginning (broken line) and ending (continuous line) of long utterances. Pooled data from ten individuals, based on a total of 68 long utterances.
Source: Kendon (1967).

away as they began a long utterance, and often a little in advance of it. Kendon showed that where the speaker failed to look up at the end of a long utterance, the listener failed to respond immediately in a significant number of cases. In this way, the changes in speakers' and listeners' gaze behaviour look as if they might provide cues which help them synchronise the change in turn.

Unfortunately, not all researchers have been able to replicate these gaze effects, and others have argued that, even though the effects may sometimes occur, they are not necessary to smooth speaker exchange in all contexts. One of the most convincing demonstrations was by Beattie and Barnard (1979) who showed that smooth speaker exchanges occurred during telephone conversations between subscribers and directory enquiries. Although all visual information was lacking, smooth and rapid exchanges were found (Beattie, 1983, p. 96)

> ...there is no evidence that the absence of visual information adversely affects the management of transitions from speaker to speaker. ... smooth transitions on the telephone are the rule rather than the exception. The basic temporal characteristics of speaker switches on the telephone are at least comparable with those of face-to-face interaction. In fact ... the data suggest that speaker switching ... is plausibly executed faster on the telephone.

It may seem paradoxical that speaker exchanges are conducted *more* smoothly when visual cues are absent, but it has been suggested (Rutter and Stephenson, 1977, p. 35) that the availability of gaze information allows participants to take risks which might lead to a breakdown in telephone conversation:

> Face to face, interruption can occur freely because the visual channel allows the communication of nonverbal signals which maintain the interaction and prevent the breakdown which interruptions might otherwise produce. Without the visual channel, such nonverbal signals cannot be communicated and speech assumes greater importance in regulating the interaction.

OTHER VERBAL AND NON-VERBAL CUES

Other cues besides gaze direction must exist if the smoothness of transitions in telephone conversations can be accounted for. Duncan (1972) suggested speakers used a range of techniques to signal that they were about to yield the turn, which are listed below.

Gaze. Like Kendon, Duncan recognised the importance of gaze direction. He found that a speaker's head turned toward the listener was associated with a substantial increase in the probability of the listener taking a turn.

Syntax. Like Sacks *et al.*, Duncan suggested that grammatical completion of a clause was an important cue.

Intonation. Certain changes in pitch were associated with turn endings.

Loudness. A drop in loudness occurred at the very end of a turn, sometimes associated with a drop in pitch.

Drawl. The final syllable of a turn was often lengthened.

Stereotyped tags. Certain formulations such as 'but ah' or 'you know' were typically tagged onto the end of turns.

Gesture. Many kinds of gesture were synchronised with speech and completion of a body movement often coincided with turn completion.

Duncan suggested, quite simply, that the more cues displayed simultaneously, the more likely a rapid and smooth exchange would occur. Beattie (1983) tested this hypothesis but found that most smooth exchanges were associated with a specific combination of up to three cues. The most frequent case was that where grammatical completion was associated with intonational cues and drawl (Beattie, 1983, p. 155):

> Clause completion accompanied by a falling intonation with drawl on the stressed syllable seems to operate effectively in conversation to inform the listener that it is their turn to speak.

Denny (1985) has since suggested that the most rapid and predictable turn exchanges occur when both listener (through looking behaviour) and speaker actively co-operate in the manoeuvre. After analysing eight video-taped dyadic conversations between university students, she concluded (Denny, 1985, p. 51):

> 'Turn exchange can be maximally predicted, and virtually ensured, by a co-occurrence of elements which consists of both speaker and auditor actions.'

CONCLUSION

The research which has been described suggests that a complex mechanism regulates smooth turn exchange. A turn contains a number of transition-relevance places (potential turn-yielding points) whose arrival can be projected roughly by a hearer who draws on both discourse and syntactic knowledge. A variety of non-verbal cues are then used by the speaker both to indicate at which turn-relevance place he or she intends to yield the turn, and to synchronise precisely the smooth change.

Turn allocation

So far, the research we have examined has considered only the case of talk between two people. Where more than two people are involved then a further problem arises of which person it is who speaks next. Sacks *et al.* (1974) suggested that on some occasions the choice of next speaker is effectively predetermined by the nature of the speech event. This would happen in, say, a formal debate or court proceedings. In fact, Sacks *et al.* suggested that there existed a continuum of speech events according to how far turn allocation was predetermined. One of the features of informal conversation, they argued, was that the allocation of next turn was not predetermined at all but was locally accomplished on a turn-by-turn basis. Other speech events were intermediate in this respect (Sacks *et al.*, 1974, p. 729):

> In contrast to both debates and conversation, meetings with chair persons partially pre-allocate turns, and provide for the allocation of unallocated turns via the use of the pre-allocated turns. Thus, chair persons have rights to talk first, and to talk after each other speaker, and they can use each such turn to allocate next speakership.

In the case of casual conversation, where turns are not preallocated, one of three situations may arise.

The current speaker may select the next speaker by name, by gaze or merely by directing a particular question or comment appropriate to one rather than another hearer. The current speaker seems to have special rights to the selection of the next speaker, perhaps because the alternative of self-selection by a next speaker cannot be done until a transition-relevance place and hence is easily pre-empted by a selection by the current speaker.

Where a speaker gives signs of yielding a turn without selecting a next speaker, someone may self-select. In this case, the maxim seems to be 'first starter gets the floor'. Although brief overlaps are common, it is nearly always the case that whoever comes in second gives up the turn to the first in.

If the speaker has selected no one, and no one self selects, then the current speaker may continue the turn to another transition-relevance place.

Although the next speaker is, as a general rule, selected on a turn-by-turn basis, it is not by any means random. Turn organisation is very sensitive, for instance, to distributions of expertise and experience amongst the participants. Two people who draw upon a mutual experience will be able to sustain an extended dialogue which excludes a third party from the conversation. There is also a strong bias for the previous speaker to be selected again as the next, thus setting up a pattern of dialogue between two participants which may extend over several turns and which a third person may find difficult to break into. One reason for this pattern is that any queries, requests for clarification and so on (from whatever source) will require the previous speaker to take a further turn. Another is that a speaker may embark upon a discourse structure which is recognisable as requiring several turns to complete, and which therefore reserves speaking rights several turns ahead. Many attention-getting strategies are of this kind. For example, a turn such as:

Julia: Hey, Fred, guess what happened to me today?

immediately removes any third party from the conversation for several turns and ensures the next turn but one will also be Julia's. It has the effect of legitimising (by obtaining Fred's approval) Julia's bid for an extended turn. Furthermore, Julia can present her next turn in such a way that it will set up the expectation of a further response from Fred. Such devices, therefore, can organise the allocation of turns to both parties several turns ahead.

It is often suggested that 'fair shares for all' is an ideal principle in casual conversation amongst equals. It can be seen that such a principle is potentially very vulnerable. The dynamics of turn allocation are such that two or more people can collaborate (perhaps unwittingly) to exclude other members from taking turns. Furthermore, the maxim of 'first in gets the turn' which applies to self-selection, implies that there is a certain cut and thrust in ordinary talk. Any member who hesitates or who lacks self-confidence in the slightest degree will lose the turn whenever it is contested or, more embarrassingly, will make a bid to speak and have to withdraw.

Problems of disfluency

Disfluencies in conversation (whether they are hesitations, interruptions or overlaps) constitute potential problems for both conversation participants and conversation analysts. The former, because they may represent a breakdown in the smooth flow of talk which requires remedial action, the latter because they pose problems of explanation and interpretation.

OVERLAPS AND INTERRUPTIONS

Activity 6.1

At this point you might pause to consider
 a) what you think constitutes an interruption
 b) why interruptions occur (or, what functions they serve).

Brief overlaps between speakers occur quite commonly in conversation. The model presented by Sacks *et al*. explained these in two ways. First, a speaker may wrongly anticipate the arrival of a transition-relevance place because the speaker has unexpectedly delayed it by adding extra material. Second, the 'first in gets the floor' maxim for self selecting speakers encourages a very rapid entry which may briefly overlap with either the end of the current speaker's turn, or with a competing bid for the next turn by another would-be speaker. Such brief overlaps are, in fact, actually predicted by the model. Sacks *et al*'s explanation of overlapping speech fits in with their notion of talk as a collaborative activity — but other researchers have identified *interruptions* as a category of overlapping speech that indicates conversational dominance on the part of the perpetrator. Whilst categories of 'simultaneous talk' or 'overlap' are potentially simply and empirically identified, a category such as 'interruption' is in fact far less straightforward. For instance, certain kinds of simultaneous talk are systematically understood (by analysts and, probably, by speakers) not to count as interruptions.

Minimal responses, such as 'mmm' or 'yeah', when contributed by a listener, seem not to be counted as interruptions. The meaning attributed to minimal responses is quite variable, and probably depends as much as anything else upon the intonation pattern with which they are uttered. A speaker can say 'mmm', for instance, in a variety of ways to express a range of meanings from surprise/great interest through to a simple indication of attention. In general, however, minimal responses are heard as expressing some level of support rather than as a bid for the floor:

```
Doctor:   If there's any doubt we can always do a blood test
          to ⌈er confirm the ⌈situation.
Patient:    ⌊mm              ⌊mm
Doctor:   but provided you've had the vaccine you can forget it.
```

These so called *back channel* cues form one instance where simultaneous speech is tolerated and does not threaten a current speaker's right to complete a turn. However, it is not always clear where a minimal response ceases to be minimal, and longer, but supportive, sequences can occur in conversations.

There have been several attempts to establish formal criteria for the identification of interruptions. For instance, Zimmerman and West (1975) classified as interruptions instances of simultaneous speech (excluding minimal responses etc.) that began *before* the word immediately preceding a transition relevance place in the first speaker's utterance. Overlaps, on the other hand, began at a transition-relevance place, or the immediately preceding word. This measure seems to take account of the second speaker's ability (or willingness) to recognise syntactic cues to a legitimate entry-point and probably reflects Zimmerman and West's concern with interruption as an indicator of conversational dominance.

Beattie (1983), on the other hand, has a more complex model that distinguishes three types of interruption in addition to overlaps and smooth speaker switches (see figure 6.6)

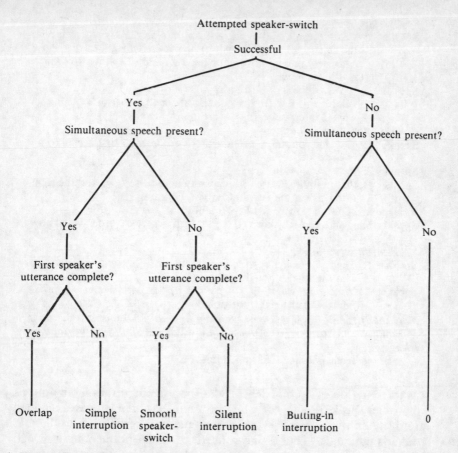

Figure 6.6   Classification of interruptions and smooth speaker switches.
Source: Beattie (1983)

The following are examples of Beattie's classification:

1. *Smooth speaker-switch*
Speaker 1: But i-i-i-it's important within (.) within the confines of the
    figure
        (300)
Speaker 2: Within the confines of the figure yes, but not (.) in the general
    visual field...

2. *Simple interruption*
Speaker 1: ...so he (.) he gives the impression that he he wasn't able to
    train them up.   ⌈Now⌉
Speaker 2:   ⌊He ⌋   didn't try
    hard enough heh heh heh.

3. *Overlap*

Speaker 1: ... it doesn't matter where it is, if it's on the edge (.) near near the edge of your periphery (.) or you know right at the centre because you can move your head (.) and it'll move you know ⎡it'll move with it⎤

Speaker 2: ⎣Yes, I   ⎦don't

I don't think we're disagreeing about that, because I think (.) what I interpreted this to mean ...

4. *Butting-in interruption*

Speaker 1: ... and you know he said that's rubbish (.) that seems to go back to

Speaker 2:   ⎡well   ⎤

Speaker 1: that really⎣because⎦ I mean why does he say ... and the right side was on the left and (.) you (.) know

Speaker 2: ⎡oh oh you you still you still⎤

Speaker 1: ⎣and you still keep   ⎦ that sort of order you know so I (.) will you know

5. *Silent interruption*

Speaker 1: Yeah I thought you meant its position with respect to everything else not the actual (.)

Speaker 2: You know wherever you've got (.) the parts I mean approximately in the right positions ...

Note that (.) indicates a pause of $\frac{1}{5}$ second or less; (300) means a pause of 300 milliseconds (i.e. 3/10 second); square brackets indicate overlapping speech

Adapted from Beattie (1983) pp. 115–116

It is the criterion of 'completeness' that best distinguishes interruptions from other speaker switches in Beattie's model. Completeness is judged intuitively on the basis of several verbal and non-verbal cues in the first speaker's utterance — but the classification is made at the point at which the first speaker *stopped* speaking, not the point at which the second speaker *began* to speak. Beattie's measure therefore seems to be an indicator of whether the first speaker might 'feel' interrupted but, unlike Zimmerman and West, it does not necessarily take account of those cues present (in the first speaker's utterance) at the point at which a potential interruption begins.

In another study, Beattie (1982) has argued that interruptions may indicate a breakdown in the normal turn-yielding mechanisms. An interruption may occur, for instance, where a listener mistakenly hears the speaker to be giving out turn-yielding signals. Beattie demonstrated that Margaret Thatcher was interrupted frequently and unsuccessfully in one television interview at points where she gave out the classic turn-yielding signals (grammatical completion, drop in pitch and drawl) without intending to relinquish the turn.

We have seen that it is possible to establish formal criteria for interruptions, and that different criteria have been adopted in different studies. It is also important to note that the *interpretation* of interruptions depends very much on the context in which they occur. While they are often thought of as an infringement of the original speaker's right to speak, frequent 'interruptions' may occur in the speech of close friends as a form of collaborative talk.

The Cassette (Band 7) contains examples of overlapping speech. If you are able to listen to them, you should be able to reassess your responses to Activity 6.1 above.

FILLED PAUSES AND RESTARTS

Beattie (1977) showed that *filled pauses* ('mmm's and 'ah's) protected the speaker from interruption for a short while. Another extremely effective tactic identified by Duncan (1972) was an incomplete gesture which indicated that a speaker wished to continue. Even when accompanied by otherwise effective turn-yielding cues, such a turn suppression signal would rarely be associated with a change in speaker. Many political speakers (though not Margaret Thatcher, it seems) use such devices to hold on to the floor. Michael Foot used a more idiosyncratic, but effective, technique of pausing in the middle of clauses where an interruption would be heard as most offensive and running fast through the transition-relevance place and into the next sentence.

Filled pauses and false starts may also indicate that a speaker is not yet convinced that the full attention of the audience is commanded. Goodwin (1981) has demonstrated that speakers will often restart an utterance when gaze has been obtained from a listener so that the whole utterance is properly attended to. Such restarts can be interpreted as 'requests for gaze attention'. Speakers also use pauses and filled pauses near beginnings of utterances, instead of a restart, to delay the effective beginning of their turn until gaze has been achieved.

A similar effect has been observed (Atkinson, 1984) in skilled public speakers, who will repeatedly restart during audience clapping until they can be heard again. Such speakers give the impression that they are battling against unsolicited applause whilst ensuring that nothing of their message is lost.

In these various ways, behaviour which at first sight seems to be disfluent or incompetent behaviour by speakers, can be seen as part of a systematic and competent mechanism for synchronising their performance with listeners' behaviour.

Cultural variability

The turn-taking mechanism described here is one which seems to work for much conversational data in English. The features and norms (such as the ones listed at the beginning of this section) which characterise such conversation may not, however, apply to all cultures and contexts. Reisman (1974) has described how public talk by Antiguan villagers may routinely involve loud and simultaneous talk, often repetitive. Basso (1972) has reported that a conversation in Western Apache may in some contexts involve completely silent turns by one of the participants. Such silences, by contrast, are taboo and embarrassing in all but the most intimate English conversations. Denny (1985) has argued that norms of turn exchange are, in fact, more variable in Western culture than has been supposed and that, as we suggested above, the perception of simultaneous talk as interruption or as rude is situation-dependent.

6.4   OBSERVING AND TRANSCRIBING CONVERSATION

How an investigator sets about observing, recording and analysing an interaction depends on the type of interaction, on the aims of the investigation and on the questions which the investigation is intended to answer. There is, in other words, no such thing as a perfect all-purpose method of observation and analysis. Two kinds of analysis of talk (*conversation analysis* and *discourse analysis*) are discussed in Chapter 7. These, however, do not fully demonstrate the range of approaches available. Two rather different examples, the first from social psychology and the second from education, will show how different goals will give rise to different techniques of investigation and record-keeping.

Bales interaction analysis

Bales (1970) was interested in the interpersonal dynamics of small groups. He developed 'a simple method by which one may train himself to pay attention to the quantity and direction of interaction, apart from its content' and showed 'how this method may be helpful in analyzing the relations of persons in a particular group' (Bales, 1970, p. 62).

Bales claimed that much of participants' behaviour can be understood in terms of their attempting to establish their status within the group, and the negotiation of power relationships. In particular, he suggested that the amount an individual speaks in the group is partly based upon, or regulated by the status he has in the outside world and which he brings into the group:

> A rank [status] order from the outside, with the rank order of total [talk] initiated will probably show a noticeable similarity. But it may also show some notable exceptions, and this is really more interesting, since it raises the question of 'power' as distinct from 'legitimate status' based on outside criteria.

So, Bales argued, the time spent talking by a given member in a given session is really a 'direct index of the amount of power he has attempted to exercise in that period'. Power was defined as the 'actual ability, whether legitimate or illegitimate, to control or dominate the actions of others' (Bales, 1970, p. 77). A full account of power relationships within a group could be achieved, not just by estimating the amount of each

Table 6.1

Scores	Implied Meaning
1.0	Person 1 speaks to the group as a whole.
1.0	Person 1 speaks (again) to the group as a whole.
1.0	Person 1 speaks (again) to the group as a whole.
2.1	Person 2 speaks (replies) to person 1.
1.2	Person 1 speaks (replies) to person 2.
1.2	Person 1 continues speaking to person 2.
3.1	Person 3 speaks (replies) to person 1.
3.1	Person 3 continues his reply to person 1.
4.0	Person 1 speaks (let us say, jokes) to all.
0.4	Each person speaks (for example, laughs) to person 4.

Source: Bales (1970, p. 66)

person's contribution, but by analysing how much talk was directed to and received by each participant.

We will not provide here a detailed discussion or criticism of Bales' theory, but we can see how such interests will affect the kind of field-work which is carried out. An investigator who proposed to carry out Bales's analysis would make a record of the group's interaction by noting who initiated each communicative act and to whom it was directed. For this purpose, each person might be allocated a number. The number 0 was used to signify the whole group, although for the purposes of later analysis any record of the whole group initiating talk would be reinter-preted as each individual member initiating an act with the exception of the one to whom the group act (such as laughter) was directed. This would be the only written record needed for this part of the analysis and it might look like that in Table 6.1.

The Flanders analysis of teacher–pupil interaction

Flanders (1970) developed a system for analysing teaching behaviour in classrooms. All events were classified as belonging to one of ten categories. Seven categories referred to teacher's talk (for example, category 2 was 'praise'; category 6, 'giving commands'); two categories referred to pupil talk (category 8 was a 'response'; category 9 was an 'initiation') and the tenth category was for 'silence or confusion'. The procedure was as follows (Flanders, 1970, p. 37)

An observer sits in the classroom in the best position to hear and see the participants. Almost as often as possible, he decides which category best represents the communication events just completed. He then writes down

Table 6.2

Category Number		Completed Tally Marks Made by an Observer	Total Tallies	Percent
Teacher	1	III	3	0.8
	2	THL I	6	2.5
	3	THL THL II	12	5.0
	4	THL THL THL THL II	22	9.2
	5	THL THL THL THL THL THL THL THL THL THL THL THL THL THL THL THL THL THL THL THL THL THL THL THL THL THL	130	54.2
	6	THL THL THL I	16	6.7
	7	IIII	4	1.6
Pupils	8	THL THL THL THL II	22	9.2
	9	THL THL II	12	5.0
Silence	10	THL THL IIII	14	5.8
		Total	240	100.0

Source: Flanders (1970, p. 38)

this category number while he simultaneously assesses the continuing communication. Observation continues at a rate of 20 to 25 tallies per minute, *keeping the tempo as steady as possible*. This usually works out to about one tally every 3 seconds. There is nothing magical about a 3-second period. An experienced observer, after considerable practice, tends to classify at this rate with this particular category system. A gifted observer might settle down to a faster rate after considerable experience, and another category system might force a slower rate, even for a gifted observer. Having a regular tempo is much more important than achieving a particular rate because most conclusions depend on rate consistency, not on speed.

The record made by an observer using Flanders' system would look like that in Table 6.2.

We can see from the examples of Bales and Flanders that, in each case, what they saw fit to transcribe and record was determined very much both by their own interests as well as their pre-existing theories regarding interpersonal interaction. In practice, an investigator will have developed sets of categories and observation methods in earlier pilot stages of the study, but the process of 'interrogating the data' never really finishes. Whenever a transcript or analysis is made an investigator not only learns more about the phenomenon under investigation but also more about the limitations of the system of analysis and how it might be refined.

Problems with live observation

Both Bales and Flanders made use of live observation techniques. You may be surprised, therefore, that we do not recommend this as an appropriate method here. Making live observations is difficult for several reasons.

It is very difficult to attend to *how* people are speaking when you are taking part in an interaction yourself and your attention is taken up with *what* they are saying. Even if you are present as an independent observer, it is often only apparent what details are interesting after some preliminary analysis of the data has been made.

Participants in conversation have to process a large amount of information through many channels (verbal, paralinguistic, non-verbal and so on) and most of this processing is necessarily unconscious — when such data are reflected upon consciously it takes considerable time.

Conversational interaction is so rich and complex that the only satisfactory way of preserving it is on a video or sound recording which can be returned to again and again to extract and transcribe new partial descriptions as the analytical need arises.

Keeping an enduring record enables others to check and agree with your analysis or discuss it with you. In large studies such as those of Bales and Flanders, observers were given a lengthy training and checks were regularly made to ensure that their scoring behaviour remained similar. Neither of these methods of ensuring reliability are appropriate to the kind of analysis you are likely to be interested in.

In this section we assume, therefore, that you already have an audio recording of the interaction in which you are interested. (Though the activities that follow can be done using the sample recordings supplied on the cassette). We give two methods of dealing with the recordings. Method 1 provides a systematic way of approaching a recording when you do not have enough time to make a transcript. Method 2 shows how a written transcript can be made. You should work through both methods, doing activities 6.2–6.5.

Let us assume, for the purposes of this illustration that we are interested, for reasons similar to Bales perhaps, in how much each person talks in a conversation. How can we set about measuring this?

We could try to count how many words each person spoke — but this is surprisingly difficult without a complete transcript.

We could try to time each person's contribution with a stop watch — but this is much more time consuming and difficult than you might think. It requires one pass through the recording for every participant, for instance, and some utterances are so short that they cannot be timed with any accuracy. (It can take less than half a second to say *yeah*, for example). It is also sometimes difficult to know exactly when someone has begun or finished because someone else's speech overlaps.

We could count the number of turns each person gets to speak. This is quite often done, in fact, but it suffers from the disadvantage that no account is taken of how long each turn is.

There are also other estimates of amount of talk which depend on a prior analysis of the interaction into certain kinds of events. One could find out how many topics a person introduced, for example, or how many complete exchanges (see the discussion of discourse analysis in section 7.3) one person got with another. These are extremely difficult to analyse without a written transcript.

The method described below is a relatively quick way of analysing a recording whenever a particular category of event can be identified as being of interest. Here, the event is simply whether someone is talking or not, but it could just as well be something more specific, such as 'question' or 'interruption'. It could even be extended more along the lines of Flanders's system to allow several coded categories of event to be included.

Method 1. Sampling the recording

Two principal methods of time sampling a recording exist. In the first, a specific time interval is chosen and an observation is made — like a camera flash — at the expiry of each interval (*instantaneous sampling*). In the second, the recording is partitioned into sections each having the duration of the chosen time period (*partition sampling*). An observation is then made of events which have occurred within this time period. Normally, one is concerned only with whether an event has occurred or not, not how many times it has occurred. Both methods provide a basis for quantitative assessments of how often particular events occur, as Figure 6.7 indicates. The study by Flanders used a three-second sampling interval, but it is not entirely clear which kind of sampling was used.

Figure 6.7(a) is a record of when three participants (a teacher, a boy, and a girl) are talking. Figure 6.7(b) shows the effect of instantaneous sampling every five seconds and Figure 6.7(c) shows the effect of partition sampling. Where the sampling interval is very small in comparison to the duration and frequency of the events being recorded then there will be very little difference between the two methods in the results they yield. The methods differ, however, in how they distort the data when sample intervals are lengthened. This is an important consideration, since you will always be interested in making the minimum number of observations necessary (to save time in analysis) and because the duration and frequency of certain events may not be known before the analysis begins.

Activity 6.2

Assess the effect of using a 20-second time interval on the data given in Figure 6.7a.

Instantaneous sampling: This is easiest to recalculate as you just have to take every fourth observation shown in figure 6.7(b) and count the new totals for each participant.

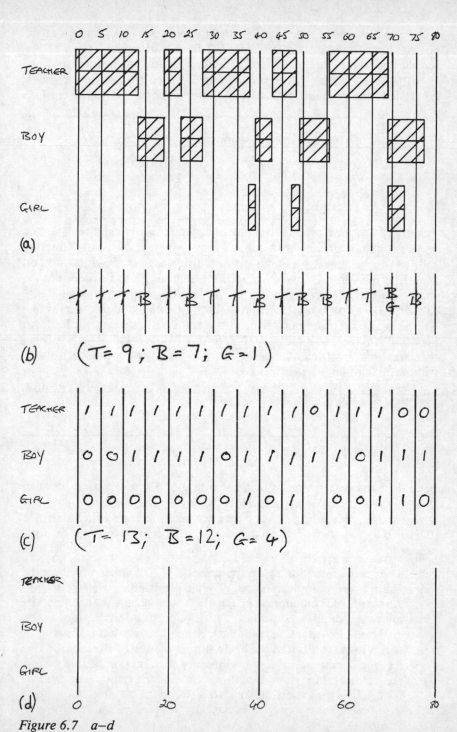

Figure 6.7 *a–d*

Partition sampling: Use Figure 6.7(d) to help you recalculate the effect of partition sampling. If a 1 is recorded for a participant in any of the four intervals in Figure 6.7(c) which correspond to your new partition in 6.7(d) then a 1 should be recorded. Only if a participant never spoke throughout the duration of the longer interval should a 0 be recorded.

My totals for the longer sample interval were as follows:

Instantaneous sample	Partition sample
Teacher = 3	Teacher = 4
Boy = 1	Boy = 4
Girl = 0	Girl = 3

Activity 6.2 shows that instantaneous sampling will tend to 'lose' or underestimate short and infrequent events, whereas partition sampling will tend to become more insensitive to differences in the duration and frequency of events. On balance, partition sampling is to be preferred for conversational interactions. It has the added advantage of making it easy to add general comments in a systematic manner about other events which may be happening in the interaction. It does, however, suffer from the disadvantage that increasing the number of observations (shortening the sample interval) cannot be done once the analysis has been made without reanalysing the entire recording.

The next activity introduces you to one practical way of using partition sampling to analyse a conversation.

Activity 6.3

Band 7 of the cassette contains a recording of a conversation between four children which can be used as the basis of this activity if you do not have a suitable recording of your own to hand. In the worked example (Figure 6.8) we show the analysis of a different recording of four children.

1   The revolution counter on the cassette player you are using provides a very simple method of time-partitioning the recording. Although such counters vary greatly from machine to machine, the important thing is to establish a *regular* partition length for a given analysis. How many seconds each counter revolution takes will, in fact, vary slightly from the beginning to the end of the tape, so this method is most suited to a preliminary examination of fairly short recordings rather than a rigorous analysis of many long recordings. Using the tape counter rather than a stop watch does, however, make it very easy to replay any selected part of the tape at leisure.

First of all you should time how long it takes your counter to make one revolution (ours took 2.5 seconds). Zero the counter at the beginning of the sequence to be coded. Treat each complete revolution as a new time interval.

2 Take a blank sheet of paper and draw two more columns than there are participants. The example in Figure 6.8 shows six columns, since there were four people involved in this group. In the first column enter the counter number for each interval; in the next columns record whether each of the participants talked during a particular interval; the last column is for notes and comments.

3 Begin playing the first section of the tape and record on the first line who spoke during the first counter revolution by putting a 1 in the appropriate column. Add any relevant comments in the right-hand margin. For example, our example in Figure 6.8 shows comments like 'T (Tony) interrupts'.

4 When you have finished, count up the number of 1's for each participant and enter the total at the foot of each column. Add all the totals together and enter a grand total at the foot of the comments column. Work out what percentage of the grand total each participant's total represents and enter it under each column total. This gives an *estimate* of the proportion of the talk contributed by each person.

The analysis in Figure 6.8 shows that although Lisa was in the chair for this discussion, most of the talk came from Tony. The analysis also shows that although the boys together occupied more of the talk than the girls, this was due mainly to the activity of one boy — Michael spoke least of any of the children. Differences of this kind show up very clearly using this technique, even though the analysis can be done fairly quickly — you may even be able to keep up with the tape and find there is rarely any need to pause or replay it.

Method 1 provides a very good way of deriving a simple quantitative analysis from a recording. It also has the important advantage of allowing you to get to know your data better, and may raise other more interesting questions which can form the basis of a more detailed and considered analysis. Its main failing, perhaps, is that it cannot measure the frequency and duration of a speaker's contributions separately. This might be an important consideration in some cases. For example, if you are investigating 'power' and 'dominance' in interactions, it may be that frequent very short turns have a very different significance from few long turns. The method also prevents any more detailed analysis of the structure of the interaction along the lines of the methods described in section 7.3.

Very little more can be done, however, without making some kind of transcript. Method 2 shows you how a systematic transcript can be made.

COUNTER	LISA (CHAIR)	STEPHANIE	MICHAEL	TONY	COMMENTS
0				1	
1	1				
2	1	1			S-'Yeah, they can....'
3			1	1	M-gives support
4	1		1	1	L-attempts turn, T-interrupts
5				1	
6	1			1	L-'mmm'
7				1	
8	1			1	L-'yeah'
9				1 1	
10				1	
11	1				
12				1	
13	1				
14	1				
15	1			1	
16					Pause - topic exhausted
17	1		1		L-reads new topic question
18		1		1	S-'no' in resp to Q
19	1			1	T-'no' but gets turn
20				1	L-curly do you think'— <u>encouragement</u>
21		1			
22	1	1			
23	1			1	T-'Yeah' - <u>support</u>
24		1	1		
25				1	T-takes topic 'another thing'...
26				1	
27				1	
28				1	
29				1	
30				1	
TOTAL	13	5	4	21	42
%	30%	12%	9%	50%	
	42%		59%		

Figure 6.8.

Method 2. Making a transcript

TRANSCRIPTS AS ANALYSIS

An audio or video recording gives prominence to certain aspects of an interaction and ignores others, just as a live observer fails to register a comprehensive and accurate record of events. A video recording, for example, will point in a certain direction and fail to record such invisible things as participants' prior states of knowledge, expectations and intentions. A written transcript continues the process of selection and partial analysis. You may imagine that making a transcript is a fairly straightforward, if somewhat tedious, job. Transcripts, however, are not neutral representations of what occurs in an interaction. They select certain phenomena as being of interest and give prominence to them and they embody many assumptions and expectations of a theoretical kind. Although a transcript is extremely valuable in giving the overall shape of an interaction and in postponing certain kinds of analysis and coding until later, it does already move in the direction of analysis and will anticipate and facilitate the analysis you intend to make next. It is worth quoting Kendon (1982, p. 478–9) at length:

> The transcription system one adopts itself embodies a set of hypotheses and assumptions that will thereafter structure one's inquiry. It is of the greatest importance to know what these hypotheses are, and whether they are appropriate to the question one is engaged upon, before adopting any system of transcription. It is a mistake to think that there can be a truly neutral transcription system, which, if only we had it, we could then use to produce transcriptions suitable for any kind of investigation ... Transcriptions, thus, *embody* hypotheses.
>
> As soon as one puts pencil to paper in making a map, as soon as one makes a transcription, one is thereby making a decision, a theoretical decision, about what is important. For no transcription, no matter how fine grained, can ever be complete. One must inevitably make a selection. Thus the map one makes, the transcription one produces, is as much a product of one's investigation as a means of furthering it. But only by laying out on paper a map of the event can one come to perceive its structure; only in this way can one come to 'see' one's formulation. ... One works in continual dialogue with the specimen.

Kendon makes the point that no transcript is ever complete. In fact, it is a complete waste of time attempting to make a complete and accurate transcript of all your data. It is far better to make a rough and ready transcript which will allow you to see the approximate shape of the interaction, in the respects of interest to you, and which you can use to identify sections of further interest. You can then return to revise your rough transcript according to the particular needs of your analysis system. So, for example, you may make a finer and more accurate analysis of overlaps or interruptions and later add details about intonation or (in the case of a video recording) non-verbal behaviour such as gaze direction.

Activity 6.4

Using the recording you used for Activity 6.3, make a rough transcript of each child's (or other participant's) talk. You should give some thought to the layout and presentation of such a transcript before you start. For example, you will need to identify the speakers in some way, and will need to include a reference system so that you can find both the place on the tape again, and the place in the transcript. A suggested layout is shown in Figure 6.9. Use only about half the width of the page to make the transcript — this leaves plenty of room for adding other comments — and leave space between each of the lines for revisions. This may seem wasteful of paper, but it is more wasteful of time and resources to recopy a whole transcript when revising it. Put a speaker's name or identification to the left of each utterance in the transcript, rather as in a dramatic script.

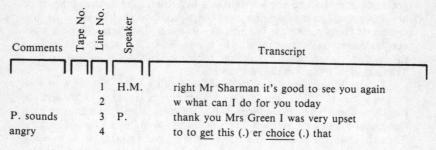

Figure 6.9. A recommended layout for transcripts

As you work through the tape, make a note of any problems which arise or any aspects of transcription which cause difficulty. Time how long it takes you to make the first rough transcript and compare it with the actual duration of the tape. You should expect to take at least 3 times the duration of the recording, and perhaps nearer 6 if the recording is of poor quality or if there are several speakers. Try not to spend any longer at this stage.

You may have been surprised at how difficult it can be to make an accurate transcription of a dialogue. Below, we've listed some of the problems transcribers frequently meet:

Poor recording quality. Most tapes which require transcription are made in less than ideal circumstances and in ways which are designed not to inhibit the movement or naturalness of the interaction. Not infrequently there will be sections of recordings which are difficult to make out, or where speech is masked by noise such as coughing or furniture movement.

Timing. Making judgements about who spoke first, or where an interruption occurred, is sometimes remarkably difficult, and you may have to replay a section of tape many times to satisfy yourself that you have it right.

Punctuation. Punctuation is, of course, a convention of written language. But you will almost certainly have found yourself using some kind of punctuation nevertheless. What function do capital letters or commas have when transcribing speech? Here there will be an important trade-off between accuracy and legibility of your transcript. We suggest that you do not worry too much about including punctuation at the stage of rough transcript, since legibility is more important. You should be aware, though, that in using it you are making an immediate analysis of such things as sentence boundaries, speech acts (question marks), and so on, which you will need to revise later when making a careful transcript.

Intonation, etc. Certain aspects of speech, such as intonation, stress, loudness, hesitation and so on, are not normally represented in writing. Some way of recording such information using special conventions is needed.

There exist a very wide range of conventions for representing the details of spoken dialogue accurately in transcripts and it may seem unfortunate that there is no internationally agreed system which could be used for features of dialogue in the way that the International Phonetic Alphabet can be used for individual sounds. However, many investigators find they have to adopt or design a set of conventions which fit the needs and interests of their own study. Inevitably, some detail of the spoken dialogue has to be sacrificed — if you were to attempt a full representation the resulting transcript would be unreadable and largely unuseable. Nevertheless, there is a core of transcription problems which face all investigators. Below is given one set of conventions for dealing with these which have a fairly wide currency amongst conversational analysts.

Conventions of transcription

you~~~~   wavy lines indicate comment in margin

you   underlining indicates emphatic stress.

(.)   indicates a very short pause

(3.0)   indicates the duration of a pause in seconds.

(we)   indicates that the utterance is unclear and hence the transcription is tentative.

( )   indicates that the utterance is very unclear and hence cannot be transcribed.

[giggle]   description of part of utterance which cannot be transcribed

[yes we / do you]   indicates that a turn at talk overlaps with the next, and the points at which the overlap begins and ends.

Activity 6.5

Using your rough transcript as the basis, make as accurate and detailed a transcript as you can using the transcription conventions given above. You should expect to spend up to six times the duration of the recording making this transcript, even though you already have a rough version. Note how many errors you find in your rough transcript.

Figure 6.10 gives an example of a transcript using these symbols, showing how it is laid out on the page. The conversation on which this transcript is based is included on the cassette (Band 8). If you are able to, you should listen to this band as you read through the transcript.

Remember that, in practice, you will normally make a transcript which is only as accurate and detailed as the occasion warrants. You may sometimes need to invent extra symbols of your own, or you may even prefer to move into a full phonetic transcription in particular sections, if you have the training.

Transcribing children's language

The extent to which a transcription system imposes certain assumptions and categories on the data is nowhere more apparent than when dealing with data from young children. Even the layout of the transcript on the page (such as in Figure 6.10) makes the assumption that there exists a basic dialogic structure, and this assumption may not be appropriate for young children. Turns between children may not be exchanged smoothly, but, more importantly, it is not always clear to whom children's speech is directed. However, the 'dramatic script' transcript model may mislead us into seeing alternating speech as a series of exchanges which occasionally overlap. For this reason, many researchers working with

```
1    H.M.    right Mr Sharma it's good to see you again w what can I do
2            for you today
3    P.      thank you Mrs Green I was very upset to get this (.) er
4            choice (.) that my daughter Nehemulla (.) is doing c s e
5    H.M.    just a minute (.) can I see this form
6    P.      yes sure (.) here ⌈yes
7    H.M.                      ⌊ah oh yes yes this is the this is the form
8            that we sent out last week (.) we've asked every parent just
9            to tick the er (.) the subjects that they would like
10           their (.) children to do ⌈(.) is there any problem ⌈about that
11   P.                              ⌊ah but do               ⌊oh yes
12           yes erm (.) I don't want my (.) er daughter to do c s e I want
13           her to do o level
14   H.M.    yes but Mr Sharma I thought we resolved this on your last
15           visit (.) and the situation hasn't changed (.) Nehemulla is
16           ideally suited to the class she's in and this class will do c s e
17           in two years time
```

Figure 6.10.   An example of a detailed transcript

children often use a different way of laying out the transcription, using a separate column for each participant, as shown in Figure 6.11.

Conventional transcription methods not only assume adult-like discourse structure, they impose linguistic categories (some so familiar that they pass unnoticed) at all levels of analysis. Quite often it will be found that the vocabulary of adult English is insufficient to record children's talk. In these cases analysts normally use a phonemic or phonetic script to transcribe problematic utterances in a way which records more faithfully what the child actually uttered and which leaves open its status as a word or phrase. Even the IPA alphabet, however, imposes adult articulation categories on the data. In fact, most transcripts of child language proceed on the tacit assumption that it is convenient and reasonable to assume that children are behaving like adults except in those respects of particular interest to the investigator. A fuller discussion of some of the problems of transcribing data from children can be found in Ochs (1979) and MacWhinney and Snow (1985).

Mark (27 months) is in the lounge with his mother.

MARK	MOTHER
'ot Mummy	[standing by central heating radiator] Hot? Yes, that's the radiator.
Been? ... (? = burn) Burn?	
	Burn?
Yeh.	
	Yes you know it'll burn don't you?
Oh [putting his hand on Ooh radiator]	
	Take your hand off it.
Uh?	
	What about the other shoe? [Mother is asking whether he needs his other shoelace tied]
a all done Mummy.	
	Mm?
It done Mummy.	
	It's done is it?
Yeh.	

Fig 6.11.   An example of transcription of children's talk
Source: Wells (1985)

7 Discourse and text

7.1 INTRODUCTION

This chapter is concerned with the description of *discourse* and *text*. Traditionally, the distinction between discourse and text was similar to that between 'spoken' and 'written', but this simple correspondence has been eroded over the years by two things. One is the increasing range of forms which written and spoken material may take in modern media; the other is the way theoretical perspectives have evolved. Let us take each in turn.

Written texts traditionally came in a limited range of forms and implied both a limited range of linguistic styles and particular relationships with the reader. A reader, for example, was usually remote from the writer and had limited, if any, possibilities for interacting and responding to the writer. Spoken language, on the other hand, usually implied the actual presence of a listener who was able to intervene in the flow of discourse and help determine later utterances. One can easily think of exceptions to this simple distinction — even in classical times — and the Greek and Roman rhetoricians were not entirely blind to the theoretical implications. By and large, however, whether something was written or spoken implied a particular relationship with a reader or hearer, a particular range of linguistic styles and communicative functions.

Such a simple distinction is now impossible, rather than merely difficult, to sustain as we demonstrate in section 7.2. Virtually the entire language output of television and all that of radio, for example, is spoken rather than written and yet the viewer or listener is usually incapable of intervening and altering the flow of the discourse. At another extreme, a new genre of computer adventure games is appearing in which the player determines the flow of the story by making decisions and responses at critical points. Where once a distinction between 'spoken' and 'written' could be viewed as a shorthand for a cluster of important distinctions, we now need to be more precise about which distinctions are of interest to us.

Theory has also evolved over the years, perhaps partly in response to changing circumstances. Literary theory, for example, which once required students to evaluate works of literature as artefacts with intrinsic qualities now views a work of literature as being generated at the point of consumption, where it results from an interaction between the reader and the text. This has the effect of making texts more like a discourse — meanings are negotiated, as it were, between author and reader, even if each plays a rather different role. In other scholarly traditions ranging from semiotics to artificial intelligence, a similar rehabilitation of the role of the reader has occurred, as is discussed more fully in section 7.4 below.

Both culture and theory have altered to the point where the simple notions which underpinned the discourse/text distinction have been undermined. How, then, are the terms now used? The old senses have not been entirely discarded, but they seem to be associated with a further conceptual distinction which is reminiscent of a traditional one made in linguistics between the language system and language use. One form of this is the *langue/parole* distinction (discussed in section 1.3) proposed by Saussure.

According to this usage, a text belongs to the realm of the linguistic system and can be described in terms of its underlying structure and the rules used to organise it. Discourse belongs to the realm of *parole* — it describes the way meanings are generated and exchanged by people in real-life contexts. Within a particular discourse, utterances are understood by making reference to a particular set of ideas, values or conventions which lie outside the actual words or tokens exchanged. The notion of text embodies notions of *grammar* and *semantics* (see Chapters 3 and 4) but discourse embodies the notion of *pragmatics* (see section 1.3).

It must be admitted that there is still some confusion in the way the terms are used in the literature. Different authors may even use 'discourse' and 'text' in interchangeable or contrary ways. Other authors use 'text' to refer to the outward material form of a language event, and 'discourse' to the more abstract exchange of meanings it represents. At first sight, this distinction seems to contradict that of *langue/parole*, but this is not entirely true. If meanings result from an interaction between context (which includes background knowledge, social relationships, etc.) and 'text', then it will readily be seen that the notion of 'discourse' is still located in the field of pragmatics. 'Text', however, has been used ambiguously to refer either to the grammatical system which underlies the material product, or to the product itself as it exists before it has been activated by situated interpreters to yield meaning.

Both the sections on spoken language and written language internally distinguish between analytical approaches which take a discourse view and those which take a textual view of their subject matter. This reflects the fact that this distinction (however evasive it may be), rather than that between spoken and written, is of greater current theoretical interest.

7.2 DIFFERENCES BETWEEN SPEECH AND WRITING

The primacy of speech

There is a view of language, probably derived from traditional (classical) grammars of English but still with wide currency, that speech is somehow an inferior version of writing: less polished, full of errors and hesitations. Many prescriptions about speech imply that this is, in some sense, a derivative of writing — as when a speaker's pronunciation is corrected: '"las' week" is sloppy — you should pronounce the *t*'. Modern linguistics, on the other hand, has sought to rehabilitate speech (Palmer, 1984, p. 28):

> A moment's reflection will soon make it clear that speech cannot in any serious sense be derived from writing and cannot therefore depend on it for correctness or non-correctness. Not only did the spoken language precede the written language historically (and even with a language like English only in very recent times has writing been at all widespread), but also every one of us learnt to speak long before we learnt to write. All the patterns of our language were quite firmly established before we went to school, and when we learnt to write we learnt only to put into written symbols what we already knew. If there is priority it is in the spoken, not the written, form of language.

Speech quite clearly preceded writing historically: the oldest known writing system, Sumerian cuneiform, appeared only towards 3000 BC. (See the discussion of writing systems in section 5.1.)

The idea of the 'priority' or 'primacy' of speech is a key notion in contemporary linguistics, which has tended to take spoken language as its major source of data. A recent debate between linguists (recorded in Hudson, 1984) reaffirmed this stand, whilst recognising that the relationship between speech and writing was rather more complex than had previously been acknowledged. Although it is clearly wrong to regard speech as derived from writing, it is also misleading to regard writing as simply a derivative of speech. For instance, some constructions found in writing do not occur, or occur rarely, in speech. The 'past historic' verb tense in French occurs only in writing. English has no such major categorical differences but constructions such as *Jane supposes Susan to be happy* are rare in speech. Many educated speakers spend as much time reading and writing as they do listening and talking — and indeed their speech may be influenced by written language; it is even possible for a spoken language to develop from a language that was restricted to writing, as in the case of modern Hebrew.

It is, in fact, not easy to draw a straighforward distinction between speech and writing. The sections below discuss differences between the two channels, and also how they are interrelated.

Speech and writing as different communication channels

Table 7.1 summarises some of the more obvious differences between speech and writing, due simply to the fact that they operate as different

Table 7.1 Some differences between speech and writing (from Czerniewska, 1985)

The oral channel	The written channel
1 Sounds	Letters
2 Intonation patterns, changes in pitch and stress to convey attitudes and some grammatical distinctions	No direct counterpart though underlining words, parentheses, punctuation (e.g. exclamation marks) and capital letters can convey similar meanings
3 Non-verbal gestures, eye contact.	No direct counterpart though different types of handwriting might express similar meanings
4 No direct equivalents though changes in pitch and speed may express equivalent meanings	Punctuation marks such as dashes, question marks and dots; different types of handwriting or type faces
5 Pauses and silence	Gaps and dashes
6 Expressions to indicate topic changes, e.g. *right then*, *now*	Headings, new chapters, paragraphs, etc. Words like *firstly*; *in conclusion*
7 No direct equivalent	Capital letters for names and beginning of sentences
8 Gap-fillers. e.g. *you know*, *er*	Hesitations not shown in final form of writing
9 Checks on listener attention and to maintain interaction such as *do you know what I mean?*	Perhaps less common but checks on reader involvement employed, e.g. *try to bear in mind . . . if you have followed my arguments so far . . .*

channels of communication. Even here, though, the differences are not absolute. For instance, telephone conversations cannot rely on gestures and eye contact.

Differences in structure and function

Activity 7.1

Here are two examples of discourse, one (orignally) spoken and one written.

(a) How do they differ?
(b) How far do you think their differences reflect more general differences between spoken and written language?

The first is a conversation between two lecturers

A   [Picks up book] Jack's this is Jack's
B   Yes he gave it to me (.) he was clearing out (.)
A   Oh (.) well I don't know whether to check through the references or just to leave it (.) for you to do
B   Don't don't leave anything else for me to do (.) can't you do it
A   Will the editors mmh check references
B   They should do
A   I think someone should mmh go through before anyway uhh to check the photocopies of all the quotations (.) can you do that?
B   Yeah (.) OK [takes photocopies]
A   OK I think that's everything then
B   Right
A   OK see you then
B   See you
A   Bye

The second is a description of a university sickness scheme.

An employee is able to insure himself or herself for up to 75% of gross income less the Single Person's State Benefit, at present £1,781. Should an employee suffer long term sickness or injury, he or she would receive this amount beginning 26/52 weeks, according to the waiting period selected, from the date of becoming unable to work up until reaching the normal retiring date.

These may perhaps be regarded, in terms of style, as archetypal instances of speech and writing. The conversation is produced by two people. It is spontaneous, and informal. Its collaborative nature is evident in its structure — in the way the two speakers need to 'negotiate' the close of the conversation, for example. Similarly, the fact that it is made up on the spot is evident in the short sequences, hestitations and fillers such as *mmh* (which amongst other things, allow speakers to plan ahead as they speak). The informality of the occasion can also be seen in the use of more 'casual' forms of speech such as *yeah* and *OK*.

The two speakers can see each other and are talking about the here and now. Hence the use of *deictic* expressions such as *this is Jack's* which refer to items in the physical context. Finally, the conversation is ephemeral (or would be, if it had not been recorded for research purposes).

The written extract is from a published document. It has probably been through at least one draft before being finalised and printed. There is no direct contact between the writer, or writers, and reader. In this case the writer is unknown and, while the document is intended for university staff, the actual reader, on any one occasion, cannot be predicted; nor can the specific context in which the document is read. The style is formal, with constructions such as *should an employee suffer*. The second sentence, in particular, is long and complex, with several dependent clauses. The complexity of this sentence is related to the formal style of the passage, but is only possible because the sentence has been pre-planned (probably reflected upon at length!). The language is explicit (there are no deictic expressions referring outside the text). Finally, while the document is unlikely to last for centuries, its status is at least more permanent than that of the casual conversation.

However, although such differences may characterise 'typical' forms of speech and writing, they cannot be said to characterise speech and writing *per se*. A spoken lecture may be carefully planned — even rehearsed; in a radio talk there is no direct contact between speaker and listener; a computer program will allow a user to interact, in writing, with the machine. It has been suggested that rather than simply distinguishing speech from writing, a continuum should be envisaged between speech that is hardest to match with writing (for instance, speech closely integrated with non-verbal behaviour) and writing that is hardest to match with speech (such as graphs and tables) — see Hudson (1984). As a general rule, however, such differences as there are between the structures of spoken and written language are probably related as much to the different *functions* associated with each channel as to any inherent channel differences.

Dimensions underlying speech and writing

Comparisons between speech and writing are, then, unlikely to be very fruitful unless one specifies what kind of speech is being compared with what kind of writing. Table 7.2 shows a number of dimensions along which instances of language use can be ranged. Examples of writing

Table 7.2 Some dimensions by which language use can be classified (based on Hudson, 1984)

1. *Transitoriness*

Permanent record	Printed book	Note for milkman	Ephemeral
	Recording of a parliamentary debate	Conversation	

2. *Degree of formality*

Formal	Act of parliament	Shopping list	Informal
	Queen's speech	Informal conversation	

3. *Use of standard English*

Standard	School textbook	Poem in local dialect	Non-standard
	BBC News	Parent–child conversation	

4. *Degree of interaction between producer and receiver*

Low interaction	Telephone directory	Notes passed between children in classroom	High interaction
	Radio talk	Telephone conversation	

5. *Type of interaction between producer and receiver*

Message-oriented	Recipe	Christmas card	Socially-orientated
	Football commentary	'How do you do?'	

6. *Dependence on context*

Context-independent	A story	Instructions for self-assembly kit	Context-dependent
	Poetry recitation	Oral directions	

(above the lines) and speech (below the lines) are given for the 'extremes' of each dimension.

Relationships between the two channels are highly complex and interact with a range of other factors. However, because of the sets of factors typically associated with each channel, they differ in status. For instance, the university document quoted above is probably legally binding — and it is often the case that formulations with legal status are written and not spoken. Lexicographers compiling the *Oxford English Dictionary* give priority to written sources when collecting citations. One justification for this has been that such sources are 'verifiable' — but clearly a recording of a radio interview is just as verifiable as a written source.

Ironically, despite their protestations about the primacy of speech, exposure to higher status written forms may also affect linguists' perceptions of language. For instance the adoption of the sentence as the largest unit of syntactic analysis (see section 3.2) was probably affected by writing: sentence-like structures are less likely to occur in speech. Even descriptive grammars tend to be biased towards the kind of formal language conventionally associated with writing. The *Grammar of Contemporary English* (Quirk *et al*,. 1972) describes 'the grammar of educated English current in the second half of the twentieth century in the world's major English-speaking communities'. However, the emphasis is on 'the English of serious exposition' and illustrative examples are normally edited. Examples such as:

A: John gave the girl an apple
B: *Gave the girl an apple*! How kind he is!

and *What a present he had given the girl*! (Quirk *et al.*, 1972, pp. 57–8) seem to owe more to written than spoken norms.

7.3   SPOKEN LANGUAGE

Introduction

In this section we will review briefly two scholarly approaches to the analysis of spoken language which have become particularly important since the early 1970s. In each case only a summary of the main features of each tradition is given. Some aspects of the analysis, such as turn-taking and speech act analysis, have been of interest to other disciplines and more detailed accounts can be found elsewhere in this book. In such cases, appropriate cross-references are given. The field is now well provided with introductory texts, however, and recommended sources are given at the end of the book.

The two approaches discussed in this section are those known respectively as *conversation analysis* (CA), which is treated at greater length, and *discourse analysis* (DA). At first glance, there may not appear to be a great difference betwen the two. Both are empirical traditions concerned with discovering order and structure in naturally occurring spoken data. Conversation analysis grew out of work by American sociologists, and is particularly concerned with how people do things in talk and understand what they are doing. Discourse analysis is in origin a British tradition founded by linguists and provides a formal framework of analysis. There are many differences of emphasis and approach between the two traditions, and yet they also share many concerns. Both agree on the importance of sequencing in structure, for example, yet one insists that no formal framework of analysis can be achieved, and the other sets out to provide one.

The essential difference, perhaps, lies in their respective notions of 'structure'. Discourse analysis conceives of structure as 'linguistic structure' — each stretch of discourse has a particular inherent structure which can be made visible by studying the organisation of linguistic units. Conversation analysts, by contrast, claim that in order to make visible the organisation of conversation, one needs to know the functions of utterances, and these are more indeterminate than discourse analysis will allow, appearing as a result of negotiation between participants. 'Structure', then, is a more fluid phenomenon which emerges from people's attempts to make sense of each other's utterances. This distinction should become more fully apparent in the description of each approach given below.

Conversation analysis

Conversation analysis, in the form which we discuss here, began in the United States in the 1970s and grew out of attempts by sociologists (in particular Harold Garfinkel) to explain how people made sense of ordinary everyday behaviour. It quickly became apparent that conversation was an ideal subject for such analyses. Although people seem to find conversation an easy enough task, a closer examination showed that it was rather difficult to explain exactly how people understand what is going on in a conversation. Conversation analysis recognises that conversation is not only complex but also fluid in structure. It developed interests in both the question of how that structure manifested itself to participants, and in the way participants co-ordinate their behaviour in order to allow the interaction to progress smoothly.

The ideas of co-ordination and co-operation are fundamental to conversation analysis and can be illustrated by considering a non-verbal example. If someone wishes to pass an object to another person — whether a ball or a pair of scissors — the success of the manouevre depends on co-operation between both people. The person who is passing needs to signal that they are about to pass, and the person receiving must not only get ready to receive but must also demonstrate this in a manner which allows the person passing to synchronise their actions. One way in which such synchronisation can be easily accomplished is if the patterns of behaviour are structured in a routine and familiar way. We can then see not only that someone is about to pass us an object, but also predict precisely when the moment of transfer is to come. If we could not do this, then the object would, of course, end up on the floor.

Conversation analysts suggest we do somewhat similar things when talking. We need to make our behaviour familiar and predictable in structure. The person who wishes to tell bad news, or tell a joke, or ask a favour needs to display by some means that they are about to do so. Without such warning, the recipient may not make the correct or timely response and the topic might end, metaphorically speaking, on the floor.

An important claim by conversation analysts, then, is that conversational activity may be fluid, but that it is organised in an orderly way. In particular, certain things are said in a particular order, or said in a particular format.

A second claim is that although conversation is orderly, it is by no means transparent in its structure. Participants constantly need to work at making sense, at checking or clarifying what is going on, and at helping co-operatively with others to produce an orderly structure. In this respect the structure of conversation is very unlike that of a written sentence, say, in that at least two people work together to improvise the finished product.

It will be obvious from this summary that conversation analysts are interested in both detailed management problems, such as the minutiae of smooth turn-taking, and in larger organising principles and structures in conversation. In this section, we will deal only with the latter. A discussion of turn-taking can be found in section 6.3.

OVERALL ORGANISATION

Although conversations may seem to meander without great structure or direction, conversation analysts have noted that they share certain similarities in overall organisation. All conversations, for example, need to be started and finished. Starts and finishes happen in a fairly regular manner which partly reflects basic interactional problems (like attracting someone's attention at the beginning, or checking that they have no more to say at the end), and is partly a cultural convention. Rather like a game of chess in which opening moves and endgames are more highly constrained than the middlegame, so openings and closings in conversations seem to be ritualised.

Sandwiched, as it were, between the opening and closing sequences, a large range of things may happen. People may give invitations, tell stories, make compliments, tell about troubles, and so on. Each activity, however, has been shown by conversation analysts to have a recognisable and regular organisation. We can tell whether someone is offering a compliment or asking a favour, it is argued, not so much from what is said, as from the format in which it is said, and the way in which it has been led up to. Two kinds of organisation have been identified: *sequential organisation* and *preference organisation*.

SEQUENTIAL ORGANISATION

The closing sequences of a conversation form a good example of an activity which is clearly sequentially organised. Schegloff and Sacks (1973) suggest that how a telephone conversation can be brought jointly and smoothly to a close represents a technical problem of co-ordination. Unexplained silences during telephone calls are generally avoided. If one person stops talking then the other will take over, or at the very least give some minimal response which shows that they are still there and attending. So, the problem is one of:

how to organise the simultaneous arrival of the co-conversationalists at a point where one speaker's completion will not occasion another speaker's talk, and that will not be heard as some speaker's silence.

One way of ensuring this might simply be to say 'goodbye' and to put down the phone. In practice, this very rarely happens. Schegloff and Sacks argued that participants first went through a sequence which established that both parties had said all they wished to say. If speaker A finishes a turn, then there is normally an obligation on speaker B to start a new one. If, however, B gives only a minimal response, such as 'OK', then effectively speaker B returns the obligation to speak to A, indicating that he or she has nothing to add at that stage. If A now also gives a minimal response, yielding the turn again, then a situation has arisen in which both participants have indicated a readiness to finish the call. Schegloff and Sacks demonstrated that 'goodbye' sequences were preceded by such reciprocal 'OK's or similar responses.

The following examples illustrate how closings are made. Each call was recorded (with permission) on internal telephones at the Open University. They appear on Band 9 of the cassette.

```
 1 A. the thing is we are receiving pages later this week
 2    um of with all the corrections in
 3 B. yeah
 4 A. but I just wanted to see how many it came to anyway
 5 B. mmm
 6 A. so there's probably index on top of that then
 7 B. yeah it will be  ⌈yeah
 8 A.                  ⌊yes right
 9 B. O.K.?
10 A. Thanks very much
11 B. right bye bye
12 A. bye.
```

Note how B is, throughout this extract, giving no more than noises of affirmation. These serve to indicate both that she is still there and listening, and that she has nothing herself to say. Hence discussion of the topic will end when A has nothing more to say himself. This point seems to be reached in line 8 where A gives the first *right*. In line 9, B asks for confirmation that A has finished which A gives in line 10. At this point, an 'opening for a close' has been made, and one of two things can happen. If B has something to say on another topic, then now is the time for her to introduce it, but she initiates instead the closing sequence. B's *bye* is returned by A and the call is ended.

```
 1 B. can you still potter on coz I'm actually you know got something I'd
 2    quite like to sort of get on with this morning
 3 A. O.K.
 4 B. if that's all right
 5 A. yeah
 6 B. I'll I'll come over this afternoon
```

```
 7 A.  right O.K. then
 8 B.  right
 9 A.  bye
10 B.  bye
11 A.  bye
```

The structure of this sequence is rather similar to the first, although two different speakers are involved. You may wonder why there are so many turns involved in closing the conversation. This is common in telephone conversations, and probably reflects the fact that participants are going through several stages of closure. At the very least, closure of the topic in hand must be distinguished from the closure of the call itself. The last repeated *bye* by A may be because, in English, it is often the person who initiates the call (A in each case) who gets the last 'goodbye'. This convention is not quite as strict as the one which operates at the beginning of conversations, which requires the person who is called to speak first.

This description of closing sequences assumes that the two parties have equal status. There may be contexts, for instance, where both people do not have equal rights to bring the call to a close. A powerful person may curtail the call more abruptly, without ensuring that the other person had fully finished.

Closure sequences demonstrate a number of features of conversational structure. They show one way in which participants can prepare each other for an upcoming event (in this case closure) and co-ordinate its successful arrival. They also show how, in parts of a conversation things get said in a particular order.

Elsewhere in the conversation the actual utterances may not be quite so predictable, but nevertheless there are sequential patterns. For example, of the following two hypothetical sequences, (1) sounds more plausible than (2):

```
(1) A.  It's cold in here
    B.  The door's open
(2) A.  It's cold in here
    B.  The light's on
```

The interesting thing about such sequences, however, is not whether they are plausible or not, but how we set about understanding them. In practice, conversations are full of sequences that would look extremely implausible if a researcher produced them as hypothetical examples. Sequence (1), however, seems to have a greater *coherence* than sequence (2). We can see easily how B's utterance follows from A's. In some way or other, we can hear B providing an explanation of A's observation. If sequence (2) seems more implausible then perhaps it is because we have expended more effort in trying to envisage a context in which B's utterance appears relevant to A's.

One pervasive feature of talk is that each contribution should accord with what Grice (1975) has termed *conversational maxims*. (These are discussed more fully in section 4.3). One such maxim is the criterion of *relevance*. The criterion of relevance suggests that any utterance will be understood by reference to what has preceded it, but it does not in itself indicate *how* it should be relevant. If, in sequence (1), we hear A as making an indirect *request* to close the door, then we might hear B's response as a refusal of that request. If, on the other hand, we hear A as making a *complaint* that the fire has not been lit, then we might hear B to be explaining why it was not necessary.

Exactly which interpretation we arrive at will normally depend on a number of other aspects of the context not supplied in this extract, which may include the relative status of the speakers and their perceived rights to make complaints or requests. In each case, however, we have traded upon an expectation that certain kinds of utterance follow others. Schegloff and Sacks (1973) suggested that such utterances formed *adjacency pairs*: these are sequences of two utterances that are: (a) adjacent (b) produced by different speakers; (c) ordered as a first part and a second part; and (d) of particular types, so that a particular first part requires a particular second (or range of second parts). Common adjacency pairs include greetings and questions and answers. If I say 'hello' to someone, then their next utterance or gesture is likely to be interpreted as a response to that greeting; if I ask a question, I will evaluate the speaker's next utterance as a potential answer. Many a politician has given the appearance of answering unwelcome questions simply by responding with bland irrelevant talk.

The way any utterance is taken in a conversation crucially depends on its location within a recognisable sequence. Whether the utterance *right* is taken to be an agreement or a preclosing manoeuvre will very much depend on what kind of turn preceded it (cited in Atkinson and Heritage, 1984):

> The point is that no analysis, grammatical, semantic, pragmatic, etc., of these utterances taken singly and out of sequence, will yield their import in use, will show what co-participants might make of them and do about them.

PREFERENCE ORGANISATION

Some adjacency pairs may take more than one kind of response, but have only one as the common pattern. Such a response is said to be a *preferred response*. The existence of a *preference organisation* of this kind sets up a stronger pattern of expectation and helps reduce uncertainty about how to take the next utterance. For example, many utterances which seek action on the part of the listener may logically be met with either compliance or refusal, yet the latter is a strongly dispreferred response. People need to go on special assertiveness training courses, it seems, in order to 'learn how to say no'. If a hearer wishes to refuse a request, then he or she is more likely to accede to a lesser request, or provide the future grounds for granting it. It is by no means impossible for

Table 7.3. Preference organisation of adjacency pairs

FIRST PARTS:	Request	Offer/Invite	Assessment	Question	Blame
SECOND PARTS:					
Preferred:	acceptance	acceptance	agreement	expected answer	denial
Dispreferred:	refusal	refusal	disagreement	unexpected answer or non-answer	admission

Source: Levinson (1983, p. 336)

a speaker to give a dispreferred response, but if one is given it is likely to be marked in some way (Levinson, 1983, p. 307):

> Dispreferred seconds are typically delivered: (a) after some significant delay; (b) with some preface marking their dispreferred status, often the particle *well*; (c) with some account of why the preferred second cannot be performed.

Table 7.3 shows the preference organisation of a number of adjacency pairs.

PRESEQUENCES

It is not just the sequential location which affects how an utterance will be taken. Precisely the same utterance may function one way in a *blaming* episode, say, and another way in a *request* episode. Or, to put it another way, the function of an individual utterance or turn depends very much on the prior understanding of what kind of activity the participants are engaged in. This is one reason why it is so important for participants to approach such activities in an orderly and predictable way.

Presequences are one way of doing this. If someone asks '*Are you doing anything tonight*?', it probably heralds some kind of invitation. Such a presequence anticipates the organisation of an invitation sequence in which a refusal is dispreferred and must be supported by a reason. The presequence orients to the most likely grounds for a refusal and thus clears the way for the invitation to go ahead. Similarly with requests. If you go into a shop and ask, '*Do you sell matches*?', the shopkeeper may reach directly to serve you, anticipating the forthcoming request. Such formulations are not routinely taken to be enquiries about the shop's stocking policy.

Presequences, then, help flag the nature of the upcoming activity. They do this by being seen to anticipate the known organisation of the particular activity.

PARTICIPANT ORIENTATIONS

Presequences demonstrate that participants are themselves aware of the local organisation of particular kinds of conversational activity. Such an awareness allows them to check regularly on each other's understandings of what is going on. A compliment and a blaming both form the first part of an adjacency pair, for example, but they have different second parts. If I say something which is intended as a compliment, I can quickly tell whether it has been misconstrued as a criticism by monitoring the kind of response which it elicits.

Conversation analysts put great stress on the fact that participants are themselves aware of the organisational structure of conversation (Schegloff and Sacks, 1973, p. 290):

> We have proceeded under the assumption (an assumption borne out by our research) that in so far as the materials we worked with exhibited orderliness, they did so not only to us, indeed not in the first place for us, but for the co-participants who had produced them.

This is put into methodological practice by insisting that on every occasion a claim is made about how participants understood an event, then a 'warrant' for such a claim must be found in the data. In other words, if an interactional detail or feature of organisation is regarded as important by conversation analysts then there is a requirement to show that participants themselves orient to that feature (Atkinson and Heritage, 1984, p. 1):

> The analyst is not required to speculate upon what the interactants hypothetically or imaginably understood, or the procedures or constraints to which they could conceivably have been oriented. Instead, analysis can emerge from observation of the conduct of the participants.

Conversational data provide various kinds of evidence for such participant orientation. We have already suggested that the organisation of presequences demonstrates an awareness of the organisation of the activity which they herald. Another source of evidence comes from misunderstandings which result in a participant's seeking or giving a clarification.

THE ROLE OF EMPIRICAL DATA

Perhaps the most notable feature of conversation analysis is the great emphasis it puts on empirical data. In this it can be contrasted with other traditions in linguistic research which have taken the analyst's recollections or intuitions as data and provided invented examples as illustration. Conversation analysis also differs from other empirical traditions in sociological and psychological research which use either interview or experimental techniques. Conversation analysts set out to discover what people actually do and, restricting themselves to naturally occurring conversations in all their messiness and apparent imperfection, they often find that people do some surprising things.

This empirical emphasis is, in principle, commendable and it guards against premature and speculative theory-building. It also leads to particular insights and observations about people's everyday behaviour which were unobtainable in other ways. Even so, it still gives rise to one or two problems of both a methodological and theoretical kind.

Conversation analysts claim the raw data are precisely that — the actual event as it happened. Recordings and transcriptions are mere mnemonics of that original event. In practice, however, recourse is made to transcriptions and recordings for the purpose of analysis. There is, of course, no way around this. The close detail in which they need to observe interactions — which may include the precise relative timing of a head shake with someone else's interruption, for example — demands a recording which can be played again and again. It is occasionally the case, however, that this requirement for detail proves to be a source of difficulty.

First, it is futile to suppose that there could exist a single and authoritative version of the original event. Different participants will have experienced rather different things. Perhaps one person was looking in the other direction, or simply blinked when the head shake occurred. Again, one must be careful about supposing that interactional nuances which emerge only after hours of painstaking study by a diligent researcher were particularly salient to the original participants. Any explanation of participants' behaviour cannot delve further and further into the detail of the interaction without bearing these things in mind.

Second, there is an important respect in which, at this level of detail, the transcript represents an analysis generated by the transcriber. Given the difficulties which professional linguists experience when trying to notate intonation (see section 2.4), conversation analysts appear to put remarkable confidence in somewhat crude representations of prosody. The fact such transcriptions appear intimidatingly detailed does not mean they are not already digested. Rather than raw data, the analyst has already selected, organised, and partially analysed the material.

Conversation analysts rightly warn against attempts to provide a definitive and authoritative analysis of 'what is going on' in an interaction. Their own search for an authoritative and immensely detailed transcription may, however, be similarly misguided.

It is not just at the level of detail that a problem about the analyst's relationship to the data appears. As has been seen in the discussion above, the structures and organisations which are described by conversation analysts are not identifiable through independent linguistic or formal criteria. Before the regular organisation of, say, an invitation sequence can be perceived, the functions of certain individual utterances must be identified. Conversation analysts often resort to what they call 'member's knowledge' (which seems to be similar to the linguist's 'intuition', see section 1.4). If *they* can hear something as an invitation, then this requires explanation, and the warrants or cues for that interpretation will lie in the data. This is claimed to be a legitimate exercise, since the analyst is like an ordinary member of the community in this respect, applying 'common-sense' knowledge.

But if analysts generate a text on the basis of their own interpretive skills, then there is a very definite sense in which they are investigating their own, rather than the participants', strategies of understanding. This may not amount to a very important consideration when they investigate data taken from their own speech community. In other instances, in anthropological research or work with child-conversation, it may become a much more worrying issue.

It would be wrong to suggest that conversation analysts have no answers to this kind of criticism. It is a canon of conversation analysis that data should not only be given where appropriate to support analyses, but that in principle such data should be made available for public inspection in its most raw form. In principle, then, if colleagues wished to object on the grounds laid out above, they could inspect and analyse the data themselves.

More importantly, conversation analysis guards itself against the charge of constructing its own data through the claim that any organisational structures visible to the analyst must also be available to the participants. It is in order to demonstrate such participant orientations that conversation analysts must rake through so much data in such detail (French and Local, 1986, p. 159):

> As the analysis proceeds it will become apparent that the search for evidence of participant orientations may involve the analyst in protracted examination of small fragments of data. The claim that one's analysis is more than a purely analytic construct but reproduces and explicates the bases of participants' understandings is a strong one. In view of this, the painstaking, 'inch-by-inch' approach to interactional data that CA recommends becomes understandable not as a matter of quirk or indulgence, but as one of necessity.

However, it is not always the case that orientations and understandings will be visible in subsequent talk. The evidence provided by conversation analysts often relies more on its plausibility than on provision of proof.

One further problem with a strict and laborious empiricism of this kind is that it makes it very difficult to illuminate the relationship between what happens in individual interactions and larger patterns in social structure, or patterns of social inequality. For example, it might be tempting to explain certain episodes in a conversation between, say, an employer and an employee, in terms of differential institutionalised power. Conversational analysis, in its strictest form, would not allow as legitimate any discussion which appealed to abstract notions of power or of social identities except in so far as the workings of such constructs were visible in the empirical data. In this, they may be open to the charge that their explanations of conversational behaviour are, in an important respect, impoverished ones.

We have discussed some of the methodological problems with conversation analysis in order to indicate where the technique can best be used. Many of the apparent limitations can be circumvented by the use of other techniques, and there exist many researchers who employ the techniques of conversation analysis in a flexible and eclectic manner.

Discourse analysis

The *discourse analysis* approach to the analysis of talk is a clear embarrassment for the distinction between 'discourse' and 'text' which we made in section 7.1. Discourse analysis was devised by two British linguists, John Sinclair and Malcolm Coulthard, and was an attempt to produce a structural linguistic analysis of spontaneous conversation. It can therefore be reasonably regarded as a *textual* approach within the terms we have described, despite its name.

Discourse analysis is based on speech act theory (see section 4.3) and assumes that, within discourse, there is a finite set of identifiable functions that utterances can perform. Sinclair and Coulthard suggest that these functions can be reliably correlated with specific linguistic items or non-verbal events (that is, it should always be clear exactly how to categorise an utterance); that sequences of functional units occur in a restricted set of possible combinations; and that any discourse can be exhaustively described in terms of its component-functional units and their patterns of combination.

THE HIERARCHICAL ORGANISATION OF TALK

The system of analysis was meant to handle classroom talk, of the type where a teacher interacts with a group of children. A lesson, like any other example of talk, can be analysed sequentially (as a series of turns) but Sinclair and Coulthard posited a hierarchical organisation. A lesson consisted of topically coherent units, termed *transactions*. These could be further segmented into sequences of speaker turns or part-turns, termed *exchanges*. Exchanges consisted of *moves* (speaker turns or part-turns). And moves were composed of functional units called *acts*. This hierarchical structure can be represented as a tree diagram (Figure 7.1), rather like those you saw used for sentence analysis in Chapter 3. As an example of Sinclair and Coulthard's analysis, and what it can reveal about classroom discourse, we shall look in more detail at the exchange and its component parts.

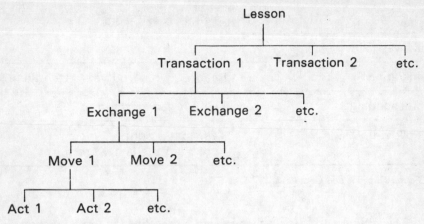

Figure 7.1   The hierarchical organisation of talk

EXCHANGES IN CLASSROOM TALK

During a transaction, a teacher can direct a pupil to carry out a task, try to elicit from a pupil some verbal contribution to a discussion, or provide information. Sinclair and Coulthard found that these activities gave rise to characteristic patterns of speaking turn. These different patterns suggested the category 'exchange', which can be defined as a minimal interactive unit of conversation (for example, a question followed by its answer; or a statement followed by an acknowledgement). Four main types of teaching exchange were identified (see Sinclair and Coulthard, 1975, pp. 63ff.):

1. Directive
   Teacher: The first quiz is this.
                Can you fill in this sentence?
                See if you can do it in your books.
                (The pupils write in their books).
2. Check
   Teacher: Finished Joan?
                (Pupil provides non-verbal response).
3. Informative
   Teacher: And — when I can find my chart — here it is.
                Here are some of the symbols that they used.
4. Elicitation
   Teacher: Read us what you've written, Joan.
   Pupil: The cat sat on the rug.
   Teacher: Yes that's right.
                I changed the last word.

Table 7.4. The elicitation exchange

Moves	
Initiating	Read us what you've written Joan.
Responding	The cat sat on the rug.
Follow-up	Yes, that's right. I changed the last word.

Source: Sinclair and Coulthard, (1975, p. 63).

The structure of these exchanges can be described in terms of component 'moves', which are respectively *initiating*, *responding* and *follow-up* moves (these are often termed I, R and F). The 'elicitation' exchange above contains all three sorts of move, and can be represented as in Table 7.4

Other exchanges show different (characteristic) sequential patterns.

The moves that make up exchanges can themselves be segmented into acts (according to the functions they perform in the discourse). For instance, part of the teacher's initiating move in the exchange above is concerned to nominate one pupil (from the whole class) to answer. The constituent acts of this exchange can be represented as in Table 7.5.

Sinclair and Coulthard identified twenty-two acts, which they claimed were sufficient to describe all classroom discourse.

This system of analysis provides a way of describing classroom talk between teacher and pupils, and the different discourse patterns that this may contain. Below are two rather differently organised sequences of classroom talk, the first of which is relatively easy to fit into Sinclair

Table 7.5. The elicitation exchange

Moves		Acts
Initiating	Read us what you've written, Joan	(elicit) (nominate)
Responding	The cat sat on the rug	(reply)
Follow up	Yes, that's right I changed the last word	(evaluate) (comment)

Source: as Table 7.4

and Coulthard's framework, the second less so. To the right of each transcript is an analysis into moves and exchange types. If you wish to check your understanding of the discussion so far you could cover up the right-hand columns and attempt your own analysis of the data before reading the ones we give.

Extract 1

		Moves	Exchanges	
T	what do you notice there — what's special about that particular section of tape — what's the child doing — anybody	I	Teacher elicitation	1
P	trying to say something	R		
T	er, right Rosita	F		
	what's he actually trying to say	I	Teacher elicitation	2
P	trying to get a word out of his mouth	R		
T	and what's the word he's trying to get out	(F)I	Teacher elicitation	3
P	mm daddy	R		

In exchange (1) the teacher produces a string of initiations. Teachers often do this, and pupils operate a rule that they only answer the final one. So here the teacher's utterance is just coded once. In exchange (2) one could assume either that there is no F or that I in exchange (3) is simultaneously an F in exchange (2). The IRF patterns evident here occur very frequently in classroom discourse.

Extract 2

		Moves	Exchanges	
P	and that's er what do you call it — what you have for breakfast	I	Pupil elicitation	1
T	what you have for breakfast	I	Teacher check	2
P	sometimes	R		
	oranges — what do you call them — red things	I	Pupil elicitation	3
T	what you have for breakfast	I	Teacher check	4
P	sometimes	R		
T	oh — it is — it isn't a living thing this	I	Teacher check	5
P	no	R		
T	strawberry	I	Teacher informative	6
P	yes	F		
T	you have strawberries for breakfast	I	Teacher check	7
P	yeah	R		
T	do you really	F		

This interchange is unusual partly because it is the pupil who is initiating, but also because the teacher is asking genuine questions, not test questions: hence a series of teacher checking exchanges, and not teacher elicitations. The pupil's initiations in (1) and (3) do not get immediate answers. The initiation in (6) could alternatively be taken as an answer to the pupil's question, but separated from it. The pupil appears to evaluate the teacher's remark in (6), giving an uncharacteristic teacher informative exchange: IF. The analysis of Extract 2 is not intended as the 'definitive' version: the point is to show how the organisation of the interchange is different from Extract 1, and more difficult to fit into the system.

LIMITATIONS OF DISCOURSE ANALYSIS

Discourse analysis was initially devised for the type of tightly structured talk that is often found between a teacher and pupils in classrooms, where the teacher is in control (normally) of information that has to be conveyed to pupils. While later attempts were made to adapt it to other contexts (see, for instance, Coulthard and Brazil, 1979) it is not really suitable for more casual conversation.

Discourse analysis is a general analytical model and, when applied to actual data, some interpretation will be required on the part of the analyst. Although the aim was to produce a system in which the categorisation of utterances would be clear and unambiguous, in practice there is unlikely to be agreement about all coding decisions.

The system is comprehensive in that all utterances are coded from beginning to end, but only one level of function is coded (the function of an utterance *within* the discourse); the analysis has nothing to say about the way language is used to convey irony, threats, humour, etc. If one accepts this limited notion of function, it is still unlikely that utterances can be analysed unambiguously in terms of a single function. Consider the following example:

A. What are you doing tonight?
B. Nothing. Why?
A. I was thinking of going to a movie, wanna come?

A's first utterance is undeniably a question but it also functions as a pre-offer (i.e. it signals that an offer is about to be made. A is not really requesting a detailed account of B's planned evening activities). B's response, *nothing*, indicates an awareness of this second function.

A further problem is that, while the analysis relies on the possibility of correlating discourse functions with specific linguistic items or non-verbal events, it is not always possible to identify utterances independently of their functions. For instance, virtually anything can function as a bid at an auction — a call of 'Here!', a wave, even a scratch of the head or a wink. Knowing whether something counts as an 'utterance' (in the sense of being part of the interaction) relies on prior recognition that it has fulfilled a particular function.

Finally, it is not possible to specify general sequencing rules (i.e. to specify what sort of functional units can follow one another). Permissible combinations will be heavily dependent upon particular contexts. For instance, consider the following:

(A is a shopper in search of a pullover to go with a beige jacket; B is a shop assistant serving A)

A. Yes mm. Do you think that blue would stand a chance with mm beige?

B   Well, try that one on (selecting a grey pullover).

A's utterance functions as a question, and it has been supposed that this requires the provision of information as an adequate response. B's response does not do this — it seems, rather, to function more as a suggestion, in imperative form. Yet in this context the sequence seems quite acceptable.

7.4   THE ANALYSIS OF WRITTEN LANGUAGE

Written language has a much longer history of analysis than spoken, and there exists a much wider variety of approaches. Once again, approaches have been distinguished here according to whether they treat the subject as properly an interaction between the written forms and a reader (who applies a knowledge of the world as well as a knowledge of language to the task); or whether they restrict themselves to an analysis of intrinsic structural or more superficial properties of written passages.

Among discourse approaches to written language, undoubtedly the most influential has been that developed by cognitive psychologists. The concepts and framework described here will be found referred to in many apparently unrelated traditions. For comparison, we also include a brief description of a kind of *political discourse analysis* known as *critical linguistics* which represents a rather different attempt to describe the meaning of discourse as a culturally situated phenomenon. Amongst the textual approaches we have described several which have been influential in educational circles. The selection is by no means comprehensive, and, if it appears fragmented, this reflects the fact that many techniques of textual description have been developed for particular, and often very limited, applications.

Discourse approaches to written language

COGNITIVE PSYCHOLOGY

Our understanding of what kinds of things texts are, and how people perceive their internal structure, owes a great deal to work over several decades in cognitive psychology. Much of this research, in principle, could apply equally well to both spoken and written language, and indeed, many of the experimental methods used by psychologists involve reading texts aloud. The contribution of cognitive psychology is discussed here, however (rather than in section 7.3), for two reasons.

First, nearly all the material investigated has, in practice, been in the form of continuous prose or two or three connected sentences. The reason why experimenters often present such passages by reading them aloud is simply because it helps ensure all subjects have been given exactly the same information and time. Although it might be possible to generalise the findings to elucidate the structure of talk between two or more people, to do so would introduce complexities which have not yet been tackled. The models discussed are therefore particularly applicable to continuous prose.

Second, some of the concepts and terminology developed by cognitive psychologists have been widely taken up by researchers in text linguistics, and an understanding of them is most useful when reading research papers and literature in this area.

Research in cognitive psychology can nevertheless be regarded as a contribution to the study of *discourse* as opposed to *text* in the more abstract sense of the terms outlined in section 7.1. That is, such research is characterised by a concern for how real people in particular contexts and states of knowledge arrive at understandings through the use of inference and general world knowledge.

Memory for meaning   When people read or hear some piece of continuous prose, they store some kind of representation of it in memory — that is, they can, at some future time, recall things about it. Psychologists have often used experiments on recall to gain insights into the kinds of structures people perceive in text. What has been found is that people do not normally remember words and sentences verbatim. Instead they seem to form a general memory of the objects and happenings referred to in the text, which might be termed a *semantic representation*.

Kintsch (1974) reported an experiment in which, from the same basic story, he constructed two written texts, one syntactically complex and one simple. Although subjects took longer to read and understand the complex version, they could not be distinguished from those who read the simple passage in terms of the kind or speed of their responses to questions made later. Kintsch concluded that subjects from both groups stored the meaning of each paragraph in a similar abstract form which was independent of the form of the original sentences.

The role of world knowledge   In a well known experiment by Bransford, Barclay and Franks (1972), one group of subjects heard sentences such as (1) read aloud, and another group sentences like (2):

(1)   Three turtles rested beside a floating log and a fish swam beneath them.

(2)   Three turtles rested on a floating log and a fish swam beneath them.

In (2), but not (1), it is possible to infer that the fish swam underneath the log. This inference is arrived at as a result of our general experience and knowledge of how things work in the world. It is not a strict logical entailment (see section 4.3) in the way propositions (3) and (4) are:

(3)   Logs float
(4)   Fish can swim

Subjects were later given a list of sentences and asked to pick out those which they had originally heard. The list included new sentences such as (5) and (6):

(5)   Three turtles rested beside a floating log and a fish swam beneath it.
(6)   Three turtles rested on a floating log and a fish swam beneath it.

The experiment showed that subjects who had heard (2) often claimed, incorrectly, that they had heard (6), but those who had heard (1) did not confuse it with sentence (5) in the same way. The researchers concluded that the semantic representations which people made when reading or hearing a text could only be arrived at by making inferences based on ordinary world knowledge — that is, information which lies outside of the text.

Schemas, frames and scripts The finding that people apply their knowledge of the world to generate representations of a text in their memory is a most important one. Amongst other things, it has given rise to a whole new movement in Artificial Intelligence (AI), since it demonstrated that in order to get machines to understand text properly, it was insufficient to build in a grammar and vocabulary which would allow the computer to recognise the words and the syntactic structure of the sentences. In addition it is necessary to build in a vast store of world knowledge, and a set of principles for making inferences.

The finding gave rise to a more specific problem, however, of how people actually selected and activated one rather than another segment of their world knowledge when they read a particular text.

An experiment by Bransford and Johnson (1972) showed that it was possible to prevent people from successfully accessing their general knowledge. A text could then appear incoherent and incomprehensible. Subjects were read the following passage:

> The procedure is actually quite simple. First you arrange things into different groups. Of course one pile may be sufficient depending on how much there is to do. If you have to go somewhere else due to lack of facilities that is the next step, otherwise you are pretty well set. It is important not to overdo things. That is, it is better to do too few things at once

than too many. In the short run this may not seem important but complications can easily arise. A mistake can be expensive as well. At first the whole procedure will seem complicated. Soon, however, it will become just another facet of life. It is difficult to foresee any end to the necessity for this task in the immediate future, but then one never can tell. After the procedure is completed one arranges the materials into different groups again. Then they can be put into their appropriate places. Eventually they will be used once more and the whole cycle will then have to be repeated. However, that is a part of life.

Comprehension and recall scores were very low when the passage was presented in this way. Another group of subjects were given a title beforehand, 'washing clothes'. Their scores were very much higher. A third group, who were given the title after hearing the passage, obtained even lower scores than the group who had no title at all.

This experiment showed that a very small clue (that the passage was about washing clothes) seemed to make an enormous difference to the subjects' ability to form representations of the passage in memory. It was as if this single clue acted as the key which gained them access to a whole area of world knowledge and which allowed sense to be made of descriptions such as 'going somewhere else if there is a lack of facilities'. The experiment also showed that people constructed their mental representations of the text as they went along — otherwise the group who were given the title after hearing the passage would have performed as well as those who heard it first. The process of building a representation of text structure was not a retrospective one peculiar to long-term memory.

If it is possible to interfere with the process of accessing relevant world knowledge by witholding a single key, then this suggests that world knowledge is itself structured in some way. It is as if all the relevant information was filed on a single filing card somewhere which could not be located until the reference code had been discovered. Bartlett (1932) proposed a solution rather like this, and which is basically the one adopted in AI today. Human memory, he suggested, organised the various pieces of knowledge and experience into cognitive structures called *schemas*. When people recalled a text, then events and descriptions which could be related to an existing schema were better remembered. If a text related events which were similar to, but not identical to, a familiar schema, then the memory of the text was often distorted so that it became more like the existing schema.

A modern development of schema theory is that of *cognitive frames* proposed by Minsky (1975):

> A *frame* is a data-structure for representing a stereotyped situation, like being in a certain kind of living room, or going to a child's birthday party. Attached to each frame are several kinds of information. Some of this information is about how to use the frame. Some is about what one can expect to happen next. Some is about what to do if these expectations are not confirmed.

We can think of a frame as a network of nodes and relations. The 'top levels' of a frame are fixed, and represent things that are always true about the supposed situation. The lower levels have many *terminals* — 'slots' that must be filled by specific instances or data. Each terminal can specify conditions its assignments must meet. (The assignments themselves are usually smaller 'subframes'.) Simple conditions are specified by markers that might require a terminal assignment to be a person, an object of sufficient value, or a pointer to a subframe of a certain type. More complex conditions can specify relations among the things assigned to several terminals.

In practice, the terms schema and frame are now used almost interchangeably in the literature. A frame is essentially a stereotype of a particular object or event which shows those characteristics which are essential, those which are variable, and those which past experience has shown are likely to be present. Figure 7.2 illustrates what a frame for *dog* might look like. Whenever the word *dog* appears in a text, then the reader can fill in the unstated facts that a dog has four legs, ears, etc. Where the text gives information about optional values, these are filled in. If not, they are filled in by the *default values* supplied by the stereotype.

The use of the definite article sometimes betrays the existence of a frame. Normally, one only uses and expects to see the word *the* in connection with something already referred to in the text, or whose existence is otherwise explained. But objects may be used with the definite article when they appear in a familiar and relevant frame even if they have not appeared in the text: *Whenever Joyce walks into a room she opens the window*. All rooms are expected to contain at least one window and hence there is no problem about which window is being referred to.

Schank and Abelson (1977, p. 422) proposed a further elaboration of the notion of frame to describe our knowledge of sequences of events:

> A *script* is a predetermined, stereotyped sequence of actions that define a well-known situation. A script is, in effect, a very boring little story.

A restaurant frame, for example, might contain information about a door leading off a street, windows, tables, menu cards and so on. A restaurant script on the other hand, would include the sequence of actions that a customer might expect to do. These would include 'enter', 'wait', 'be shown seat', 'look at menu', right through to 'pay bill', and 'leave'. Bower, Black and Turner (1979) have shown that in several cases people do agree on what the main events in particular scripts are, and that in their recall of stories often erroneously include events which appear in the script but not in the original story.

Cognitive psychologists have shown that people's understanding of texts not only depends on a general knowledge of the world, but involves strategies of comprehension which are not peculiar to language. Scripts and frames will help us understand peoples' actions in the world as much as written descriptions about them.

Part I   Language and Knowledge

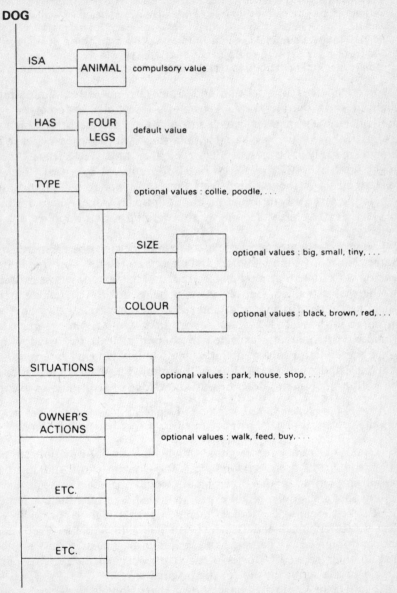

Figure 7.2. A 'dog' frame
Source: Greene (1986)

It might be thought that cognitive psychologists' work is more relevant to how people understand prose than to descriptions of the texts they attempt to comprehend. This, however, is by no means true. Such research demonstrates that any description of the structure of a text in terms which have psychological reality must take into account the role of an intelligent and informed interpreter. It also suggests that perceived structures will be different for different readers, depending on what knowledge schemas are triggered and what their content might be.

Political discourse analysis

The term *political discourse analysis* has been used (Seidel, 1985) to refer to types of analysis that, rather than looking simply for patterns and structures in discourse, see it as a form of social practice. For this sort of approach both the immediate and wider social contexts in which language is produced are all-important. Language is seen as reflecting and sustaining the values of a culture. Seidel (1985, p. 44) discusses the assumptions underlying such an approach:

> It is my contention that discourse of any kind — text as a suprasentential unit of meaning, an extension of the syntactic and logical structuring of a sentence — is a site of struggle. It is a terrain, a dynamic linguistic, and above all, semantic space in which social meanings are produced or challenged. This is most clearly, but not exclusively, the case with political discourse, since the theory and practice of politics and political talk is seen to be primarily concerned with power. This of course assumes a conflict, not a consensus model of society, and a model of language use seen as part of social action and concerned with the relation between action and structure.

One may compare this with *sociolinguistics*, which also explores the relationship between language and society (see section 1.4) but often seems to regard both as neutral. Such neutrality would be contested by researchers working within a 'political discourse analysis' tradition. Seidel (1985) gives an overview of these traditions. Here, by way of example, we shall look briefly at one approach that has been termed *critical linguistics*.

CRITICAL LINGUISTICS

Consider the following two extracts from British newspapers, reporting an incident in which police in Rhodesia (as it was in 1975) killed eleven black people:

Rioting Blacks Shot Dead by Police as ANC Leaders Meet
Eleven Africans were shot dead and 15 wounded when Rhodesian police opened fire on a rioting crowd of about 2,000 in the African Highfield township of Salisbury this afternoon.
    The shooting was the climax of a day of some violence and tension during which rival black political factions taunted one another while the

African National Council Executive committee met in the township to plan
its next move in the settlement issue with the government.

(The Times, 2nd June 1975)

Police Shoot 11 Dead in Salisbury Riot
Riot police shot and killed 11 African demonstrators and wounded 15
others here today in the Highfield African township on the outskirts of
Salisbury. The number of casualties was confirmed by the police. Disturb-
ances had broken out soon after the executive committee of the African
National Council (ANC) met in the township to discuss the ultimatum by
the Prime Minister, Mr. Ian Smith, to the ANC to attend a constitutional
conference with the government in the near future.

(The Guardian, 2nd June 1975)

Trew (1979) carried out an analysis of these extracts using a number of
linguistic categories. His aim, however, was not simply to describe interesting discourse patterns but to see if these could reveal the ideology,
or set of values, inherent in the discourse. He argues that police shooting
innocent people is not regarded as normal, or legitimate, and therefore
needs to be explained. The newspaper articles therefore, do not simply
describe events but offer explanations or interpretations. This is often
done implicitly, through the choice of particular words or syntactic structures. Trew sets out as a table his analysis of the first sentence in each
article (Table 7.6). The linguistic features Trew draws attention to
include the following:

1) The verbs in the main clause in the *Times* article are passive
    ('Eleven Africans *were shot*') whereas the Guardian uses active verbs
    ('Riot police *shot* . . . 11 African demonstrators'). Futhermore in the
    Times article the *agents* (those who did the killing) are placed at some
    distance from the main verb in a dependent clause ('when Rhodesian

Table 7.6

	Agent	Process	Affected	Circumstance
Times		Passive		
Headline	police	shoot dead	rioting blacks	(as) ANC leaders meet
Report	—	shoot dead	eleven Africans	(when) Rhodesian police opened fire on a rioting crowd
Guardian		Active		
Headline	police	shoot dead	11	(in) Salisbury riots
Report	riot police	shoot and kill	11 African demonstrators	

Source: Trew (1979)

police ... '). The use of the passive, argues Trew, coupled with the displacement of the agent, puts this agent in a less focal position.

2) Both newspapers describe the circumstances in which the shooting took place as a 'riot', which can provide a framework for explaining police action, and makes at least their intervention, if not the actual killing, legitimate.

Trew analyses further developments in the press treatment of this story, including an editorial in *The Times* of the same day and subsequent articles in both *The Times* and the *Guardian*. While 'riots' continue to be emphasised, the agents of the killing (the police) are not referred to again. Trew argues that it is by this sort of process that a 'favoured' interpretation is offered of events and unpalatable aspects are obscured.

He contrasts the *Times* editorial with one that appeared in the *Tanzanian Daily News*. The first sentence of each gives an impression of the different interpretations placed upon the event:

> The rioting and sad loss of life in Salisbury are warnings that tension in that country is rising as decisive moves about its future seem to be in the offing.
>
> > (*The Times*)

> Rhodesia's white supremacist police had a field day on Sunday when they opened fire and killed thirteen unarmed Africans, in two different actions in Salisbury; and wounded many others.
>
> > (*Tanzanian Daily News*)

For examples of other work carried out within a critical linguistics framework see Kress and Hodge (1979) and Fowler, Hodge, Kress and Trew (1979). The overall aim of the method is to identify and describe 'the social, interpersonal and ideological functions' of a range of linguistic constructions used in a variety of contexts. Although we have given an example from a newspaper, in principle any discourse, spoken or written, can be analysed.

An important point to note about this kind of analysis is that the theory underlying it is explicitly *determinist*: it suggests that the (varieties of) language used in a culture affect the way people perceive and interpret events. Linguistic determinism has a chequered history. One of the major early exponents was the anthropological linguist, Whorf, who argued that different languages caused their speakers to interpret the world differently. The argument has since been applied to different varieties within a language, but it is by no means uncontroversial and perhaps merits more detailed and cautious consideration than critical linguists such as Fowler *et al.* are inclined to give it (at least in their 1979 volume).

The method of analysis has other limitations. We mention here one that seems to us to be particularly important. (This is not a criticism of Trew's analysis, which is a good example of its kind, but of the tradition in general.) The researchers are clearly politically committed and this will

affect the sort of discourse they choose to analyse, the features they select
for study and, arguably, the interpretations they come to. (While this
contrasts with the objective intentions of other research on language and
society it should be borne in mind that no such research can be absolutely
objective. Even if never articulated, the beliefs or sets of values held by
researchers are likely to influence what they study — or do not study! —
and how their research is conducted.) Fowler *et al.*, however, tend to
offer single 'correct' interpretations for the linguistic categories they
identify in certain types of discourse — and to imply that these are
somehow not apparent to 'lay' readers, who will be deceived by the
discourse. So, passivisation obscures the agent from lay readers, but not
from the professional analyst who, presumably, has been able to escape
from the ideological straitjacket of his/her culture.

This criticism could be levelled also at other forms of linguistic
analysis where the linguist works directly from his/her own intuitions (see
section 1.4). In practice, the assignation of meaning is rather more
complex, with people producing a range of interpretations of discourse,
depending upon their previous experience, political commitment, etc.
(see also the discussion of 'cognitive frames' above). Some readers, for
instance, may accept the 'legitimated' portrayal of police killing offered
by the *Times* not so much because they are *deceived* by the passivisation
as because their political convictions lead them to prefer this interpretation. Others, with different political beliefs, would probably manage to
focus on the agency.

This is not to suggest that a particular type of portrayal of an event
will have no effect upon how it is perceived (nor that constant exposure
to particular uses of language will have no effect in the long term upon
a speaker/listener's set of values). It is, however, too crude an analysis
to suggest that linguistic structures have one correct interpretation and
that those from whom this is hidden are somehow being duped.

Textual approaches to written language

The approaches to the description of text which are described below are
all concerned with intrinsic structural or presentational qualities. It may
seem strange that so many researchers in such a variety of traditions
should attempt to analyse and characterise texts without taking into
account the audience or contextual factors, particularly when cognitive
psychologists and others have demonstrated the crucial role of the
reader. However, not all of the approaches discussed below are incompatible with the view of written language as discourse.

In some cases they simply make certain assumptions about the shared
world view, experience and expectations of readers which makes it unnecessary (in their view) to take readers into account when examining
distinctive differences between texts. Other approaches are unashamedly

concerned with somewhat superficial aspects of texts, simply because their purposes — which are less ambitious than those of cognitive psychology — do not seem to require anything more.

An example of this is as follows. Claude Shannon developed a theory of textual properties which allowed him to create a series of texts which bore more or less resemblance to real English. In doing so, he was modelling the statistical probabilities of certain sequences of letters or words occurring in the text. He produced one text (Shannon, 1948) which displayed within it all the transitional probabilities of English. That is, if it were repeated many times, it would display the same overall characteristics as a very long sample of any English text:

THE HEAD AND IN FRONTAL ATTACK ON AN ENGLISH WRITER THAT THE CHARACTER OF THIS POINT IS THEREFORE ANOTHER METHOD FOR THE LETTERS THAT THE TIME OF WHO EVER TOLD THE PROBLEM FOR AN UNEXPECTED

The Shannon text, as it is called, is now used as a test routine for electronic typewriters (and other communication links), since it simulates not only the relative frequencies of letters but also the likely rotational operations in the print head which occur when moving from one letter to another. Predictions of failure in the machine under long periods of normal use can be made much more accurately than by using familiar sentences such as *The quick brown fox jumped over the lazy dog*.

This demonstrates that even apparently superficial characterisations of text may have important uses. It follows that in assessing the adequacy of a particular approach one must bear in mind the practical application, which may warrant the use of assumptions which are on theoretical grounds somewhat unsatisfactory.

COHESION

One factor that distinguishes text from a random collection of sentences is the existence of links between one sentence and another. Consider, for example, the following pair of sentences (from Halliday and Hasan, 1976, p. 2):

Wash and core six cooking apples. Put *them* into a fireproof dish.

Them refers to *six cooking apples*: the words form a cohesive relation constituting an *anaphoric* tie. That is to say, the relation is backwards (anaphoric). The tie is grammatical rather than lexical. If, instead of *them* the example had *the apples*, then *apples* would be a lexical tie and *the* (defining *which* apples we are talking about) a grammatical tie.

Cohesive relations need not require reference to something earlier in the text. *Reference* may be forward (cataphoric) as in the first word of this example (from Halliday and Hassan, 1976, p. 17):

> *This* is how to get the best results. You let the berries dry in the sun, till all the moisture has gone out of them. Then you gather them up and chop them very fine.

Sometimes reference is not to the text at all. In that case it is *exophoric* (related to a context or situation) as in 'Here *she* comes', as an isolated statement, rather than endophoric (related to the text) as in 'We've been waiting a long time at the bus stop for *Linda*. Here *she* comes at last.' Types of reference are set out by Halliday and Hasan as shown in Figure 7.3. On this basis, Halliday and Hasan build a considerable scheme taking account of personal reference (she, me, etc.), demonstrative reference (this, that, here, etc.) and comparative reference (better, more similar, different, etc).

To reference they add other cohesive relations. These include *substitution* and *ellipsis*. In substitution, but not in reference, the item substituted is a replacement for an item that must have occurred earlier in the text and whose meaning is not 'recoverable from the environment' as are pronouns. Halliday and Hasan acknowledge that the distinction between reference and substitution is blurred at the edges. However, they contrast the reference items *she* 'some person (female), other than the speaker or addressee, who can be identified by recourse to the environment' with the use of *one* as 'a sort of counter' in, for example, *My axe is too blunt. I must get a sharper one* (Halliday and Hasan, 1976, pp. 88–9). They stress that reference is a semantic relation, whereas substitution is grammatical and so is *ellipsis* (which involves omission, e.g. *Joan bought some carnations, and Catherine some sweet peas —* where the verb is not repeated but the two clauses are linked). Another grammatical relation is *conjunction*, which links in various ways (e.g. by cause and effect relationship as in: *He was knocked down by a car. As a result he spent two months in hospital*). *Lexical cohesion* (already mentioned in the example of the apples) is more complicated because it is established through semantic relations in vocabulary though grammatically constrained.

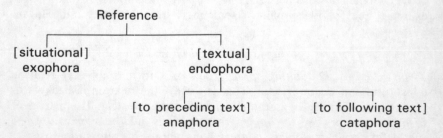

Figure 7.3.   Types of reference
Source: Halliday and Hasan (1976).

The full system of cohesive analysis provides a very detailed coding system developed for the analysis and description of text. The book *Cohesion in English* also gives a discussion of the relationship between cohesion and register (roughly, style and tone of language), for Halliday and Hasan (1976, p. 23) consider that the two taken together 'effectively define a text'. We have given here no more than an introduction to their work in the form of a broad outline of the system of cohesion, a system based on examination of intersentential ties.

QUANTITATIVE APPROACHES

Quantitative approaches to text analysis largely disregard both the role of the reader and the importance of conventions that readers and writers share. Their emphasis is on the text itself. However, they tend to have less concern for the overall structure of texts, than for low-level elements, notably words. Nevertheless, quantitative methods possess a rigour less apparent in other approaches and they are fairly readily replicable. The problems come in interpreting the data obtained and in assessing the validity of findings.

Here we consider two quantitative approaches that are related to each other. The oldest and simplest approach involves counting how frequently each word occurs in a text; sometimes a record is made of where each word is used, and these data are the basis for a *concordance*. Concordances for the Bible have been available for several centuries. However, the growth of computing has made the study of word frequencies and the compilation of concordances much less time-consuming and has led to more, and more sophisticated, work. The second approach we discuss is that of readability formulae, which are in fairly widespread use for assessing the difficulty of educational and technical texts.

Word-frequency studies   Texts have been examined to produce word-frequency lists for several purposes. In education, for example, the lists compiled by West (1927) and Thorndike (1932) have been widely used in preparing and assessing reading materials. Such lists are associated with the approach to foreign-language teaching that considered a 'controlled vocabulary' to be of importance. For beginning readers in Britain, the 'Ladybird Reading Series' is based on a word-frequency list (McNally and Murray, 1962), so that the most frequent words are learnt first in reading.

Another use of word-frequency studies is to help establish authorship, both in literary studies (such as the 'Who wrote Shakespeare?' controversy) and in historical and criminal investigations. Examples given in a most useful guide to linguistic computing by Susan Hockey (1980) include establishing the authorship of twelve of the 88 *Federalist Papers* written in 1787–8 to persuade New York citizens to ratify the constitution. Here, all but twelve of the 88 papers were known to be by one or other of three authors, though published under one pseudonym. One of the three authors was known not to have written the twelve papers whose attribution was in question. The claims of the other two, Alexander Hamilton and James Madison, were investigated by manual counting of sentence length. Mean sentence lengths and ranges in length were compared, but inconclusively. Subsequent computer analysis revealed that Hamilton always used 'while' but Madison preferred 'whilst' in papers known to be by them, and that relatively frequent use of 'upon' and 'enough' also marked Hamilton's style. This provided strong evidence, which was later corroborated by further detailed work. More recent analyses have been more sophisticated and have taken into account imagery, such items as conjunctions, certain grammatical patterns, and so on. The purpose of this work has been largely to give objective evidence for speculations on an author's work and to compare authors. An interesting application to Open University texts is reported by Whalley (1980) who computed the frequency of conjunctions and related this to the occurrence of new main themes in the OU texts.

Word-frequency analyses need not be restricted to literary texts, of course. One corpus which has been studied consists of the 100,000 words of Richard Nixon's conversations on tape, the so-called 'White House Tapes'. As reported by Stokes (1974), a computer concordance program was used to examine what words were used by Nixon in what context. About one-third of the tapes are rehearsals of public speeches, the remainder mostly private conversation. Analysis by Parrish and Shames at Cornell University showed the word 'cooperate' was used 23 times in the public mode but only six times in the private mode, and on two of these occasions Nixon was indicating he preferred not to cooperate in investigations. It was also found that 'I' was used about ten times as often as would be expected in a corpus of contemporary American English such as that of Kučera and Francis (1967) and that there was a predominant pattern of military and hunting imagery.

Readability formulae Readability formulae attempt to provide a description of some of the linguistic properties of texts in a very rough and ready manner which obscures syntactic, and particularly semantic, complexities. Nevertheless they have been very influential — at least in education — as predictors of the difficulty which a text will present to a reader. Readability formulae do at least have the virtue of being precisely specified and replicable in use.

Most formulae work on the principle that long sentences and long words make for a difficult text, but they vary on how exactly they take such features into account. Examples of two formulae commonly used, taken from Klare (1974) are given below.

Fog Index
Reading grade level = 0.4 × (average sentence length + percentage of words of 3 or more syllables).

Note that a passage of 100 words of text is usually taken as a sample for convenience. 'Reading grade level' refers to American school grade. Grade 1 = 6 years of age.

Example A passage of 100 words contains $6\frac{2}{3}$ sentences. Average sentence length is therefore: 100 divided by $6\frac{2}{3} = 15$ words.

The passage contains 18 words of 3 or more syllables. Reading grade level is, therefore: 0.4 of (15 + 18).

that is, $\dfrac{4}{10} \times 33 = 13.2$

Flesch Reading Ease Formula

Reading ease $= 206.835 - 0.846 \times wl - 1.015 \times sl$, where wl = number of syllables per 100 words and sl = average number of words per sentence. Samples of 100 words are again taken in applying this formula, as is usually the case.

Example Taking the hypothetical passage of 6 sentences (i.e. $sl = 15$) and, say 210 syllables ($wl = 210$) we substitute as follows:

$$\text{Reading ease} = 206.835 - (0.846 \times 210) - (1.015 \times 15)$$
$$= 206.835 - 177.66 - 15.225 = 13.95$$

Stokes (1978) compared seven readability formulae on samples from eleven British text books. He found that the different formulae give significantly different results and concluded that none could be regarded as more reliable than the others.

There are several reasons why readability formulae are, in practice, poor predictors of the difficulty which children will actually experience. One is that, as Stokes has shown, many textbooks (though not fiction) are extremely inconsistent in readability level from page to page. No single measure could therefore satisfactorily characterise a whole book. A second, and more important reason, is that the difficulty a particular child will experience will depend on many things associated with that child's personal experience, knowledge and motivation. Readability formulae make no attempt to characterise the conceptual difficulty in text.

STORY GRAMMARS AND RHETORIC

A very long and varied tradition exists which views various kinds of texts as having a hierarchical internal structure rather like the phrase structure of a sentence (see section 3.3).

Rhetoric, a subject of study in schools and universities for over two thousand years, was intended primarily to help in the composition of texts and speeches rather than with their analysis. Nevertheless, such rules — in so far as the conventions were followed — allow us to describe internal structures. Classical rhetoric provided three things:

(a) A means of classifying texts into certain types according to their internal structure. Examples might be judicial, deliberative, or dramatic.

(b) A means of describing the internal structure of such texts. For example, a judicial speech should, according to Cicero, comprise six parts: exordium, narration, partition, confirmation, refutation and conclusion. Each part may, in turn, be subdivided into smaller sections. The conclusion contained three parts: summing up, inciting indignation against the opponent and arousing sympathy for the client.

(c) A means of classifying the stylistic devices and conceits which comprise each part of the speech. Such devices as speakers saying they will finish and not bother their listener with certain matters (which are thus introduced and then dealt with) were explicitly taught in Roman times.

In this way, a law speech might be regarded as having a tree structure as is partially displayed in Figure 7.4.

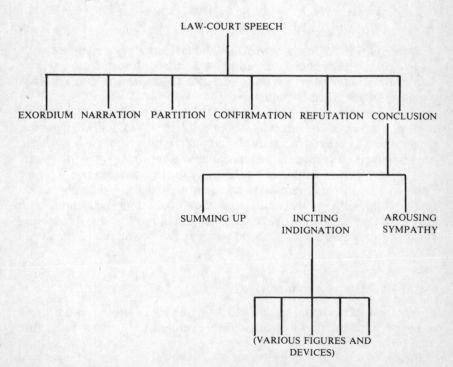

Figure 7.4. Partial rhetorical structure of a law court speech according to Cicero.

Story grammars   More than half a century ago, V. I. Propp analysed a great number of fairy tales and proposed an analysis according to the functions of characters. Although fairy tales contain a vast number of characters, Propp claimed that the basic structures of such tales are of a type and that the number of 'spheres of action' is finite. 'Spheres of action' correspond to performers, not exactly particular characters, because a character may have more than one role or any role may be taken by more than one character. These spheres of action are: the villain, the donor, the helper, the princess (or other sought-for person) and her father, the dispatcher, the hero, the false hero.

Propp's work became well known only through translation (Propp, 1958). A useful, readily available, brief account is in Hawkes (1977), who also discusses attempts by structuralists to use this and other work in devising grammars for stories.

A more recent approach, which has been used in studies of recall, is more obviously (and consciously) like modern sentence grammar. Mandler and Johnson (1977) give an analysis which can provide a hierarchical representation, based on a series of rewrite rules. For instance, their first rule is:

Story → setting + event structure

(→ is a symbol conventionally used to mean may 'be expressed as'). They used *states* and *events* as their basic units ('terminal nodes' in their nomenclature) and consider there are three kinds of relationship between these units, namely *and*, *then* and *cause*.

An example of Mandler and Johnson's representation of the structure of a short story is shown in Figure 7.5. The dog story on which it is based (Mandler and Johnson, 1977, p. 119) is given below.

Dog story
1 It happened that a dog has got a piece of meat
2 and was carrying it home in his mouth.
3 Now on his way home he had to cross a plank lying across a stream.
4 As he crossed he looked down
5 and saw his own shadow reflected in the water beneath.
6 Thinking it was another dog with another piece of meat,
7 he made up his mind to have that also.
8 So he made a snap at the shadow,
9 but as he opened his mouth the piece of meat fell out,
10 dropped into the water,
11 and was never seen again.

Cognitive psychologists have shown that where a story conforms to a well-known pattern it is more easily remembered and understood. Such findings seem to lend some validity to story grammars, but they are equally compatible with the schema and script theories discussed in

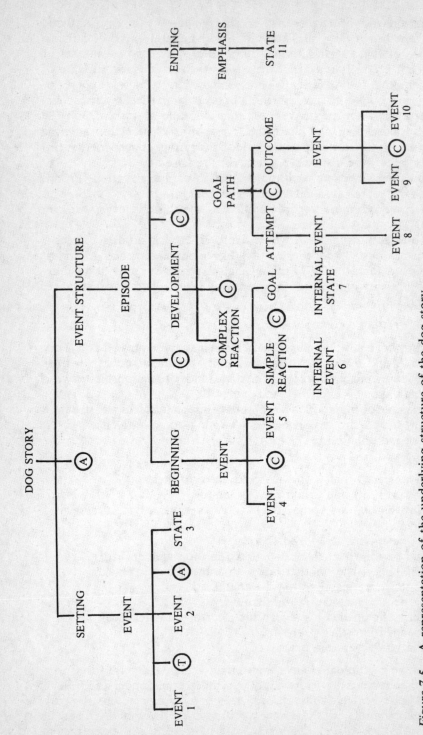

Figure 7.5. A representation of the underlying structure of the dog story.
Note: the connections *and, then* and *cause* have been abbreviated to A, T, and C, and circled. The numbers under the terminal modes refer to the surface statements of the story.
Source: Mandler and Johnson (1977).

section 7.2. In other words, a story grammar can be regarded as a cognitive script which people use for certain kinds of text. Van Dijk and Kintsch (1978, p. 75) comment:

> We have hypothesized that the reader approaches a narrative with a narrative schema in mind, and that part of the process of comprehending the narrative consists of filling in the empty slots in that schema with appropriate information from the text.

They tested this hypothesis by asking college students to make abstracts of two stories, one from Boccaccio's *Decameron* and a second from an Apache myth. The first had a familiar narrative structure, but the Indian story was regarded as 'weird' by the students. 'The story, of course, does follow a well-developed schema, but known only to Indians and anthropologists.' The researchers found that most students made very similar summaries for the Decameron stories, but gave very varied responses for the Indian story. They concluded that the process of writing a summary is directed by the schema which a person has applied to the text.

Appendix 1
Cassette contents

For purchasing details on this *Describing Language* cassette please contact:

> Open University Educational Enterprises Ltd.
> 12 Cofferidge Close,
> Stony Stratford,
> Milton Keynes,
> MK11 1BY

CONTENTS SUMMARY

Band 1 Illustrations of sounds mentioned in Activity 2.1
Band 2 Illustrations of sounds mentioned in Activity 2.2
Band 3 'Mini-tutorial' on consonant sounds (Activity 2.3)
Band 4 'Mini-tutorial' on vowel sounds (Activity 2.5)
Band 5 'Mini-tutorial' on phonemes and allophonic variation (Activity 2.7)
Band 6 Interruptions in discourse
Band 7 Partition sampling and transcription exercise (Activity 6.4)
Band 8 Interview between parent and teacher
Band 9 Telephone closings
Band 10 Conversation fragments for transcription practice

Appendix 2

Answers to activities in Chapter 2.

ACTIVITY 2.2

(a) The sound is voiced.
(b) The tongue makes contact with the soft palate or velum; the sound produced is thus said to be velar.
(c) The manner of articulation would be plosive.
(d) The three-part description of the sound is voiced velar plosive. The symbol for this is [g].
(e) The symbol for a voiceless velar plosive is [k].
(f) The manner of articulation would now be fricative not plosive.
(g) The symbol for a voiced velar fricative is [ɣ]. The symbol for a voiceless velar fricative is [x].
(h) These sounds are not normally used in English. [x] is found in some Scots and, more rarely, in some English dialects. [ɣ] is used in some continental European languages, such as Danish.

Activity 2.4

(a) (i) The tongue is higher in the mouth for [i] than for [ɑ].
    (ii) The highest point of the tongue is nearer the front of the mouth for [i].
(b) (i) The tongue is higher for [u] than for [a].
    (ii) The tongue is highest nearer the front for [a].
(e) (i) [u] is produced with the lips rounded and is hence referred to as a rounded vowel.
    (ii) The other rounded vowels shown on Figure 2.8 are [o] and [ɔ].

Further reading and references

CHAPTER 1. THE NATURE OF LANGUAGE

Further reading

There are many good introductory books on linguistics which cover the issues raised in this section. The following are particularly recommended:

Brown, K. (1984). *Linguistics*, London, Fontana.
Hudson, R. (1980). *Sociolinguistics*, Cambridge, Cambridge University Press.
Trudgill, P. (1983). *Sociolinguistics*, Harmondsworth, Penguin.

The following books describe particular investigations of the relationship between language and society, discussing methodological as well as theoretical issues.

Gal, S. (1979). *Language Shift*, New York, Academic Press
Milroy, L. (1980). *Language and Social Networks*, Oxford, Blackwell.
Le Page, R. B. and Tabouret-Keller, A. (1985). *Acts of Identity*, Cambridge, Cambridge University Press.

References

Bloomfield, L. (1933). *Language*, London, George Allen & Unwin.
Chomsky, N. (1965). *Aspects of the Theory of Syntax*, Cambridge, MIT Press.
Chomsky, N. (1957). *Syntactic Structures*, The Hague, Mouton.
Fowler, H. W. (1926). *A Dictionary of Modern English Usage*, Oxford, Clarendon Press.
Gumperz, J. J. (1972). 'Introduction' in J. J. Gumperz and D. Hymes

(eds), *Directions in Sociolinguistics*, New York, Holt Rinehart and Winston.

Harris, R. (1980). *The Language-Makers*, London, Duckworth.

Hudson, R. (1980). *Sociolinguistics*, Cambridge, Cambridge University Press.

Hymes, D. (1972). 'Models of the interaction of language and social life' in J. J. Gumperz and D. Hymes (eds), *Directions in Sociolinguistics* New York, Holt Rinehart and Winston.

Katzner, (1977). *The Languages of the World*, London, Routledge and Kegan Paul.

Labov, W. (1972). *Sociolinguistic Patterns*, Oxford, Blackwell.

Labov, W. (1975). *What is a Linguistic Fact?*, The Hague, Reidel.

Linguistic Minorities Project (1983). *Linguistic Minorities in England: Summary Report*, London, London Institute of Education.

Lyons, J. (1968). *Introduction to Theoretical Linguistics*, Cambridge Cambridge University Press.

Lyons, J. (ed) (1970). *New Horizons in Linguistics*, Harmondsworth, Penguin.

Orton, H., Sanderson, S. and Widdowson, J. (eds) (1978). *The Linguistic Atlas of England*, London, Croom Helm

Palmer, F. (1984). *Grammar*, Harmondsworth, Penguin.

Parlett, D. S. (1967). *A Short Dictionary of Languages*, London, English Universities Press (Teach Yourself Books).

Romaine, S. (1982). 'What is a Speech Community?' in S. Romaine (ed), *Sociolinguistic Variation in Speech Communities*, London, Edward Arnold.

Sapir, E. (1949). *Culture, Language and Personality: Selected Essays* (ed. David G. Mandelbaum), Berkeley, University of California Press.

Spencer, N. J. (1973). 'Differences between Linguists and Non-Linguists in Intuitions of Grammaticality-Acceptability' *Journal of Experimental Psycholinguistics*, 83–98.

Saussure, F. de (1974). *Course in General Linguistics*, London, Fontana-Collins.

Trudgill, P. (1983). *Sociolinguistics*, Harmondsworth, Penguin.

Voegelin, C. F. and Voegelin, F. M. (1977). *Classification and Index of the World's Languages*, New York Elsevier.

CHAPTER 2. THE SOUNDS OF LANGUAGE

Further reading

A good general introduction to phonetics is:

O'Connor, J. D. (1973), *Phonetics*, Harmondsworth, Penguin.

A standard phonetic description of Received Pronunciation is given in:

Gimson, A. (1962). *An Introduction to the Pronunciation of English*, London, Edward Arnold.

A good all-round discussion of prosody can be found in:

Couper-Kuhlen, E. (1986). *An Introduction to English Prosody*, London, Edward Arnold.

References

Atkinson, J. M. and Heritage, J. (eds) (1984). *Structures of Social Action*, Cambridge, Cambridge University Press.

Bolinger, D. (1985). *Intonation and its Parts*, London, Edward Arnold.

Cooper, W. E. and Sorensen, J. N. (1981). *Fundamental Frequency in Sentence Production*, New York, Springer Verlag.

Crystal, D. (1969). *Prosodic Systems and Intonation in English*, Cambridge, Cambridge University Press.

Fry, D. B. (1955). 'Duration and Intensity as Physical Correlates of Linguistic Stress', *Journal of the Acoustical Society of America*, vol. 27, pp. 765–8.

Fry, D. B. (1958). 'Experiments in the Perception of Stress', *Language and Speech*, vol. 1, pp. 126–52.

Gussenhoven, C. (1986). 'The Intonation of George and Mildred: Post-nuclear Generalisations' in C. Johns-Lewis (ed.), *Intonation in Discourse*, Beckenham, Croom Helm.

Ladd, R. (1978). *The structure of Intonational Meaning*, Bloomington, Indiana University Press.

Liberman, M. Y. and Prince, A. (1977). 'On Stress and Linguistic Rhythm', *Linguistic Inquiry*, vol. 8, pp. 249–336.

Lieberman, M. K. (1986). 'The Acquisition of Intonation by Infants: Psychology and Neural Control' in C. Johns-Lewis (ed.), *Intonation in Discourse*, Beckenham, Croom Helm.

O'Connor, J. D. (1973). *Phonetics*, Harmondsworth, Penguin.

O'Connor, J. D. and Arnold, G. F. (1961). *Intonation of Colloquial English*, London, Longman.

Umeda, N. (1982). 'F_0 Declination is Situation Dependent', *Journal of Phonetics*, vol. 10, pp. 279–290.

CHAPTER 3. SENTENCE AND WORD STRUCTURE

Further reading

The account given in this chapter has necessarily been brief and simplified. For a fuller account of grammatical structure you are recommended to read the following book, on which much of the discussion in

Chapter 3 is based:

Palmer, F. R. (1984). *Grammar*, Harmondsworth, Penguin.

The following books and articles are recommended for further details on different grammatical frameworks.

Transformational-generative grammar:

Lyons, J. (1977). *Chomsky*, London, Fontana (2nd ed).
Smith, N. and Wilson, D. (1979). *Modern Linguistics*, Harmondsworth, Penguin.

Systemic grammar:

Berry, M. (1975, 1977). *An Introduction to Systemic Linguistics*, vols 1 & 2, London, Batsford.

Case grammar:

Fillmore, C. (1968). 'The Case for Case' in E. Bach and R. T. Harms (eds), *Universals in Linguistic Theory*, New York, Holt, Rinehart and Winston.

References

Clark, H. H. and Clark, E. V. (1977). *Psychology and Language*, New York, Harcourt, Brace, Jovanovich.
Crystal, D., Fletcher, P. and Garman, M. (1976). *The Grammatical Analysis of Language Disability*, London, Arnold.
Klima, E. and Bellugi, V. (1966). 'Syntactic Regularities in the Speech of Children' in J. Lyons and R. J. Wales (eds), *Psycholinguistic Papers*, Edinburgh, Edinburgh University Press, pp. 183–219.
Quirk, R., Greenbaum, S., Leech, G. and Svartvik, J. (1972). *A Grammar of Contemporary English*, Harlow, Longman.

CHAPTER 4. MEANING

Further reading

An easy introduction to many of the issues discussed in this chapter can be found in:

Lyons, J. (1981). *Language, Meaning, and Context*, London, Fontana.

A much fuller treatment also exists in two volumes:

Lyons, J. (1977). *Semantics*, Cambridge, Cambridge University Press.

A demonstration of how semantic feature analysis can be used in child-language research:

Clark, E. (1973) 'What's in a word? On the Child's Acquisition of

Semantics in His First Language' in T. E. Moore (ed.), *Cognitive Development and Child Language Acquisition*, London, Academic Press.

The original book on speech act analysis remains a very readable introduction:

Austin, J. L. (1962). *How To Do Things with Words*, Oxford, Clarendon Press.

References

Biggs, C. (1982). 'In a Word, meaning' in D. Crystal (ed.) *Linguistic Controversies*, London, Edward Arnold.

Bolinger, D. (1965). *Aspects of Language*, New York, Harcourt, Brace, Jovanovitch.

Coulthard, M. (1977), *An Introduction to Discourse Analysis*, London, Longman.

Eco, U. (1984). *Semiotics and the Philosophy of Language*, London, Macmillan.

Gannon, P. and Czerniewska, P. (1980). *Using Linguistics: An Educational Focus*, London, Edward Arnold.

Geis, (1982). *The Language of Television Advertising*, London, Academic Press.

Grice, H. P. (1975). 'Logic and Conversation' in P. Cole and J. Morgan (eds), *Syntax and Semantics*, **3**: Speech Acts, New York, Academic Press.

Gumperz, J. (1982). *Discourse Strategies*, Cambridge, Cambridge University Press.

Kempson, R. (1977). *Presupposition and the Delimitation of Semantics*, Cambridge, Cambridge University Press.

Kent, G. A. and Rosenoff, A. J. (1910). 'A Study of Association in Insanity', *American Journal of Insanity*, vol. 67, pp. 317–90.

Lyons, J. (1977). *Semantics*, Vol. 1 and 2, Cambridge, Cambridge University Press.

Quine, W. (1953). 'Two Dogmas of Empiricism' in W. Quine (ed.), *From a Logical Point of View*, New York, Harper Torchbooks.

Quine, W. (1960). *Word and Object*, Cambridge, Cambridge University Press.

Palmer, F. R. (1981). *Semantics*, Cambridge, Cambridge University Press, (2nd edn).

Stork, E. C. and Widdowson, J. D. A. (1974). *Learning about Linguistics*, London, Hutchinson.

Todasco *et al.* (1973). 'An Intelligent Woman's Guide to Dirty Words: English Words and Phrases Reflecting Sexist Attitudes towards Women in Patriarchal Society, Arranged According to Usage and Idea', Vol. 1 of *The Feminist English Dictionary*, Chicago, Feminist Writers, Workshop, Loop Center YWCA.

CHAPTER 5: WRITING SYSTEMS

Further reading

Two standard descriptions of the development of writing systems are:

Diringer, D. (1962). *Writing*, London, Thames and Hudson.
Gelb, I. J. (1963). *A Study of Writing*, Chicago, University of Chicago Press.

A fuller account of the history of English spelling is given in:

Scragg, D. G. (1974). *A History of English Spelling*, Manchester, Manchester University Press.

A good discussion of the relationship between sound and spelling can be found in:

Stubbs, M. (1980). *Language and Literacy*, London, Routledge and Kegan Paul.

Examples of most writing systems used in the world today are included in:

Katzner, K. (1977). *The Languages of the World*, London, Routledge and Kegan Paul.

References

Algeo, J. (1972). *Problems in the Origins and Development of the English Language*, New York, Harcourt Brace Jovanovich.
Bradley, H. (1913). *On the Relations between Spoken and Written Language with Special Reference to English*, London, British Academy.
Chomsky, N. and Halle, M. (1968). *The Sound Pattern of English*, New York, Harper and Row.
Gelb, I. J. (1963). *A Study of Writing*, Chicago, University of Chicago Press.
Smith, P. T. and Baker, R. G. (1976). 'The Influence of English Spelling Patterns on Pronunciation', *Journal of Verbal Learning and Verbal Behaviour*, Vol. 15, pp. 267–285.
Stubbs, M. (1980) *Language and Literacy: the Sociolinguistics of Reading and Writing*, London, Routledge and Kegan Paul.
Venezky, R. L. (1970). *The Structure of English Orthography*, The Hague, Mouton.

CHAPTER 6. FACE-TO-FACE INTERACTION

Further reading

There are no popular introductions to non-verbal communication which can be safely recommended. Two more advanced overviews are given in:

Weitz, S. (ed.) (1974). *Nonverbal Communication: Readings with Commentary*, New York, Oxford University Press.

A useful collection of seminal articles, but at present out of print:

Laver, J. and Hutcheson, S. (eds) (1972). *Communication in Face to Face Interaction*, Harmondsworth, Penguin.

Various aspects of the relationship between gesture and speech, and of smooth turn-taking, will be found in:

Beattie, G. (1983). *Talk*, Milton Keynes, Open University Press.

References

Addis, B. R. (1966). *The Relationship of Physical Interpersonal Distance to Sex, Race, and Age*, MA thesis, University of Oklahoma.

Argyle, M. and Dean, J. (1965). 'Eye-contact, Distance and Affiliation', *Sociometry*, Vol. 28 pp. 289–304.

Atkinson, M. (1984). *Our Masters' Voices: The Language and Body Language of Politics*, London, Methuen.

Bales, R. F. (1970). *Personality and Interpersonal Behaviour*, New York, Holt, Rinehart and Winston.

Basso, K. (1972). '"To give up on words": Silence in Western Apache Culture' in P. P. Giglioli (ed.), *Language and Social Context*, Harmondsworth, Penguin Education.

Beattie, G. W. (1977). 'The Dynamics of Interruption and the Filled Pause', *British Journal of Social and Clinical Psychology*, vol. 16, pp. 283–4.

Beattie, G. W. and Beattie, C. A. (1981). 'Postural Congruence in a Naturalistic Setting', *Semiotica*, vol. 35, pp. 41–55.

Beattie, G. W. (1982). 'Turn-taking and Interruption in Political Interviews: Margaret Thatcher and Jim Callaghan Compared and Contrasted', *Semiotica*, vol. 39, pp. 93–114.

Beattie, G. W. (1983). *Talk: An Analysis of Speech and Non-verbal Behaviour in Conversation*, Milton Keynes, Open University Press.

Beattie, G. W. and Barnard, P. J. (1979). 'The Temporal Structure of Natural Telephone Conversations (Directory Enquiry Calls)', *Linguistics*, vol. 17, pp. 213–30.

Bell, D. C. and Bell, A. M. (1892). *Bells Standard Elocutionist*, London, Hodder and Stoughton.

Birdwhistell, R. L. (1970). *Kinesics and Context: Essays on Body-motion Communication*, Harmondsworth, Penguin.

Boucher, J. D. and Ekman, P. (1975). 'Facial Areas of Emotional Information', *Journal of Communication*, vol. 25, pp. 21–9.

Darwin, C. (1872) *The Expression of the Emotions in Man and Animals*, London, Murray.

Denny, R. (1985). 'Marking the Interactional Order: The Social Constitution of Turn Exchange and Speaking Turns', *Language in Society*, vol 14, pp. 41–62.

Duncan, S. (1972). 'Some Signals and Rules for Taking Speaking Turns in Conversations', *Journal of Personality and Social Psychology*, vol. 23, pp. 283–92.

Ekman, P. (1973). *Darwin and Facial Expression: A Century of Research in Review*, New York, Academic Press.

Ekman, P., and Friesen, W. V. (1967) 'Head and Body Cues in the Judgment of Emotion: A Reformulation', *Perceptual and Motor Skills*, vol. 24, pp. 711–24.

Ekman, P., Friesen, W. V. and Ellsworth, P. (1972). *Emotion in the Human Face: Guidelines for Research and an Integration of the Findings*, New York, Pergamon Press.

Ekman, P., Sorenson, E. R. and Friesen, W. V. (1969). 'Pan-cultural Elements in Facial Displays of Emotion', *Science*, vol. 164, pp. 86—8.

Fisher, J. D., Ryttine, M. and Hesling, R. (1976). 'Hands Touching Hands: Affective and Evaluative Effects of an Interpersonal Touch', *Sociometry*, Vol. 39, pp. 416–21.

Flanders, N. A. (1970). *Analyzing Teaching Behaviour*, Reading, MA, Addison-Wesley Publishing Co.

Goodwin, C. (1981). *Conversational Organization: Interaction between Speakers and Hearers*, New York, Academic Press.

Hall, E. T. (1963). 'A System for the Notation of Proxemic Behaviour', *American Anthropologist*, vol. 65, pp. 1003–26.

Henley, N. M. (1973). 'Status and Sex: Some Touching Observations', *Bulletin of the Psychonometry Society*, vol. 2, pp. 91–3.

Jellison, J. M. and Ickes, W. J. (1974) 'The Power of the Glance: Desire to See and Be Seen in Competitive Situations', *Journal of Experimental Social Psychology*, vol. 10, pp. 444–50.

Jourard, S. M. (1966). 'An Exploratory Study of Body Accessibility' *British Journal of Social and Clinical Psychology*, vol. 5, pp. 221–31.

Kendon, A. (1967). 'Some Functions of Gaze Direction in Social Interaction', *Acta Psychologica*, vol. 26, pp. 22–63.

Kendon, A. (1982). 'The Organization of Behaviour in Face-to-Face Interaction: Observations on the Development of a Methodology' in K. R. Scherer and P. Ekman (eds), *Handbook of Methods in Nonverbal Behavior Research*, Cambridge, Cambridge University Press.

Mackey, W. C. (1976). 'Parameters of the Smile as a Social Signal', *Journal of Genetic Psychology*, vol. 129, pp. 125–130.

MacWhinney, B. and Snow, C. (1985). 'The Child Language Data Exchange System', *Journal of Child Language*, vol. 12, pp. 271–96.

Mehrabian, A. (1969), 'Significance of Posture and Position in the Communication of Attitude and Status Relationship', *Psychological Bulletin*, vol. 71, pp. 359–72.

Morris, D., Collett, P., Marsh, P. and O'Shaughnessy, M. (1979). *Gestures*, London, Jonathan Cape.

Nguyen, T., Heslin, R. and Nguyen, M. L. (1975). 'Meanings of Touch: Sex Differences', *Journal of Communication*, Summer, pp. 92–103.

Ochs, E. (1979). 'Transcription as Theory' in E. Ochs and B. B. Schieffelin (eds), *Developmental Pragmatics*, New York, Academic Press.

Reisman, K. (1974). 'Contrapuntal Conversation in an Antiguan Village' in R. Bauman and J. Scherzer (eds) *Explorations in the Ethnography of Speaking*, Cambridge, Cambridge University Press.

Rutter, D. R. and Stephenson, G. M. (1977). 'The Role of Visual Communication in Synchronizing Conversation', *European Journal of Social Psychology*, vol. 7, no. 1, pp. 29–37.

Sacks, H., Schegloff, E. A. and Jefferson, G. (1974). 'A Simplest Systematics for the Organization of Turn-taking for Conversation', *Language*, vol. 50, No. 4, pp. 696–735.

Scheflen, A. E. (1964). 'The Significance of Posture in Communication Systems', *Psychiatry*, vol. 27, pp. 316–31.

Schegloff, E. A. (1984). 'On Some Gestures' Relation to Talk' in J. M. Atkinson and J. Heritage (eds) *Structures of Social Action*, Cambridge, Cambridge University Press.

Sommer, R. (1962). 'The Distance for Comfortable Conversation: A Further Study', *Sociometry*, vol. 25, pp. 111–16.

Stier, D. S. and Hall, J. A. (1984). 'Gender Differences in Touch: An Empirical and Theoretical Review', *Journal of Personality and Social Psychology*, vol. 47, pp. 440–59.

Thompson, J. J. (1973). *Beyond Words: Non-verbal Communication in the Classroom*, New York, Citation Press.

Wainwright, G. R. (1985). *Teach Yourself Body Language*, London, Hodder and Stoughton.

Wells, G. (1985). *Language Development in the Pre-School Years*, Cambridge, Cambridge University Press.

Zimmerman, D. H. and West, C. (1975). 'Sex Roles, Interruptions and Silences in Conversation', in Thorne, B. and Henley, N. (eds) *Language and Sex: Difference and Dominance*, Rowley, Massachussetts, Newbury House.

CHAPTER 7.   DISCOURSE AND TEXT

Further reading

A good and eclectic introduction to conversation and discourse analysis, with a useful discussion of methodology is:

Stubbs, M. (1983). *Discourse Analysis*, Oxford, Blackwell.

The best introduction to the more linguistic approach to discourse analysis is:

Coulthard, M. (1977). *An Introduction to Discourse Analysis*, London, Longman.

A very accessible treatment of approaches in cognitive psychology and artificial intelligence is:

Greene, J. (1986). *Language Understanding: A Cognitive Approach*, Milton Keynes, Open University Press.

A more advanced collection of papers, representative of current thinking in the analysis of spoken and written discourse is:

Van Dijk, T. A. (ed.) (1985). *Handbook of Discourse Analysis vol. 4: Discourse Analysis in Society*, London, Academic Press.

A similar collection including papers in conversation analysis is:

Atkinson, J. M. and Heritage, J. (eds) (1984). *Structures of Social Action*, Cambridge, Cambridge University Press.

References

Atkinson, J. M. and Heritage, J. (1984). *Structures of Social Action*, Cambridge, Cambridge University Press.

Bartlett, F. C. (1932). *Remembering*, Cambridge, Cambridge University Press.

Bower, G. H., Black, J. B. and Turner, T. J. (1979). 'Scripts in Text Comprehension and Memory', *Cognitive Psychology*, vol. 11, pp. 177–220.

Bransford, J. D., Barclay, J. R. and Franks, J. S. (1972). 'Sentence Memory: A Constructive versus Interpretive Approach', *Cognitive Psychology*, vol. 3, pp. 193–209.

Bransford, J. D. and Johnson, M. K. (1972). 'Contextual Prerequisites for Understanding: Some Investigations of Comprehension and Recall', *Journal of Verbal Learning and Verbal Behaviour*, vol. 11, pp. 717–26.

Coulthard, M. and Brazil, D. C. (1979) *Exchange Structures*, (Discourse Analysis Monographs 5), Birmingham, University of Birmingham English Language Research.

Czerniewska, P. (1985). 'The Experience of Writing' in Open University, *Every Child's Language: An in-service pack for primary teachers*, Clevedon, Multilingual Matters.

French, P. and Local, J. (1986). 'Prosodic Features and the Management of Interruptions' in Johns-Lewis, C. (ed.), *Intonation in Discourse*, London, Croom Helm.

Fowler, R. G., Hodge, R. I. V., Kress, G. R. and Trew, A. A. (1979). *Language and Control*, London, Routledge and Kegan Paul.

Greene, J. (1986). *Language Understanding: A Cognitive Approach*, Milton Keynes, Open University Press.

Grice, H. P. (1975). 'Logic and Conversation' in P. Cole and J. Morgan (eds), *Syntax and Semantics 3: Speech Acts*, New York, Academic Press.

Halliday, M. A. K. and Hasan, R. (1976). *Cohesion in English*, London, Longman.

230   *Describing Language*

Hawkes, T. (1977). *Structuralism and Semiotics*, London, Methuen.
Hockey, S. (1980). *A Guide to Computer Applications in the Humanities*, London, Duckworth.
Hudson, R. (1984). *Higher-level Differences between Speech and Writing*, London, Committee for Linguistics in Education.
Kintsch, W. (1974). *The Representation of Meaning in Memory*, Hillsdale, Erlbaum-Wiley.
Klare, G. (1974). 'Assessing Readability', *Reading Research Quarterly*, vol. 10, pp. 62–102.
Kress, G. R. and Hodge, R. I. V. (1979). *Language and Ideology*, London, Routledge and Kegan Paul.
Kučera, H. and Francis, H. N. (1967). *Computational Analysis of Present-day American English*, Providence, Brown University Press.
Levinson, S. (1983). *Pragmatics*, Cambridge, Cambridge University Press.
McNally, J. and Murray, W. (1962). *Key Words to Literacy*, London, Schoolmaster Publishing Company.
Mandler, J. M. and Johnson, N. S. (1977). 'Remembrance of Things Parsed: Story Structure and Recall', *Cognitive Psychology*, vol. 9, pp. 111–51.
Minsky, M. (1975). 'A Framework for Representing Knowledge' in P. Winston (ed.), *The Psychology of Computer Vision*, New York, McGraw-Hill.
Palmer, F. (1984). *Grammar*, Harmondsworth, Penguin, (2nd edn).
Propp, V. I. (1958). *Morphology of the Folktale* (trans. L. Scott), Austin, University of Texas Press.
Quirk, R., Greenbaum, S., Leech, G. and Svartvik, J. (1972). *A Grammar of Contemporary English*, Harlow, Longman.
Schank, R. C. and Abelson, R. P. (1977). 'Scripts, Plans and Knowledge' in P. N. Johnson-Laird and P. C. Wason (eds). *Thinking: Readings in Cognitive Science*, Cambridge, Cambridge University Press.
Schegloff, E. and Sacks, H. (1973). 'Opening up Closings', *Semiotica*, vol. 8, pp. 289–327.
Seidel, G. (1985). 'Political Discourse Analysis' in T. A. Van Dijk, (ed.), *Handbook of Discourse Analysis vol. 4: Discourse Analysis in Society*, London, Academic Press.
Shannon, C. E. (1948). 'A Mathematical Theory of Communication', *Bell System Technical Journal*, vol. 27, pp. 379–423, 623–56. (Extract reprinted in 1968 in R. C. Oldfield and J. C. Marshall (eds), *Language*, Harmondsworth, Penguin.)
Sinclair, J.McH. and Coulthard, R. M. (1975). *Towards an Analysis of Discourse*, London, Oxford University Press.
Stokes, A. (1978). 'The Reliability of Readability Formulae', *Journal of Research in Reading*, vol. 1, pp. 21–34.
Stokes, G. (1974). 'The Story of P: A Computer Unmasks the Man behind the Transcripts', *Harpers Magazine*, vol. 249, pp. 6–12.

Thorndike, R. L. (1932). 'Reading as Reasoning', *Reading Research Quarterly*, vol. 9, pp. 135–47.

Trew, A. A. (1979). 'Theory and Ideology at Work' in R. G. Fowler, R. I. V. Hodge, G. R. Kress and Trew, A. A., *Language and Control*, London, Routledge and Kegan Paul.

Van Dijk, T. A. and Kintsch, W. (1978). 'Cognitive Psychology and Discourse: Recalling and Summarizing Stories' in W. V. Dressler (ed.), *Current Trends in Textlinguistics*, Berlin, W. de Gruyter.

West, M. (1927). *The Construction of Reading Material for Reading a Foreign Language*, London, Oxford University Press.

Whalley, P. (1980). 'A Partial Index of Text Complexity Involving the Lexical Analysis of Rhetorical Connectives', *A. L. L. C. Journal*.

Index